THOMAS R. PRESTON

Not in Timon's Manner

Feeling, Misanthropy, and Satire in Eighteenth-Century England

Studies in the Humanities No. 9

Literature

THE
UNIVERSITY OF ALABAMA
PRESS
University, Alabama

Copyright © 1975 by
The University of Alabama Press
ISBN 0-8173-7315-2
Library of Congress Catalog Card Number 74-2570
All rights reserved
Manufactured in the United States of America

Contents

Acknowledgments

This book could not have been written without the aid
of many friends. Thanks are due to Pender Turnbull,
Richard O'Keefe, and especially Richard Perrine—all of
the Fondren Library staff, Rice University. Ray Jones
of the University of Florida Library performed services
above and beyond the call of duty. Several friends have
read the manuscript at various stages of its development: William F. Cunningham, Jr., patiently commented
on the first draft several years ago; Michael J. Conlon
debated several chapters with me; Aubrey Williams carefully criticized the first draft; Ward Hellstrom argued
with me long into many nights, and for his many insights
I am particularly grateful; Ronald Paulson gave generous
advice and moral support. My wife and children endured
the various revisions. My debt to them all is great indeed. A special debt is owed to the late Alan D. McKillop, who warmly encouraged the writing of the initial
dissertation from which this study gradually developed.
His friendship remained constant through the years, until
his death during the correction of page proof for this
work. Gladly would he learn and gladly teach.

Parts of chapters three and five were originally published by *PMLA* and are reprinted with permission.

Part of chapter four appeared in *Quick Springs of Sense:
Studies in the Eighteenth Century*, ed. Larry S. Cham-
pion. Copyright © 1973 by The University of Georgia
Press. Reprinted by permission of the publisher.

Quotations from *Rasselas*, edited by R.W. Chapman, and
from *Collected Works of Oliver Goldsmith*, edited by
Arthur Friedman, are used by permission of The Claren-
don Press, Oxford.

Laramie, Wyoming
At the University

Not in Timon's Manner

To

MARIE PRESTON

and to the memories of

THOMAS PRESTON and LOREL McKILLOP

Introduction

The gloomy Dean of St. Patrick's, in a now famous letter to Alexander Pope, accuses himself of misanthropy
but carefully dissociates his kind of hatred from the
traditional misanthropy projected in the archetypal
Timon figure:

> I have ever hated all nations, professions, and com-
> munities, and all my love is toward individuals: for
> instance, I hate the tribe of lawyers, but I love Coun-
> sellor Such-a-one, and Judge Such-a-one: so with phy-
> sicians—I will not speak of my own trade—soldiers,
> English, Scotch, French, and the rest. But princi-
> pally I hate and detest that animal called man, al-
> though I heartily love John, Peter, Thomas, and so
> forth. This is the system upon which I have gov-
> erned myself many years, but do not tell, and so I
> shall go on till I have done with them. I have got
> materials toward a treatise, proving the falsity of
> that definition *animal rationale*, and to show it
> would be only *rationis capax*. Upon this great foun-
> dation of misanthropy, though not in Timon's manner,
> the whole building of my Travels is erected; and I
> never will have peace of mind till all honest men
> are of my opinion.[1]

All honest men are probably, at least in secret, of
Swift's opinion, for this paradoxical misanthropy, which
has a modern, existential ring to it, seems to represent an unflinching facing up to the reality of human
evil without, like Timon, despairing of the human potential for good. Unlike Timon, Swift does not reject
society nor does he wish it ill; as he says in another
letter to Pope, his misanthropy lacks the malicious
force of anger: "I tell you after all, that I do not

1

hate mankind: it is *vous autres* who hate them, because
you would have them reasonable animals, and are angry
for being disappointed."[2]

Swift's benevolent misanthropy, to name this phenomenon of hating man and loving the individual, provides
an illuminating background to his great satiric works.
It also possesses, however, important historical significance as an early and formative expression of a tradition of benevolent misanthropy that came to flourish
in English literature and literary thought of the mid
and late eighteenth century. The purpose of this study
is to trace the development of that tradition and to
show how it provided a mode of literary satire accommodated to the prevailing antisatiric ethos of what has
been called the "Age of Sensibility."[3]

The Age of Sensibility, invoking the power of man's
supposedly innate benevolent feelings, inspired an optimistic belief in man's gradual but nevertheless certain moral progress to the utopian state of physical
and moral harmony that, according to the Christian tradition, he once possessed in Eden.[4] Beneath the bravura
surface of this faith, however, lies concealed a pessimistic fear that man suffers from a "tragic insuffi-
ciency"[5] to attain the utopia of his longing, a fear
that later resulted in Romantic irony and the character
of the Romantic rebel.[6] In *An Enquiry Concerning the
Principles of Morals*, David Hume gives explicit witness
to this underlying fear: "Why rake into those corners
of nature which spread a nuisance all around? Why dig
up the pestilence from the pit in which it is buried?
The ingenuity of your researches may be admired, but
your systems will be detested: And mankind will agree,
if they cannot refute them, to sink them, at least, in
eternal silence and oblivion. Truths, which are *perni-
cious* to society, if any such there be, will yield to
errors, which are salutary and *advantageous*."[7]

The tradition of benevolent misanthropy, delicately
balancing optimistic and pessimistic tendencies in the
Age of Sensibility, pointed to the fact of universal
human evil and the improbability of social man's moral
transformation; but at the same time it defended the
individual's potential for significant moral progress
through the development of his benevolent feelings. This

double vision of man, in effect, offered a philosophical
position that could reconcile the conflicting demands
of intellect and feeling, of the head and the heart.
Moreover, it kept open the door of satire by justifying
satire's traditional claim of exposing moral evil to
the lash of correction. Most importantly, however, benevolent misanthropy conferred psychological validity
on the satirist's frequent assertion that his attack is
benevolently motivated, for the new tradition reinterpreted misanthropy to mean the psychological state of
disappointment and frustration arising in a man of feeling attempting to exercise his benevolence in an unfeeling world. The tradition of benevolent misanthropy by
no means resolves all the contradictions of this extremely contradictory age. Rather, it is one of many
philosophical and literary forms, though certainly one
as relevant today as it was then, through which the Age
of Sensibility both expressed and grappled with its repressed but nagging awareness that beneath the "errors
which are salutary and *advantageous*" still waits the
"pestilence from the pit."

1

Traditional Misanthropy and the Man of Feeling

The Ambiguity of the Timon Archetype

Benevolent misanthropy emerged in the eighteenth century primarily as a response to problems raised by the benevolist philosophy of man. But, as the following discussion points out, the possibility of reinterpretation is in fact latent in the traditional image of misanthropy as a moral evil involving complete rejection of society and the harboring of malevolent feelings towards all mankind. This image of misanthropy became firmly established through the great Timon figures of literature.[1] According to Plutarch, the comedians of Greek Old and Middle Comedy mocked the supposedly real Timon of Athens with gusto, "calling him a vyper, and malicious unto mankind, to shunne all other mens companies."[2] Lucian's comic presentation of Timon, one of the earliest detailed treatments, emphasizes the antisocial and malevolent characteristics attributed to the real misanthrope. His Timon flees society, snarling, "I hate all alike, both gods and men.... I should be content if I could bring sorrow to the whole world, young and old alike." The god Hermes, however, quietly satirizes Timon's sweeping malice when he replies, "Don't say that, my friend; they do not all deserve sorrow."[3]

Shakespeare's Timon, Molière's Alceste, Wycherley's Manly, and Swift's Gulliver offered the Renaissance and early eighteenth century even more amplified versions of the archetype. For sheer malevolence, perhaps, no Timon figure surpasses Shakespeare's version.[4] His Timon would see all human values completely destroyed:

4

> Matrons, turn incontinent!
> Obedience fail in children! Slaves_and fools,
> Pluck the grave wrinkled Senate from the bench
> And minister in their steads! To general filths
> Convert o' th' instant, green virginity!
> Do't in your parents' eyes! Bankrupts, hold fast!
> Rather than render back, out with your knives
> And cut your trusters' throats! Bound servants, steal!
> Large-handed robbers your grave masters are
> And pill by law. Maid, to thy master's bed!
> Thy mistress is o' th' brothel. Son of sixteen,
> Pluck the lin'd crutch from thy old limping sire;
> With it beat out his brains! Piety and fear,
> Religion to the gods, peace, justice, truth,
> Domestic awe, night-rest and neighborhood,
> Instruction, manners, mysteries and trades,
> Degrees, observances, customs and laws,
> Decline to your confounding contraries
> And let confusion live!
>
> (IV.i.3-21)

Apemantus' attack on Timon suggests, however, that the
misanthrope is again satirized: "Thou has cast away
thyself, being like thyself,/A madman so long, now a
fool" (IV.iii.220-221). A few lines later Apemantus re-
news his attack in terms of the golden mean: "The middle of humanity thou never knewest, but the extremity
of both ends. When thou wast in thy gilt and thy per-
fume, they mocked thee for too much curiosity. In thy
rags thou know'st none, but art despised for the contrary" (IV.iii.300-304). Timon's indiscriminate hatred
and malice are, perhaps, most completely satirized when
countered with the discriminating justice and equity
asserted in Alcibiades' promise to the senators of Athens: "Descend, and open your uncharged ports./Those
enemies of Timon's and mine own,/Whom you yourselves
shall set out for reproof,/Fall, and no more" (V.iv.35).
The traditional image of misanthropy gained further
currency in the popular Renaissance character books,
where the Timon figure appears sometimes as a full blown
misanthrope and sometimes in the more temperate guise
of a cynic, a blunt man, or a malcontent. In the character books, however, misanthropic personalities are

usually treated as humorists suffering from excessive
melancholy or spleen.[5] Samuel Rowlands satirizes the
cynic in *The Melancholie Knight,* emphasizing his splenetic humor and resulting misanthropy:

> Like discontented *Tymon* in his Cell
> My braines with melancholy humers swell,
> I crosse mine armes at crosses that arise,
> And scoffe blinde *Fortune*, with hat ore mine eyes:
> I bid the world take notice I abhore it,
> Having great *melancholy* reason for it.[6]

Barnaby Rich sees the melancholy cynic as vainly affected, "as if he would have it said, Loe, yonder goes
the melancholy gentleman: see there vertue and wisdome
both despised and neglected."[7] To Bishop Hall the malcontent is a "querulous curre" who speaks nothing but
"Satyres, and libels." He is a slave to envy, Hall argues, and would be a conspirator if fear did not restrain him.[8] Roger Sharpe calls the melancholy cynic or
malcontent a Diogenes mocked, for he "Cals each man
knave he meets, but be it knowne,/That title he doth
give them, is his owne."[9]
 As the above "characters" suggest, although a figure
of ridicule and scorn, the traditional misanthrope was
simultaneously treated as an excellent satirist himself.
There is actually no inherent reason why he should have
been conceived as a satirist, but in R.C. Elliott's
terms, "over the centuries, as the Timon story takes on
its unique form, the convention develops that the misanthrope shall be frantically voluble in expressing his
hatred of man. Whether he is a true 'railer' or not,
the fact is that he rails superbly."[10] From the perspective of the humors, melancholy or spleen might make
a man taciturn part of the time, but eventually he would
give way to railing.[11] A satirical wit, Congreve argued, was natural to the splenetic humorist:

> The saying of humourous things does ot distinguish
> characters, for every person in a comedy may be al-
> lowed to speak them. From a witty man they are ex-
> pected, and even a fool may stumble on 'em by chance.
> Tho' I make a difference betwixt Wit and Humour, yet

I do not think that humourous characters exclude Wit.
No, but the manner of Wit should be adapted to the
Humour. As for instance, a character of splenetic
and peevish Humour should have a satirical Wit. A
jolly and sanguine Humour should have a facetious
Wit. The former should speak positively, the latter
carelessly, for the former observes and shows things
as they are; the latter, rather overlooks Nature and
speaks things as he would have them.[12]

In effect, the traditional misanthrope functioned in
literature, to use Elliott's terms again, as a "satirist satirized" and is closely associated with one of the
mainstreams in formal satire.

The traditional satirist of formal satire, unlike the
traditional misanthrope, often claims that he is a benevolent moralist out to reform vice, and certainly the
origins of literary satire can be traced to the oral
tradition of Diogenes and to the Diatribes of Cynic
moralists like Bion and Menippus.[13] Diogenes Laertius
records that Diogenes the moralist was famous throughout Greece for his vituperative and scurrilous speech:
"He was great at pouring scorn on his contemporaries
.... He would continually say that for the conduct of
life we need right reason or a halter."[14] The Cynic
moralists undoubtedly provided satirists a precedent
for attributing moral purpose to their exposures of vice
and for creating the satiric spokesman of the *vir bonus*,
the ironist, or the public defender.[15] Roman and Renaissance critics certainly insisted that satire demonstrate a clear moral purpose. Roman critical theory ap-
proved the type of humor exemplified in the Old Comedy
and *chreias* of Greece and in the Latin Plays of Plautus
because such humor presumably subjected laughter to the
restraint of reason and gave it moral direction. Unrestrained, coarse, and obscene humor, on the other hand,
was severely condemned, because it seemed to prompt
laughter merely for laughter's sake and lacked any dis-
cernible moral intent.[16] Renaissance satiric theory
claimed this same moral concern: "...practically every
critic and satirist in the Renaissance hammers out the
same monotonous theme—that satire exists only as the
fearsome Nemesis of vice."[17]

Unfortunately, however, that very freedom of speech, which Diogenes claimed is the most beautiful thing in the world and which is necessary if satire is to be effective, tends to undermine the moral purpose asserted by the satirist and to cast doubt on the reality of his benevolence. The Roman movement from the grand style to the plain style of satiric utterance is a well-known example of the attempt to remove this doubt and to confirm the moral purpose of the satirist. The literary circle about Scipio urged the ironic or Socratic manner of satire over the Juvenalian, with its *carmen maledictum ad vitia hominum carpendum*.[18] If the satirist feels the need to show anger at the vices of men, argues Paneatius, the critic of the coterie, he must also "show that this anger is designed to effect a reform in the character of the person thus reproved; real anger must be far from us."[19] Ironically, however, all the critical theory and satiric apologia seem only to increase the suspicion that the satirist may not be benevolent at all, that in reality he may be little more than a misanthrope in disguise.

The history of formal satire in fact encourages such a suspicion, for traditional satire, like traditional misanthropy, also uses the satirist satirized. Satirists have often created satiric spokesmen who, while their vision of human evil may be just, admit that their own moral indignation is merely a mask hiding many of the vices they are lashing, that there is a vast gulf between their private and public lives.[20] Cicero noted that satire had a tendency to fall into this ironic mode,[21] and the tendency was reinforced by the long confusion of the satiric spokesman with the satyr of the Greek satyr-plays and, in England, by a native tradition of cruel, even ferocious, satire.[22] Alvin Kernan and others have demonstrated that throughout the Renaissance, especially in England, satirists, although invoking Roman precedent, usually failed to see their alleged model as a well-wrought artistic structure. Using the dialogue of a satiric spokesman and adversarius, the Roman model normally exposed a single vice and advocated its opposite either directly or by implication. They instead focused on the intention of satire, treating it primarily as the utterance of a satyr-satirist who, in the process of a rambling attack on many vices, often revealed that the cracking of his satiric lash was prompted by some of the vices under attack—anger, rage, malice, envy, lechery, sadism.[23]

The ironic satirist satirized convention provides some very significant effects. The attacks on human vice expose moral evil in society, but because the satiric perspective widens to include the satiric spokesman himself the satirist satirized convention finally suggests that all men are guilty of evil. In the background, especially during the Renaissance, are analogues of the Pauline assertion that "all have sinned, and fall short of the glory of God" (Rom. 3:23). Certainly St. Paul speaks ironically through the cry of Shakespeare's Timon, "There's nothing level in our cursed natures/But direct villainy" (IV.iii.19–20). The cry, of course, damns Timon himself, for in the widened perspective of the satire Timon is as guilty of evil as those he attacks. This emphasis on the universality of human evil in effect shifts the focus from the individual's capacity for virtue (the ostensible intent of the satire) to his capacity for vice, tending to project evil primarily as individual vice threatening the moral and physical welfare of society. The ultimate satiric voice, that is, the voice behind the satiric spokesman, is the voice of "ideal society" castigating its aberrant individuals, including the satiric spokesman.

The traditional misanthrope in essence puts dramatic flesh on the satirized spokesman of formal satire. His malevolence and rejection of society, not characteristics necessarily inherent in a concept of misanthropy, in fact, reflect the ironic mode of the satirist satirized. These characteristics developed almost inevitably from the view that misanthropy derived not from moral indignation but from major vices the misanthrope attributed to others—especially pride and self-love. Misanthropy was considered a form of disillusionment engendered in an honest man whose pride and self-love are wounded when, believing the world is filled with men as honest as himself, he discovers instead that his honesty is treated with ingratitude and indifference. This psychology of the misanthrope is already assumed in the statement on misanthropy Socrates offers in the

Phaedo, perhaps the earliest extended reference to misanthropy in Western literature.

> Misanthropy arises out of the too great confidence of
> inexperience;—you trust a man and think him alto-
> gether true and sound and faithful, and then in a
> little while he turns out to be false and knavish;
> and then another, and when this has happened several
> times to a man, especially when it happens among
> those whom he deems to be his most trusted and fa-
> miliar friends, after many disappointments he at last
> hates all men, and believes that no one has any good
> in him at all.... Is it not obvious that such a one
> was attempting to deal with other men before he had
> acquired the art of human relationships? This art
> would have taught him the true state of the case,
> that few are the good and few the evil, and that the
> great majority are in the interval between them.[24]

Socrates here glosses over the evil of those who have
betrayed the misanthrope in order to focus on the overweening self-sufficiency that he thinks underlies the
misanthrope's initial failure to discover what the world
is really like. Implicitly Socrates accuses the misanthrope of wounded self-love, a moral failing that is
very much present in the great literary presentations.[25]
The accusation becomes quite explicit when Socrates,
Timon, and Alcibiades hold an imaginary discussion in
one of Archbishop Fenelon's *Dialogues of the Dead*.[26]

"That Severity, that Impatience at other Men's Vices,"
says Socrates to Timon, "proceeds from a self-love,
which grows thus impatient, when we cannot mould their
Minds just as we please" (p. 195). Fenelon points out
further that the generosity for which the misanthrope
in the Timon stories is famous before he meets ingratitude and indifference is itself a mode of self-love,
at bottom little more than a bid for the acknowledgment
of his worth. Again Socrates states the case: "Do you
know what 'tis that hinders you from loving wicked Men?
'Tis not your Virtue, but the Imperfection of your Virtue: An imperfect Virtue sinks under the weight of
other Men's Imperfections. Our Self-love hinders us
from always bearing with what is so contrary to our own
Taste and Manners. We are angry with the Ungrateful,

because through a Principle of Self-love we want our
Favours to be acknowledg'd" (pp. 197-198). The self-
love supposedly motivating Timon's famed generosity is
brilliantly revealed in the generous purpose Gulliver
attributes to the publication of his travels: "I am not
a little pleased that this Work of mine can possibly
meet with no Censurers.... I write for the noblest End,
to inform and instruct Mankind, over whom I may, without Breach of Modesty, pretend to some Superiority....
I hope, I may with Justice pronounce myself an Author
perfectly blameless...."[27] Gulliver's pride and self-
love, however, are deeply wounded, for, as he complains
to his cousin Sympson, "instead of seeing a full Stop
put to all Abuses and Corruptions, at least in this little Island, as I had Reason to expect: Behold, after
above six months Warning, I cannot learn that my Book
hath produced one single Effect according to mine Intentions...."[28]

The traditional misanthrope doubtless functions in literature as a satirist satirized, but, paradoxically, in
the great literary presentations at least, he is far
more ambiguous a person than the terms of the satirist
satirized convention suggest. If the misanthrope is
guilty of great vices—malevolence, rejection of society, wounded self-love—these vices, in turn, are viewed
as the warping of a basically magnanimous and noble soul.
In the Timon stories, these virtues are usually mani-
fested in the generosity Timon displays before his conversion to misanthropy. In terms of the total literary contexts, this generosity must finally be regarded
as prodigality, but, nevertheless, in Lucian the underlying integrity of character wins and retains the admiration of the gods as it does the admiration of Alcibiades in Shakespeare. The final lines of Shakespeare's play, spoken by Alcibiades, recall that the
dead misanthrope was "noble Timon" (V.iv.80). In the
background of the Timon stories lurks the faint suggestion that the ultimate voice behind the satirist satirized may not be the voice of "ideal society" but of the
complacent, self-serving society indicted by the misanthrope, that the vices attributed to the traditional
misanthrope may, perhaps, be merely the self-defensive
mud-slinging of this indicted society.[29]

The moral ambiguity of the Timon archetype increases
in the updated versions represented by Wycherley's Manly and Molière's Alceste. Rose Zimbardo has clearly
demonstrated that the plot of *The Plain Dealer* follows,
in dramatic form, the Roman model of formal satire and
the satirist satirized convention in the character of
Manly.[30] The rudimentary adversarius traits suggested
in Hermes, Alcibiades, and even Apemantus are fully developed in the character of Freeman. Manly is not a
complete misanthrope in that he admits the existence of
virtue in a few individuals, but he is both a satirist
and an object of satire. As a satirist he opposes dishonesty in any form and advocates absolute "plain dealing," which for Manly means hating the majority of men
because they are dishonest, acting with total candor
oneself,and launching almost brutal verbal assaults on
all varieties of deception. As he tells the temporiz-
ing Freeman,"counterfeit honor will not be current with
me: I weigh the man, not his title; 'tis not the king's
stamp can make the metal better or heavier" (I.i.214-
216). Manly cannot "wish well to pimps, flatterers,
detractors, and cowards, stiff nodding knaves, and sup-
ple, pliant, kissing fools" (I.i.274-276), and yet he
sees that, for the most part, these vices constitute
the way of the world. Although at odds with most of the
world, Manly himself quickly becomes the object of satire as his lustful attraction to the faithless Olivia
exposes in him wounded self-love and drags him into a
revoltingly dishonest game of revenge and deceit.

Despite his shocking moral failures, however, the fact
remains that Manly's hatred of the majority of men re-
wards him at the end of the play with the hand of the
devoted Fidelia. Revealing herself as a woman,Fidelia
confesses, in morality play fashion, that she had left
her inheritance to follow Manly, because in "several
public places" she had observed his "actions thoroughly, with admiration"(V.iii.187-190). Indeed, Fidelia's
dogged attachment to Manly keeps admiration for his
brand of "plain dealing" alive even during the course
of his moral decline. In the first act Fidelia tells
Manly, "Fame, the old liar, is believed when she speaks
wonders of you; you cannot be flattered, sir, your merit is unspeakable" (I.i.403-406). Later she asserts,

"There is nothing certain in the world, sir, but my
truth and your courage" (IV.i.198-199).[31]

The moral ambiguity of Manly in *The Plain Dealer* sug-
tests the possibility of favorably reinterpreting traditional misanthropy, and this suggestion in fact exists even more strongly in the play Wycherley presumably used as his model, Molière's *The Misanthrope*.[32]
Like Manly, Alceste is a satirist satirized,but at the
very beginning of the play he also claims to be a complete misanthrope:

>   All are corrupt; there's nothing to be seen
>   In court or town but aggravates my spleen.
>   I fall into deep gloom and melancholy
>   When I survey the scene of human folly,
>   Finding on every hand base flattery,
>   Injustice, fraud, self-interest, treachery....
>   Ah, it's too much; mankind has grown so base,
>   I mean to break with the whole human race.
>   (I.i.p. 20)

Philinte, Alceste's adversarius, like Hermes, quietly
satirizes Alceste's sweeping condemnation: "Must all
poor human creatures be embraced/Without distinction,
by your vast distaste?/Even in these bad times, there
are surely a few..." (I.i.p.21). "No, I include all
men in one dim view" (I.i.p.22), he insists and, then,
in a few lines reveals that his own misanthropy derives
from the disillusionment of wounded self-love. "Notice,"
he cries, "how tolerant people choose to be/Toward that
bold rascal who's at law with me" (I.i.p.22). Alceste's
self-love is almost heroic: he thinks that the loss of
his case will be an evil committed "before the universe"
itself (I.i.p. 26);he rejects praise because it cannot
distinguish him, for "This fawning age has praise for
everyone," and "every lackey's on the honors list" (III.
vii.p.97); he even treats Célimène's assumed deception
of him as a cosmic event: "Madam, I've had a mortal,
mortal blow./If Chaos repossessed the universe,/I swear
I'd not be shaken any worse" (IV.ii.p. 107).

Despite his inordinate self-love, Alceste is clearly
to be admired in part. Unlike Manly, he never stoops
to lecherous revenge on the woman he loves nor does he
ever resort to games of dishonesty and deceit with others. He also elicits the open admiration of characters

in the play who are basically decent, especially Eliante. Eliante recognizes Alceste's faults,but his character remains worthy of praise:

> His conduct has been very singular lately;
> Still, I confess that I respect him greatly.
> The honesty in which he takes such pride
> Has—to my mind—its noble, heroic side.
> In this false age, such candor seems outrageous;
> But I could wish that it were more contagious.
>
> (IV.i.p. 104)

Moreover, Alceste's misanthropy is also quite modified.
Despite his claim of all-inclusive hatred, Alceste obviously excepts in practice Eliante, Célimène, and
Philinte. Also, though his misanthropy is a mask for
wounded self-love, it definitely excludes malevolence.
It is impossible to imagine him speaking to Célimène as
Manly speaks to Olivia: "...may the curse of loving
play attend your sordid covetousness, and fortune cheat
you, by trusting to her, as you have cheated me; the
curse of pride,or a good reputation,fall on your lust;
the curse of affectation on your beauty;...and the curse
of scorn, jealousy, or despair on your love; and then
the curse of loving on!" (II.i.928-936). Finally, Alceste does not actually reject society until the very
end of the play, and even then hope exists that Eliante
and Philinte can reconcile him with society again.
Molière's treatment of Alceste, in effect, encourages
a favorable reinterpretation of traditional misanthropy, and that favorable reinterpretation occurred in
England as benevolent misanthropy. The intellectual resources for developing the new tradition were provided
by the benevolist philosophy of man, which, arising at
the Restoration, came almost to dominate English moral
thought during the Age of Sensibility.

The Man of Feeling as Natural Man

The idea that misanthropy could be informed by benevolence instead of malevolence was sparked during the
course of the eighteenth century in part by that mode
of comedy Stuart Tave has defined as "amiable humor."[33]
Where the humors were traditionally considered "follies

and vices to be lashed,"[34] they gradually became detached from morality and transformed through the influence of Benevolism into amiable eccentricities grafted onto essentially benevolent souls. This change in attitude towards the humors certainly affected misanthropy. Hume asserts in the *Enquiry Concerning the Principles of Morals* that Timon of Athens was probably "denominated the manhater" less because of any "inveterate hatred" than because of "his affected spleen."[35] Amiable humor played a large role in eighteenth-century English thought, and the English were considered, both by themselves and other nations, to be prone to humorous eccentricity in general and to the humor of misanthropy in particular.[36] When Voltaire returned from England in 1726, he wrote a comparison of English and French tastes in comedy, claiming that Molière's *Tartuffe* was a failure on the English stage: "In order to have had false piety, it would have been necessary to have had true piety.... The philosophy, the liberty, and the climate [of England] all lead to misanthropy: London, which has no Tartuffes, is full of Timons" (my translation).[37]

The comedy of amiable humor certainly assisted the growth of benevolent misanthropy, but its energy was expended on such varieties of eccentricity that it could hardly have supplied the impetus necessary for distinguishing benevolent misanthropy as a psychological phenomenon of widespread interest and concern. This impetus came primarily, I think, from the man of feeling that Benevolism thrust into the forefront of moral and literary thought.[38] Whether enunciated by Latitudinarian divines or by secular moralists like Shaftesbury and Hutcheson, Benevolism maintained that virtue consists in benevolence, that the feelings of man are so constituted that he is "naturally" inclined to act benevolently, and that acting benevolently is rewarded with pleasure. In the words of Hutcheson, "Benevolence is our *greatest Happiness*."[39] Benevolism projected the man of feeling as an ideal all men could supposedly realize with ease, for the man of feeling was simply natural man.

Moreover, if the man of feeling was natural man, then society, Benevolism contended, in opposition to Hobbes and Mandeville, represents the natural state in which

benevolent feelings can be expressed. According to
Hume, the presocial, warlike state of nature postulated
by Hobbes is a "*philosophical* fiction" corresponding to
the "*poetical* fiction" of literature's golden age, for
"Men are necessarily born in a family-society, at least;
and are trained up by their parents to some rule of conduct and behaviour."[40] Shaftesbury went even further
than Hume, identifying society as the natural effect of
the benevolent feelings in action:

> If eating and drinking be natural, herding is so
> too. If any appetite or sense be natural, the
> sense of fellowship is the same. If there be any-
> thing of nature in that affection which is be-
> tween the sexes, the affection is certainly as
> natural towards the consequent offspring; and so
> again between the offspring themselves, as kindred
> and companions, bred under the same discipline and
> economy. And thus a clan or tribe is gradually
> formed; a public is recognised; and besides the
> pleasure found in social entertainment, language,
> and discourse, there is so apparent a necessity for
> continuing this good correspondency and union,
> that to have no sense or feeling of this kind, no
> love of country, community, or anything in common,
> would be the same as to be insensible even of the
> plainest means of self-preservation, and most nec-
> essary condition of self-enjoyment.[41]

The benevolist theory of man's "natural" or "radical"
goodness is usually thought to be opposed to the orthodox Christian doctrine of Original Sin. Opposed to the
Calvinist doctrine of Total Depravity it certainly is;
but, except for the worldly happiness it attributes to
virtue, Benevolism possesses quite orthodox roots and
can in fact be viewed as the reemergence of an ancient
mode of Christian thought emphasized in the evangelical
commandment of love and in the writings of the early
Church Fathers. St. Basil's *Long Rules*, for example,
insist that the "germ" of charity is innate and that
man is by nature a social creature with natural obligations of charity.[42] Even Augustine, with all his pessimism about human nature unaided by grace, granted the
potentiality of natural goodness. In replying to Pe-
lagius, Augustine argued that "we do not deny that hu-

man nature may be without sin; nor ought we by any means to refuse to it the power of perfectibility, since we admit its capacity for progress." Augustine's point was that *in fact* a blameless man never existed, but as far as he could judge, "no great error is made, and certainly not a dangerous one, when a man indulges such an opinion, carried away by a certain benevolent feeling."[43]

The most eloquent and thorough exposition of the benevolist tradition in early Christianity is found in Origen and Clement of Alexandria. The entire extant works of Clement in particular read like a handbook to Latitudinarian theology. His famous *Pedagogus*, for example, reduces the essentials of Christianity to "The Philanthropy of the Instructor [Christ]" and to the duty of Christians to imitate this philanthropy. In the *Miscellanies* or *Stromata*, Clement devotes a chapter to expounding the thesis that men become true Christians by perfecting their benevolence, for the true Christian "is an imitator of God, especially in Beneficence."[44] The Latitudinarian divines carry on this early Christian tradition of Benevolism when, like Archbishop Tillotson, they preach that while "there is a great Degeneracy and Corruption of human Nature, from what it was originally framed when it came out of God's Hands," nevertheless, "this Degeneracy is not total. For tho our Faculties be much weakened and disordered, yet they are not destroyed nor wholly perverted." Education and God's grace can develop man's inclination to benevolence with "great ease to great Perfection."[45] In like manner, secular moralists are not necessarily unorthodox Christians when, like Shaftesbury, they argue, "A good creature is such a one as by the natural temper or bent of his affections is carried primarily and immediately ...to good and against ill," or, "When in general all the affections or passions are suited to the public good, or good of the species,... then is the natural temper entirely good."[46]

Benevolism, however, whatever its relation to Christian orthodoxy, by claiming that the man of feeling was natural man, had a very practical end in view: it sought to offer a compelling incentive to the practice of virtue. Sterne, for example, claims that thinking well of

human nature is better than thinking ill of it, because
"'tis one step toward acting well, to think worthily of
our nature; and, as in common life, the way to make a
man honest, is, to suppose him so, and trust him as
such."[47] Archbishop Secker's first Charge to the diocese of Canterbury (1758) illuminates this aspect of
Benevolism, for it laments the failure of the clergy to
inculcate the Church's theological doctrines but explains this failure on the grounds that preaching benevolence had seemed more important.

> The truth, I fear, is that many, if not most of us,
> have dwelt too little on these Doctrines in our
> Sermons: by no means, in general, from disbeliev-
> ing or slighting them; but partly from, that for-
> merly they had been inculcated beyond their Pro-
> portion, and even to the Disparagement of Christian
> Obedience; partly from fancying them so generally
> received and remembered, that little needs to be
> said, but on social Obligations....[48]

Secker is not here "whitewashing" the clergy, for his
1738 Charge to the diocese of Oxford shows how sincere-
ly he had once believed in the necessity of preaching
the "social Obligations": "No controversies, however
needful, must be suffered to divert our attention from
what is of all things the most needful, the Study of
Practical Religion, and the common Duties of Life.
These are the things, which Mankind are most apt to fail
in, and most concerned not to fail in: and therefore
spending much Time upon them, obtaining a thorough Insight into them, and having a deep Sense of them, is
the very Foundation of doing good to others and to our
Souls."[49]

 Belief in the practical moral incentive of Benevolism
was very widespread, as is suggested by the controversy
that arose in the *Gentlemen's Magazine* over Whitefield's
resuscitation of the Calvinist doctrine of Total Depravity. The argument carried over into several issues,
but the essential case for Benevolism is presented by
"Publicola" in the issue for June 1751:

> I readily acknowledge that men being abandoned to
> vicious practices become so forgetful of God, and

act so contrary to reason, that they are like brute beasts, which have no understanding; and we have sufficient cause at this time to complain of the great corruption of mankind. And if Mr. *W——field* had only arraigned the vices of men, and shewn them enemies to God as acting contrary to their reason and his laws, in following their sensual pleasures, in their covetousness and all manner of unrighteousness, he would have met with no opposition but from the irrational and vicious. But when these preachers represent human nature, as being sunk into such depravity by the fall of *Adam*, that vice is its natural and necessary production, when they assert inbred sin, and the absolute incapacity of men, either from reason or will, to do any good, according to the notions of *Austin*, they cast a reproach upon our good creator and his dispensations. (XXI, 274)

In July "Publicola" reentered the controversy, arguing that the doctrine of Total Depravity "was particularly confuted by *Origen* and *Clemens Alexandrinus*" (XXI, 305). He carefully points out that, unlike Benevolism, the Calvinistic doctrine leads to moral decay: "[Such an opinion of human nature as Whitefield's] can never do any good; but will often have bad effects, and drive men into despondency or infidelity....it gives men horrible notions of their creator, it drives them to despair, it prevents their thankfulness, because they cannot thank god [sic] for an evil nature; it furnishes unbelievers with an objection to his goodness; it occasions great contempt for morality" (XXI, 304).

The Man of Feeling in an Unfeeling World

Benevolism unfortunately could, and often did, degenerate into sentimentalism, the belief that because man is "naturally" good he can be converted back to his "natural" state by intensive exposure to benevolence in action. Both moral discourses and literature often succumbed to such sentimentalism by advocating candor, the "virtue" of putting the best possible construction on human actions, and, more importantly, by depicting the man of feeling as an exemplary character to allure mis-

guided men to the pleasures of virtue. Shaftesbury, for
example, in the *Characteristics* urged the use of exemplary characters,[50] and Richardson, perhaps his most
famous supporter, argued for exemplary characters both
in the practice of his novels and in his preachments.
According to Richardson, "Lessons of morality and dis-
interestedness, given by Example are far more effica-
cious than those endeavoured to be inculcated by pre-
cept," and again, "the Example of a beneficient spirit,
gracefully exerted, will awaken in others a capacity
to enjoy the true pleasure that arises from benevolent
action."[51] Sir Charles Grandison, Richardson informs
the reader in the concluding note to the novel, is "in
the general tenor of his principles and conduct, (though
exerted in peculiarities of circumstances that cannot
always be accommodated to particular imitation,) proposed for an example," and Richardson defends his intent
with a long quotation on the value of exemplary characters from Archbishop Tillotson.[52]
  Ironically, however, if Benevolism's claim that the
man of feeling was natural man could lead to sentimentalism, it simultaneously made urgent the problem of how
the man of feeling, exemplary though he might be, could
survive without imposition in society, where, it was almost universally admitted, the majority of men seemed
to live contrary to their nature. "It can serve no good
Purpose," argues Bishop Sherlock, "to give Men a great
Opinion of themselves and of the considerable Figure
they make in the Universe; nor can it be done with
Truth and Justice. Experience, which shews us daily our
own and the Follies of those about us, will be too hard
for Reasonings upon this Foot; and the Mind of Man,
Conscious of its own Defects, will see through the Flattery, which ascribes to it Perfections and Excellences
with which it feels itself to be unacquainted."[53]
Shaftesbury himself asserted the paradox that society,
though the natural state for expressing benevolent feelings, also works against their development. The moral
"sense of right and wrong...being a first principle in
our constitution and make," he argues, "there is no
speculative opinion, persuasion, or belief, which is
capable immediately or directly to exclude or destroy
it. That which is of original and pure nature, nothing

besides contrary habit and custom (a second nature) is
able to displace."[54] This contrary "second nature" is
acquired from society, "from the force of custom and
education in opposition to Nature." In society "marks
are set on men; distinctions formed; opinions decreed
under the severest penalties; antipathies instilled,
and aversions raised in men against the generality of
their own species. So that 'tis hard to find in any
region a human society which has human laws. No wonder
if in such societies 'tis hard to find a man who lives
naturally and as a man."[55]

  Concern for the problem of the man of feeling living
in an unfeeling world appears regularly in nearly every
form of mid and late eighteenth-century discourse,often
emerging in the very midst of arguments attempting to
prove that benevolence is natural to man. William Richardson's analysis of Hamlet's character symbolizes the
ambivalent attitude the man of feeling generated. The
virtuous man of feeling may be natural man and he should
attain worldly happiness, but, Richardson argues,he is
paradoxically unfit for the world as it is; his feeling will be rather "a fountain of bitter suffering,than
of immediate pleasure." Hamlet clearly exemplifies this
thesis: "We love, we almost revere the character of
Hamlet; and grieve for his sufferings. But we must at
the same time confess, that his weaknesses, amiable
weaknesses! are the cause of his disappointments and
early death." Richardson therefore concludes that "the
instruction to be gathered from this delineation is that
persons like Hamlet should retire, or keep aloof, from
situations of difficulty and contention: or endeavour,
if they are forced to contend, to brace their minds, and
acquire such vigour and determination of spirits as
shall arm them against malignity."[56]

  Being armed "against malignity" meant,in moral terms,
that the man of feeling needed to acquire the virtue of
prudence—not expediency or calculated self-interest,
what the schoolmen called "carnal prudence,"[57] but the
ability to discern the evil designs of others and to
exercise benevolence with discrimination. Even the
early eighteenth-century benevolist Francis Hutcheson,
whose works are primarily intended to promote the man
of feeling, pauses nervously to note the need for pru-

dence: "Our Reason can indeed discover certain Bounds, within which we may not only act from *Self-Love*, consistently with the *Good* of the *Whole*, but every Mortal's acting thus within these Bounds for his own *Good*, is absolutely necessary for the *Good* of the *Whole*; and the Want of such *Self-Love* would be *universally perni-cious*."[58] As early as 1694, however, Francis Atterbury, the nonjuring Bishop of Rochester, evidently disturbed at the rapid spread of Benevolism, pointed out the grave dangers surrounding the man of feeling:

> Charity is grafted always on Good-Nature, and a Sweetness of Disposition: which though it be a Temper of Mind very lovely and desireable; yet is it such as, in the Circumstances of our present Imperfect State, hath its Inconveniencies; and is what makes Conversation dangerous in a World, where we are surrounded with Temptations.... It makes us easy and yielding to Common Customs, and re-ceiv'd Opinions; Ready to comply with a thousand things (of which we are not exactly well satis-fied) upon the pure score of good Nature, and be-cause we cannot allow ourselves to be troublesome. And being found and known to be of this easy and complying Temper; this very thing will invite Ill Spirits, and Ill men, to make their attempts upon us.[59]

During the midcentury Fielding became one of the major expounders of prudent benevolence. In his *Essay on the Knowledge of the Characters of Men* he tries to expose hypocrisy and to "arm as well as I can, the honest, un-designing, open-hearted man, who is generally the prey of this monster, against it."[60] In the *Enquiry into the Causes of the Late Increase of Robbers*, Fielding again returned to the man of feeling's need to acquire the virtue of prudence:

> ...as it hath pleased God to permit human socie-ties to be constituted in a different manner [from Plato's Utopia], and knaves to form a great part (a very considerable one, I am afraid) of every community, who are ever lying in wait to destroy and ensnare the honest part of mankind, and to be-tray them by means of their own goodness, it be-

comes the good-natured and tender-hearted man to
be watchful over his own temper; to restrain the
impetuosity of his benevolence, carefully to select
objects of his passion, and not by too unbounded
and indiscriminate an indulgence to give the reins
to a courser which will infallibly carry him into
the ambuscade of the enemy.

Fielding concludes his admonition to the man of feeling
on a Christian note by alluding to Christ's warning that
his disciples be as wise as serpents and as innocent as
doves.[61]

The leading periodical writers of the Age of Sensibility continued Fielding's efforts, keeping the need for
prudent benevolence before the popular mind. Like
Fielding, they feared that unrestrained feeling would
harm the man of feeling, but they also feared it would
harm the cause of benevolence itself. The *Connoisseur*
wrote in 1755: "Generosity is the daughter of good-
nature. She is very fair and lovely, when under the
tuition of judgment and reason; but when she escapes
from her tutors, and acts indiscriminately, according
as her fancy allures her, she subjects herself, like her
mother, to sneer, ridicule, and disdain."[62] The Man of
Feeling himself, Henry Mackenzie, argued incessantly in
the *Mirror* and the *Lounger* for prudent benevolence. He
observed, like the *Connoisseur*, that if the man of feeling were imposed upon, he would hurt the cause of benevolence and encourage mere "drawing-room" feeling.
"In morals, as in religion," he claims in *Lounger*, No.
20, "there are not wanting instances of refined senti-
mentalists, who are content with talking of virtues they
never practice, who pay in words what they owe in actions; or perhaps, what is fully as dangerous, who
open their minds to impressions which never have any
effect upon their conduct...."[63] The primary target of
Mackenzie's attack was the novelists, who, he feared,
were depicting imprudent men of feeling being abused by
the world. Such depictions permitted a fashionably benevolent reading public to languish over the fictional
man of feeling, thus convincing itself of its own virtue, while it retained worldly wisdom enough to avoid
too much feeling in real life. In *Lounger*, No. 77,
Mackenzie argues that "in the tale of woe we savor every
part of the description, whereas in real life we may go

out of our way to avoid a sorrowful or woeful circumstance because it may interfere with our feelings or
inclinations."[64]

There was undoubtedly a literary cult of sensibility
that reveled in the sufferings of abused men of feeling,[65] but to a large extent Mackenzie was unfair to the
novelists. If many indulged in the cult of sensibility,
probably a larger number used the novel either as a vehicle for presenting exemplary characters or for simultaneously praising the man of feeling and teaching him
the need for prudence.[66] Perhaps the bluntest example
of this double theme occurs in the *Benevolent Quixote*.[67]
Squire Thornbourough, the benevolent Quixote, "equally
credulous and generous...discerned not the plans that
were often laid to ensnare him, nor saw the ridicule to
which he was so frequently exposed. Till very lately,
he had known the world by books; and expected more perfection, or at least more sincerity, than he ever found.
A dupe to his own benevolence, he was often obliged to
pay handsomely for interfering in the schemes of others,
though from the best motives, when from the malice of
fortune, or his own want of experience, they turned out
in a different manner from what he hoped" (I, 213-214).
Finally, a benevolent neighbor, Mr. Fitzwilliam, advises
him to restrain his benevolence: "But remember, my
young friend, this last maxim is addressed solely to
yourself, and is only requisite from the peculiar turn
of your character: it is not my general opinion, nor
the advice I would give to the bulk of mankind, whose
cold unfeeling apathy requires a spur to the actions of
benevolence, not a curb to restrain them" (III, 11-12).

Prudence, however, was a dangerous virtue, and, as the
last quotation from the *Benevolent Quixote* indicates, it
was recommended only with reservations. Ever since the
Renaissance the term itself had primarily meant "carnal prudence,"[68] and even true prudence—the discernment of evil designs and the discriminate exercise of
benevolence—it was feared, would easily devolve into
the selfish promotion of one's worldly interests or into an excuse for avoiding benevolence. Hannah More's
once famous verses "Sensibility" concisely express the
fears attending the recommendation of what Eleanor
Hutchens calls the "mixed virtue":

And while Discretion all our views should guide,
Beware, lest secret aims and ends she hide;
Though midst the crowd of virtues, 'tis her part,
Like a firm sentinel, to guard the heart;
Beware, lest Prudence self become unjust,
Who never was deceiv'd, I would not trust;
Prudence must never be suspicion's slave,
The world's wise man is more than half a knave.[69]

With the character of Sir Charles Grandison, Richardson
fell into the trap Hannah More describes.

Sir Charles is supposedly a model of prudent benevolence, and the reader is, indeed, continually reminded
that "A benevolent-minded man may be led into errors
and rashness even by the warmth of his Benevolence," or
that "The good man's charity is not extended indiscriminately to all that ask him." Unfortunately, Sir Charles
displays a balance between prudence and benevolence so
serene and so accompanied by worldly success that his
benevolence looks suspiciously like a coverup for the
crudest form of egoism. Richardson unwittingly implies
this when he claims that "A generous man will be thought
a weak man, if he submits to imposition."[70] Ultimately
Sir Charles seems to be more concerned with his high
opinion of himself than with benevolence, as Harriet
Byron, his future wife, shrewdly notes:

Do you think, my dear, that had he [Sir Charles] been
the first man, he would have been complaisant to his
Eve, as *Milton makes Adam* [So contrary to that part
of his character, which made him accuse the woman to
the Almighty]—To taste the forbidden fruit, because
he would not be separated from her, in her punishment, tho' all *posterity* were to suffer by it?—No;
it is my opinion, that your brother would have had
gallantry enough to his fallen spouse, to have made
him regret her relapse; but that he would have done
his own duty, were it but for the sake of posterity,
and left it to the Almighty, if such had been his
pleasure, to have annihilated the first Eve, and
given him a second.[71]

Richardson's difficulty with Sir Charles indicates
that the man of feeling's moral balance between benevolence and prudence needed to be very delicate, so delicate, in fact, that from a psychological perspective it

appeared almost impossible to achieve. In the process
of learning the need for prudence, the man of feeling,
believing the world was made up of men as benevolent as
himself, seemed more likely to undergo disillusionment
at finding it filled instead with ingratitude and indifference. And even if he achieved the desired balance, the effort required to maintain it could also result in disillusionment. Adam Smith observes in the
Theory of Moral Sentiments:

> When the sense of propriety, when the authority of
> the judge within the breast, can control this ex-
> treme sensibility, that authority must no doubt
> appear very noble and very great. But the ex-
> ertion of it may be too fatiguing—it may have too
> much to do. The individual, by a great effort,
> may behave perfectly well; but the contest between
> the two principles, the warfare within the breast,
> may be too violent to be at all consistent with
> internal tranquility and happiness.[72]

The man of feeling's disillusionment could, of course,
take several forms, ranging from simple melancholy to
the religious melancholy of an Edward Young and the
"Graveyard School" of poets to the suicide of a Wer-
ther.[73]   Misanthropy, however, almost inevitably suggested itself, for the psychological pattern of the man
of feeling's disillusionment clearly recalls that attributed to the traditional misanthrope.

The process of thought that occurred is exemplified in
Henry Mackenzie's *The Man of Feeling* (1771).[74] Walter
Allen points out that the novel is "by implication, a
statement of the case against the world, against society."[75]   But it is also a statement of the case for the
possible psychological inability of the man of feeling
to achieve the balance of benevolence and prudence.
Early in the story Mackenzie indicates the need for this
balance: there "is one ingredient, somewhat necessary
in a man's composition toward happiness, which people of
feeling would do well to acquire: a certain respect for
the follies of mankind" (p. 6). Harley's lack of respect for these follies invariably places him in pain-
ful situations, although both his aunt and a wise beggar have warned him that there is "no doing" with plain

dealing in "this world" (p. 12). Harley dies young, but his death speech sums up the man of feeling's progress towards disillusionment:

> This world, my dear Charles, was a scene in which I never much delighted. I was not formed for the bustle of the busy, nor the dissipation of the gay. ... It was a scene of dissimulation, of restraint, of disappointment.... I have been blessed with a few friends, who redeem my opinion of mankind.... The world is in general selfish, interested, and unthinking, and throws the imputation of romance or melancholy on every temper more susceptible than its own. (pp. 90-91)

As Harley himself suggests, his disillusionment has taken the form primarily of simple melancholy. Misanthropy, however, is hovering nearby. A visit to Harley's grave, his friend assures the reader, "is worth a thousand homilies; every noble feeling rises within me! every beat of my heart awakens a virtue!—but it will make you hate the world—No: there is such an air of tenderness around, that I can hate nothing; but, as to the world—I pity the men of it" (p. 93).

If Mackenzie was reluctant to draw the conclusion his process of thought implied, John Home, writing in *Mirror*, No. 39 (1779), is typical of those who did. "When a man of acknowledged honour and abilities, not unconscious of his worth," claims Home, "and possessed of those delicate feelings I have mentioned, sees himself set aside, and obliged to give way to the worthless and contemptible, whose vices are sometimes the means of their promotion, he is too apt to yield to disgust or despair; that sensibility which, with better fortune, and placed in a more favourable situation, would have afforded him the most elegant pleasures, made him the delight of his friends, and an honour to his country, is in danger of changing into a morose and surly misanthrope, discontented with himself, the world, and all its enjoyments."[76] The terms "not unconscious of his worth" and "sees himself set aside" suggest that wounded self-love may even play a part in the man of feeling's disillusionment. But it can only play a minor part, for Home carefully traces the primary cause of disillusionment to benevolent feelings or sensibility

disappointed by the evil ways of the world. The man of
feeling's misanthropy then will necessarily be informed
with benevolence. It will constitute in fact a defense
mechanism or psychological shield protecting him from
undesired imposition, his armor "against malignity." In
Kierkegaard's existential terms, it will be the "incognito" of feeling in an unfeeling world.[77]

2

The Incognito of Feeling

The concept of benevolent misanthropy followed two separate lines of development during the eighteenth century: it was projected as a subject for discursive and
imaginative exposition, and it was dramatized in the
form of a benevolent misanthrope character type whose
literary role is that of a satirist. Both lines of development took place simultaneously, so their relationship is one of mutual influence rather than of cause
and effect. The former line of development, however,
provides a kind of theoretical context for the satiric
character type and will be considered separately in this
chapter. Since the large body of discursive and imaginative writing devoted to the exposition of benevolent
misanthropy remains for the most part little known, my
treatment will rely heavily on extensive quotation and,
to show the evolution of the concept, will proceed in a
primarily chronological fashion.

In the *Inquiry Concerning Virtue*, published in the
Characteristics (1711),Shaftesbury condemns misanthropy as an "unnatural" passion, arguing that "whoever is
unsociable, and voluntarily shuns society or commerce
with the world, must of necessity be morose and ill-
natured."[1] But in the *Essay on the Freedom of Wit and
Humour*, also published in the *Characteristics*, Shaftesbury claims that many apparently misanthropic personalities may actually be motivated by a love of mankind.
"Imposters," he points out, "naturally speak the best
of human nature, that they may the easier abuse it.

These gentlemen, on the contrary, speak the worst; and had rather they themselves should be censured with the rest, than that a few should by imposture prevail on the many." Shaftesbury conducts his defense in terms that echo Epictetus' famous description of the "true" cynic:

> ...the gentlemen for whom I am apologising cannot however be called hypocrites. They speak as ill of themselves as they possibly can. If they have hard thoughts of human nature, 'tis proof still of their humanity that they give such warning to the world. If they represent men by nature treacherous and wild, 'tis out of care for mankind, lest by being too tame and trusting, they should easily be caught.[2]

Shaftesbury, of course, believes that men can ultimately rise to the universal philanthropy Theocles envisions in the *Moralists*; but Philocles defends, in Swiftian terms, the love of the individual: "I told Theocles... that I feared I should never make a good friend or lover after his way. As for plain natural love of one single person in either sex, I could compass it, I thought, well enough; but this complex, universal sort was beyond my reach. I could love the individual, but not the species."[3]

The idea that misanthropy may really be an incognito of feeling received important support from David Hume in his essay "Of the Dignity or Meanness of Human Nature," published in 1741, the same year Swift's famous letter on misanthropy was published. Hume characteristically thinks an exposure of human evil is detrimental to the cause of virtue, and yet he argues, "I am far from thinking, that all those, who have depreciated our species, have been enemies to virtue, and have exposed the frailties of their fellow creatures with any bad intention. On the contrary, I am sensible that a delicate sense of morals, especially when attended with a splenetic temper [originally, 'with somewhat of the *Misanthrope*'], is apt to give a man a disgust of the world, and to make him consider the common course of human affairs with too much indignation."[4]

By midcentury the concept of benevolent misanthropy

was gaining increasing momentum. In 1753 Elizabeth Montagu, "Queen of the Blues," wrote a description of Molière's Alceste that reflects the growing reinterpretation of traditional misanthropy:

> When virtue and wisdom live out of the world, they grow delicate, but it is too severe to call that moroseness; and, perhaps, they lose something of their purity, when they mix with the crowd, and abate in strength, as they improve in flexibility. There is a limit, and a short one too, beyond which human virtue cannot go; a hair's breath beyond the line, and it is vice.... The character [Alceste] being so entirely kept up, and the error, though every where visible, no where monstrous.... right in principle, wrong only in excess, you cannot hate him when he is unpleasant, nor despise him when he is absurd. When the groundwork of a character is virtuous, whatever fantastic forms or uncouth figures may be wrought upon it, it cannot appear absolutely odious or ridiculous.[5]

The tone of Montagu's letter indicates a movement away from holding the misanthrope up to scorn and ridicule and towards a sympathetic willingness to see virtue behind his apparent rejection of man. Elizabeth Montagu, in fact, anticipated by five years the celebrated defense of Alceste that Rousseau wrote in his "Letter to M. D'Alembert on the Theatre" (1758).[6]

Rousseau admits that Alceste is presented as a "ridiculous figure" (p. 37), but this fact only condemns Molière. Distinctions must be made, for "This name, misanthrope, must not give the false impression that the one who bears it is the enemy of humankind" (p. 37). A conscious enemy of mankind would be a monster and, if he could exist, would cause horror, not laughter (p. 37). Alceste is not an enemy of mankind, but a "good man who detests the morals [manners] of his age and the viciousness of his contemporaries; who, precisely because he loves his fellow creatures, hates in them the evils they do to one another and the vices of which these evils are the product. If he were less touched by the errors of humanity, if he suffered less from indignation at the iniquities he sees, would he be more humane himself?"

(p. 37). Rousseau thus argues that Alceste, the "true" misanthrope, is not the enemy of men but of their vices; in fact, "If there were neither knaves nor flatterers, he would love all humankind" (p. 38). As a result of this interpretation, Rousseau asserts that all good men must be misanthropes and that those who do not think like Alceste are unconsciously the enemies of mankind, the "real" misanthropes (p. 38). Whether or not Rousseau intended it, these sentiments certainly echo Swift, as does his conclusion that "true" misanthropy will be found only in the best of men: "The character of the misanthrope is not at the poet's disposal; it is determined by the nature of his dominant passion. This passion is a violent hatred of vice, born from an ardent love of virtue and soured by the continual spectacle of man's viciousness. It is, then, only a great and noble soul which is susceptible to it" (p. 39).

Rousseau does not mean, however, that the "true" misanthrope remains incapable of moral failures. Quite the contrary. Passion often renders "him weak, unjust, and unreasonable"; he even, at times, can "spy out the hidden motives of others' action with a secret pleasure at finding the corruption of their hearts"; small wrongs often fill him with anger, and by baiting him, "a clever villain" can even make "him appear to be a villain himself" (p. 40). But Rousseau does mean that wounded pride or self-love will be mostly absent from the "true" misanthrope:

> Let him be enraged at every disorder at which he is only a witness, for this is only one more detail in the picture; but make him cold in what directly concerns himself. For, having declared war on the vicious, he must expect that they in turn will declare it on him. If he had not foreseen the harm that his frankness would do him, it would be a folly and not a virtue. If a false woman betray him, unworthy friends dishonour him, or weak friends abandon him, he must suffer it without a murmur. He knows men. (p. 40)

Molière could have presented this aspect of the misanthrope by placing Philinte's "actions and those of Alceste in apparent opposition with their principles and

in perfect conformity with their characters. I mean
that the misanthrope should have always been furious
against public vices and always tranquil about the personal viciousness of which he was the victim. On the
other hand, the philosopher Philinte ought to have seen
all the disorders of society with a stoical phlegm and
set himself in a fury at the slightest harm directed
personally to himself" (p. 41).

The question of misanthropy was certainly very much in
the air by midcentury, but the distinctions emerging
were not always clear, as the essay "Of Misanthropy" in
the *Library* for 1761 indicates.[7] This essay argues, like
Plato, that "The character of the far greater part of
mankind consists in a mediocrity, somewhat inclined on
this side and the other, towards vice, or virtue" (I,
360). Because this is the way human nature seems to be,
the writer of the essay expects it to be reflected in
literature and moral discourse:

> I never wonder to find men weak, inconstant, rising
> above themselves in speculation, falling beneath in
> practice, acting their parts unequally, different
> from each other, and from themselves. This is na-
> ture; thus it hath been, and thus it will be, in
> every business where human creatures are the agents
> and contrivers: it is the perfect hero, the fault-
> less saint, the unchecked villain, which raises my
> surprise.... (I, 361)

Since the "nature and conduct of men do not permit us
to think the best of them....they equally forbid us to
think the worst" (I, 363). Therefore, the essay claims,
the misanthrope, "He who hates the name of man, is himself the first monster in nature, who quarrels not with
a few individuals, but with a whole species; who cuts
himself off from the friendship and confidence of all,
an enemy to good and bad, jealous both of his friends
and foes, and a voluntary outcast from society" (I, 364).

The *Library* thus still thinks of misanthropy in terms
of the traditional Timon figure, but in the same year
(1761) Goldsmith published the *Citizen of the World* (a
collection of essays originally published in the *Public
Ledger*), which included an essay on misanthropy that
reflects the growing reinterpretation.[8] Goldsmith,
also drawing on the Timon story, has the misanthrope

withdraw from society, but he carefully removes two of
the traditional misanthrope's major vices: wounded
pride and malicious intentions towards mankind. "It has
been said," claims Goldsmith, "that he who retires to
solitude, is either a beast or an angel; the censure is
too severe, and the praise unmerited; the discontented
being, who retires from society, is generally some good
natured man, who has begun life without experience, and
knew not how to gain it in his intercourse with mankind"
(II, 279). Goldsmith's interest in reinterpreting traditional misanthropy actually emerged two years before
the *Public Ledger* essay in his oriental tale *Asem* (1759).
Asem is also based on the Timon figure in that he retires from society, but he is also too benevolent to
wish it evil. After he is blessed with a vision of how
dull and uninspiring the world would be if God had created man to be virtuous of necessity, Asem returns to
society, where he hopes to "keep from vice myself, and
pity it in others" (III, 65). In the next chapter we
will see that Goldsmith also dramatized the concept of
benevolent misanthropy in two of his most important
fictional characters.

  Goldsmith's discussion of misanthropy in the *Citizen
of the World* was followed in 1771 by the character
Géronte, which the famous Italian playwright Carlo Goldoni, writing in French, created for his play *Le Bourru
Bienfaisant*. Géronte is basically only a choleric man,
but Goldoni recognizes that a surly exterior may hide a
benevolent interior. "Beneficience," he writes, "is a
virtue of the soul; gruffness is only a fault of tem-
perament; both are compatible in the same person" (my
translation). Goldoni's stress on the constitutional
element of his surly man indicates that he was writing
almost exclusively from the perspective of amiable humor and concentrating on the physically gruff exterior
of the traditional misanthropic personality. He thus
overlooked, for the most part, any deeper implications
inherent in a union of misanthropy and feeling. He did
feel, however, that his character possessed universal
significance and, despite the facts to the contrary,
claimed Géronte as a theatrical creation of his own: "I
had the good fortune to recognize in nature a character
who was new to the stage; a character whom one meets

everywhere, and who nevertheless had escaped the notice
of both ancient and modern authors" (my translation).[9]
  The psychology of benevolent misanthropy received a
carefully articulated statement, and one that clearly
relates the new misanthropy to amiable humor, in the
discussion of Jaques that William Richardson included
in his *Essays on Shakespeare's Dramatic Characters*
(1774).[10] According to Richardson, "The most striking
character in the mind of Jaques...is extreme sensibility. He discovers a heart strongly disposed to compassion, and susceptible of the most tender impressions of
friendship..." (p. 143). Paradoxically, however, Jaques,
"avoiding society, and burying himself in the lonely
forest, seems to act inconsistently with his constitution. He possesses sensibility; sensibility begets
affection; and affection begets the love of society.
But Jaques is unsocial" (p. 144). The paradox is resolved, Richardson argues, if we consider that "the excess and luxuriancy of benevolent dispositions, blight-
ed by unkindness or ingratitude, is the cause that, instead of yielding us fruits of complacency and friendship, they shed bitter drops of misanthropy" (pp. 144-
145).
  Richardson's defense of Jaques is based on a theory of
disrupted ruling passions. "If beneficent affections,
ardent and undisciplined, predominate in our constitution, and govern our opinions," he points out, "we enter into life strongly prepossessed in favour of mankind, and endeavour, by a generous and disinterested
conduct, to render ourselves worthy of their regard"
(p. 145). The man of feeling becomes indignant at injustice, seeks to aid the afflicted, and adopts ardent
friendships without suspicion. "This conduct may, for
a time, be flattered: our fond imaginations may height-
en every trivial act of complacency into a testimony of
unfeigned esteem," so that, continues Richardson, "deceived by delusive appearances, we become still more
credulous and profuse" (p. 146). The time of disillusionment, however, will inevitably come:

  ...the fairy vision will soon vanish: and the nov-
  ice who vainly trusted to the benevolence of mankind, will suddenly find himself alone and desolate,

in the midst of a selfish and deceitful world: like
an enchanted traveller, who imagines he is journey-
ing through a region of delight, till he drinks of
some bitter fountain, and instantly, instead of
flowery fields and meadows, he finds himself destitute and forlorn, amid the horrors of a dreary de-
sart. (p. 146)

As strange as it may at first seem, then, "our benevolent affections, considered merely as principles of action, partaking of the same common nature with other
passions and affections, if their tenor be interrupted,
occasion pain" (p. 148).
 The disruption of the benevolent affections can have
two results, depending on the purity of the affections
themselves. "When the uneasiness arises from the sudden and untoward suspension of our emotions, or from the
disappointment of some ardent affection," Richardson
asserts, "it is of a mild and dejected nature. It may
dispose us to remonstrate, but not to inveigh" (p. 150).
On the other hand, when "ambition, avarice, or vanity
are concerned, our sorrow is acrimonious, and mixed with
anger. If, by trusting to the integrity and beneficence of others, our fortune be diminished...; or if
we be not advanced and honoured agreeably to our desires,
and the idea we had formed of our own desert, we conceive ourselves injured. Injury provokes resentment,
and resentment moves us to retaliate. Accordingly, we
retaliate: we inveigh against mankind..." (p. 151).
 The result of "sorrow excited by repulsed and languish-
ing affection" (p. 152) Richardson calls *melancholy*,
while the result of the "disappointment of selfish appetites" (p. 152) he calls *misanthropy*. "Melancholy," he
argues, "is amiable and benevolent, and wishes mankind
would reform: misanthropy is malignant, and breathes
revenge" (pp. 152-153). Jaques is essentially a benevolent misanthrope, for while he is partially "moved by
a sense of injury and disappointment," melancholy actually rules his mind (p. 153). This "mixture of melancholy and misanthropy in the character of Jaques is more
agreeable to human nature than the representation of
either of the extremes," Richardson claims, "for a complete misanthrope is as uncommon an object as a man who

suffers injury without resentment" (p. 155). Jaques's
benevolent misanthropy makes him an excellent and an
acceptable satirist: "As benevolence and sensibility
are manifest in the temper of Jaques, we are not offend-
ed with his severity. By the oddity of his manner, by
the keenness of his remarks, and shrewdness of his observations, while we are instructed, we are also amused"
(p. 155).

While complete misanthropy is rare in mankind, yet
Shakespeare, Richardson points out, has provided in
Timon of Athens an excellent example of it. Timon "illustrates the consequences of that inconsiderate pro-
fusion which has the appearance of liberality, and is
supposed even by the inconsiderate person himself to
proceed from a generous principle; but which, in reality,
has its chief origin in the love of distinction" (p. 313).
Richardson shrewdly observes that a benevolent man of
feeling continually receives praise and adulation (usually insincere), so that actions that may have been
initially motivated by benevolence can gradually become motivated by "the love of praise and distinction"
(p. 320). This may have been Timon's case; but, in any
event, when we see him, he is entirely ruled by self-
love: "Timon imposes on himself; and while he is really actuated by a selfish passion, fancies himself entirely disinterested" (pp. 330-331). Thus, when he is
rejected by those he had formerly benefited, his resulting misanthropy must be blamed on wounded pride or
self-love.

Richardson's important contribution to the body of
eighteenth-century writing on benevolent misanthropy
was followed in 1775 by *Liberal Opinions; or, The History of Benignus,* a long, rambling novel that Courtney
Melmoth (Samuel Jackson Pratt) offered as his case
against a society that drives the benevolent hero into
misanthropy.[11] The book, however, is not just a satire
against society, as Lois Whitney asserts,[12] but also
against the notion that virtue will be rewarded in this
life, a "liberal opinion" that completely infuriated
the *Monthly* reviewer. Melmoth's appeal to revealed religion's promise of a future life for the experience
of happiness and the reward of virtue in no way ap-
peased the *Monthly* reviewer, who argued that revealed

religion rests on natural religion, and "if it be not
manifest from fact and experience that the general
tendencies of things are favourable to virtue and happiness: *natural religion* is a term without meaning."[13]
The conclusion was obvious.

Melmoth's satire is certainly heavy-handed, but it is
also very effective. Nurtured on the Bible and the
Spectator papers, Benignus enters the world only to
find that "Perhaps no man was ever accoutred with weap-
ons of worse defence, to struggle through the warfare
of life..." (I, 116-117). Benignus finally finds protection from a benevolent rake, Mr. Draper, who eventually dies in his defense, leaving Benignus again at
the mercy of the world. The novel thus becomes a warning for men of feeling. "I have ventured to assert,"
says Benignus, "that, an extreme tender and good mind,
ardently pursuing its propensities, is the most im-
proper mind in the world to produce T e r r e s t r i a l
felicity"(I, 119-120). When asked if goodness is against
one's worldly interest, he replies, "Nine times out of
ten" (I, 121). Continually imposed upon by the unfeeling world, Benignus finally turns misanthrope and, in
the manner of traditional misanthropy, retires from society into the forest. Benignus, however, bears no enmity towards mankind and retains his benevolence, which,
with shrewd irony, Melmoth has him lavish on the beasts
of the forest, the nonrational animals.

The concept of benevolent misanthropy received further
imaginative exposition in 1781 with the short character
sketch of the Senator that William Hayley inserted in
his tedious poem *The Triumph of Temper*.[14] The Senator
appears in Canto IV, in obvious contrast to the "Misanthropic race" (of which Swift is "High-Priest") described in Canto III:

> It chanc'd her Sire among his friends inroll'd
> A wealthy Senator, infirm and old;
> Who, dup'd too early by a generous heart,
> Rashly assum'd a Misanthropic part:
> Tho' peevish fancies would his mind incrust,
> Good-Nature's image lurk'd beneath their rust;
> And gay Serena...
> Would oft the sickness of his soul beguile.
> And teach the sullen humourist to smile.
>
>   (Canto IV, 66-74)

Hayley manages to squeeze into this brief sketch the man
of feeling's psychology of disillusionment, the resort
to misanthropy, and the benevolence that continues even
with the misanthropy.

In 1782 the *Novelist's Magazine* gave wide circulation
to benevolent misanthropy by reprinting a translation
of "The Misanthrope Corrected," one of the "moral tales"
of the French writer Marmontel.[15] Marmontel's purpose
in this moral tale is to show that benevolent misanthropy, at least, is compatible with social intercourse.
All misanthropy is so contrary to human nature, Mar-
montal argues, that "it is a factitious character; a
part which we take up out of whim, and maintain through
habit; but in acting which, the soul is under restraint,
from which we struggle to be delivered" (VI, 219). The
benevolent misanthrope, however, especially needs so
ciety, for "A misanthrope, who is such from virtue,
thinks that he hates men, only because he loves them"
(VI, 219). Alceste is for Marmontel a misanthrope from
virtue, and in the course of the tale he is "corrected"
in the sense that, without changing his hatred of man,
he rejoins society by falling in love with and marrying
the daughter of the benevolent Viscount De Laval.

The body of writing on benevolent misanthropy was significantly increased in 1783 with the publication of
Percival Stockdale's *An Essay on Misanthropy,* which was
inspired by a desire to vindicate Swift from the charge
of misanthropy recently leveled at him in James Harris'
Philological Inquiries.[16] Stockdale seeks "to distinguish between acrimonious declamation and philosophical decision" (p. 8), between what he ultimately calls
"practical" and "speculative" misanthropy. "There are
two kinds of *misanthropy*," Stockdale asserts; "the one
is to be avoided as our seducer to most odious and dangerous errors; as the foe to our dignity, and the bane
of our happiness. The other we ought carefully to
study; and our prudent conduct through life (notwithstanding the taunts of the unthinking, and the expostu-
lations of the good) should be the right and genuine
effects of our diligent speculations" (pp. 8-9). The
practical misanthrope, either "from a naturally sple-
netick disposition, or from a long series of misfortunes, and ill-treatment, which both chagrined, and
soured his mind, rails at human nature, with a child-

ish, or doating petulance, and clamour...and rashly,
or rather madly, pronounces the whole human species, a
race of monsters" (p. 10). The speculative misanthrope,
in contrast, "is as acute, and severe in his observations, as he is gentle and placid in his conduct. He
cannot but be convinced, that the great majority of
mankind are under the fatal domination of vice.... Of
whatever virtues he may be conscious that he is possessed, he is, at the same time, conscious that a noble
pre-eminence in virtue is the inestimable attainment
but of a few" (pp. 10-11).

Speculative or benevolent misanthropy, Stockdale
claims, while serving as a psychological defense against
an unfeeling world, also fosters the spirit of Christian
love:

> This latter Misanthropy will keep us calm and se-
> rene amid the tumults of life. It will arm us com-
> pletely against the selfishness, malignity, and bar-
> barity of mankind: We will not be discomposed; for
> we will not be disappointed. It will secure us es-
> teem, respect, content, and satisfaction; and, how-
> ever paradoxical the assertion may seem, it will
> tend to make us good Christians: It will even
> warm and dilate our hearts with the tenderest and
> most expanded humanity; and it will adorn our con-
> duct with universal and active benevolence. (p. 9)

Stockdale bases his argument for the speculative misanthrope's Christian love on the Swiftian distinction
between loving the individual and loving mankind.
"While the history of the human race, and his own accurate observations, are continually confirming his
Misanthropy, are convincing him, afresh, that mankind,
in the aggregate, are extremely wicked," Stockdale contends, nevertheless, that the speculative misanthrope
is so "impressed with the idea of the weakness of the
human heart; of these powerful temptations to evil,"
that he "feels every emotion of vehemence and practical
hatred to mankind, die within his breast" (pp. 12-13).
Instead of wishing harm to individual men, he is, in
fact, "inclined, to alleviate their calamities by his
good offices" (p. 13); in the final analysis, "Our sage
observer, and reasoner,...reflects, that from the num-

ber of his own select acquaintance, there must be many
worthy individuals in the world; many, relatively to
their absolute numerical amount; though few, in comparison with the infinite number of the bad" (p. 16).
Paradoxically, then, speculative misanthropy with its
love for the individual becomes a practical universal
benevolence: "Thus the very little principle of self-
love is transmuted, and expanded into the warmest sympathy with his fellow-creatures; into universal benevolence; the basest alloy of his nature is exalted, and
purified into gold, by the celestial alchymy of virtue"
(p. 11).

Stockdale's association of speculative misanthropy with
Christianity—he even attributes it to Christ himself—
may seem strange, but it is, in fact, consistent with
the traditional Christian concept of the *person*.   La
Bruyère, in a passage that may have influenced Swift,
suggests the Christian background for loving the individual and hating mankind:

> Nothing is of greater assistance to a man for bear-
> ing quietly the wrongs done to him by relatives and
> friends than his reflections on the vices of human-
> ity....he may dislike mankind in general for having
> no greater respect for virtue; but he finds ex-
> cuses for individuals, and even loves them from
> higher motives, whilst he does his best to require
> himself as little indulgence as possible.[17]

The individual has enjoyed a peculiar honor in Christian thought primarily because of the doctrine of personal salvation. As Gilson suggests, the importance of
"personalism" in Christianity is, perhaps, best summed
up in St. Thomas' statement that "Person signifies what
is most perfect in all nature...."[18] St. Thomas, however, is alluding to the Trinity, so that while he is
praising the uniqueness of the individual person, he is
simultaneously pointing to the paradox that from individual persons in dialogue arises the idea of community and human unity.

The paradox in Christian thought that individual uniqueness implies human community is classically stated by
Emmanuel Mounier:

The unity of the human race is for the first time
fully affirmed and doubly confirmed: every person is created in the image of God, every person
is called to the formation of one immense Body,
mystical and physical, in the charity of Christ.
...Even the conception of the Trinity, emerging
from two centuries of controversy, produces the
astounding idea of a Supreme Being which is an ultimate dialogue between persons,and is of its very
essence the negation of solitude.[19]

In the existential terms of Kierkegaard,the individual
as a Christian can define his uniqueness only through
universal man: "Faith is precisely this paradox, that
the individual as the particular is higher than the universal, is justified over against it,is not subordinate
but superior—yet in such a way, be it observed, that
it is the particular individual who, after he has been
subordinated as the particular to the universal, now
through the universal becomes the individual who as the
particular is superior to the universal, for the fact
that the individual as the particular stands in an absolute relation to the absolute."[20]
Benevolent or "speculative" misanthropy,to use Stockdale's term,is extremely existential and personalistic.
It thus does away with the traditional misanthrope's
rejection of society.   Indeed, it fulfills all the implications of the paradox by envisioning the misanthrope,
because of his love for individuals, remaining in an
evil and hated society for the express purpose of reforming at least some of its members.   The paradox of
individual and universal man,when put in terms of love
and hate, achieves a new significance.   By rejecting
society the Timonian misanthrope demonstrates a hatred
that destroys life itself,for it repudiates not merely
the lifeless abstraction *man*,but the individual men in
whom life and reality exist.   By remaining in society,
the benevolent misanthrope acknowledges the value of
the individual at the same time he reveals the empti-
ness of the abstract universal, man.   The final paradox is that the benevolent misanthrope's hatred is
really an expression of love that,because it is available to all individual men, is ultimately universal in
its intent.

In the late seventeenth century Locke called attention
to the paradoxical Christian relationship of the individual person to the human community when he separated
the concept of person from the body, traditionally
viewed as the principle of individuation.   By making
consciousness the principle of personal identity—not
the body—he seemed to be denying the Christian doctrine
of personal resurrection on the Last Day, or at least
Bishop Butler and other divines thought he was. In any
event, Locke was obliged to add a paragraph to the *Essay
Concerning Human Understanding* clearing up this problem:
"And thus may we be able, without any difficulty, to
conceive the same person at the resurrection, though in
a body not exactly in make or parts the same which he
had here,—the same consciousness going along with the
soul that inhabits it."[21]   And yet the personal salvation of the individual cannot be isolated from the salvation of mankind.   As Mounier points out,   "The conception of a human race with a collective history and
destiny, from which no individual can be separated, is
one of the sovereign ideas of the Fathers of the Church.
In a secularized form, this is the animating principle
of eighteenth-century cosmopolitanism.... [Personalism]
is against every form of racialism or of caste, against
the 'elimination of the abnormal....' " [22]
The Christian overtones in Stockdale's treatment of
benevolent misanthropy ultimately derive from this rich
background of Christian thought.   For the most part,
however, Stockdale and others formulate benevolent
misanthropy in the secular terms of philosophy.   "The
true philosopher," Stockdale writes, "the tenour of
whose mind I have been endeavouring to describe, sees
the forcible and extensive prevalence of vice.... He
knows that the almost infinite majority of mankind, are
wicked, and mischievous.   Therefore, as far as he dis-
likes *them,* by disliking their predominant properties,
he must, undoubtedly, be a speculative *misanthrope*.
From the theory which I have ascribed to him, it is
certainly evident, that compassion, rather than resentment, is a concomitant of his Misanthropy" (p. 17).
The "true philosopher" may even become a satirist, but
his satire is clearly motivated by benevolence: "Thus,
however zealous he may be, with all the means that he

can command, to discourage, and reform, our abuse of
power, our intemperate indulgence in sensual pleasure,
our forgetfulness of benefits received, and the other
moral irregularities which men, every day, commit; he
opposes these evil habits with a generous ardour, but
not with a cynical rancour" (p. 11).

Three years after Stockdale's *Essay,* Lord William
Craig treated the question of benevolent misanthropy
in *Lounger,* No. 91 (1786).[23] Craig argues that "There
is a certain standard of virtue and propriety, which a
man of delicacy is apt to form in his own mind, but
which, in the common events of the world, is rarely to
be met with; there are certain ideas of elevated and
sublime happiness which a man of a highly cultivated
mind has a disposition to indulge, which it is hardly
possible can be realized" (XXXI, 254). When such a man
of delicacy "comes abroad into the world" and finds
"folly where he expected wisdom, falsehood in the room
of honour, coarseness instead of delicacy,and selfishness and insensibility where he had formed high ideas
of generosity and refinement, he is apt to fall under
the dominion of melancholy....Such a man...runs some
risk of contracting a degree of habitual disgust at
mankind, and becoming misanthropical to a certain extent" (XXXI, 254-255).

The misanthropy of a man of feeling, however, will
differ greatly from that of a Timon, Craig claims, for
it will be informed by benevolence:

> It will not...be that species of misanthropy which
> takes delight in the miseries of mankind; on the
> contrary, it will be a feeling of disgust arising
> from disappointed benevolence,mingled with pity and
> compassion for the follies and weaknesses of men.
> I doubt very much if there exists in the world a
> complete *misanthrope,* in the darkest sense of that
> word, a person who takes pleasure in the wretched-
> ness of others....the misanthropy of which I speak
> is of a much softer kind,and borders nearly on the
> highest degree of *philanthropy.* It seems indeed to
> be the child of philanthropy, and to proceed from
> too much sensibility, hurt by disappointment in
> the benevolent and amiable feelings. (XXXI, 255)

Echoing Swift, Craig asserts that this benevolent type
of misanthrope, "though he may think ill of the species,
...will be kind to individuals; he may dislike man, but
will assist John or James" (XXXI, 256).

Craig illustrates his argument from Shakespeare, using
Hamlet, Jaques, and Timon as his examples. The misanthropy of Hamlet and Jaques "proceeds from excess of
tenderness, from too much sensibility to the evils of
the world, and the faults of mankind" (XXXI, 258), but
in the character of Jaques we have "a personage of a
more fixed and systematic melancholy than that of Hamlet" (XXXI, 257). In Jaques "we see a settled and confirmed melancholy, not proceeding from any misfortune
peculiar to himself, but arising from a general feeling of the vanity of the world, and the folly of those
engaged in its pursuits" (XXXI, 257). Timon, in contrast to both Hamlet and Jaques, is far "less amiable";
his misanthropy "is of a much blacker and more savage
nature" (XXXI, 258). Where Hamlet's misanthropy arises
"from a deep sense of the guilt of others" and Jaques's
"from a general impression of the follies and weaknesses
of the world," Timon's "is produced by a selfish sense
of the ingratitude of others to himself. His disgust
at the world, therefore, is not mixed with the same
gentleness and amiable tenderness which are displayed
by the other two; and he possesses as much misanthropy
of the blackest sort as it is possible for human nature
to arrive at. Shakespeare indeed holds him forth as a
person altogether bereft of reason" (XXXI, 258-259).

Craig's essay indicates that as the Age of Sensibility
drew to its close, the term *misanthropy* had almost come
to signify benevolent misanthropy alone. So common-
place in fact was the concept that in his *Philosophy of
the Moral Powers,* while arguing that an excessive refinement of moral sensibility may be "injurious to our
happiness and to our usefulness as members of Society,"
Dugald Stewart casually points to "that peculiar species
of misanthropy which is grafted on a worthy and benevolent heart." The danger of such misanthropy, however
benevolent, he worries, is that it can lead to "solitary
contemplation," which is its "great nurse and cherisher."
Referring his readers to Marmontel's "The Misanthrope
Corrected," Stewart urges "society and business."[24] By

the end of the century, however, it was even possible
to assume that the misanthropy arising from injured
pride or self-love, if the misanthrope was also a man
of feeling,would be benevolent rather than malevolent,
and the German playwright Augustus Kotzebue provided
just such a case in his *Misanthropy and Repentance,*
which was translated in 1798 as *The Stranger.*[25]

The Stranger, really Count Charles Waldbourg, becomes
a misanthrope after one of his best friends seduces and
runs away with his wife. Like the archetypal Timon,
the Stranger retreats from society,but though he hates
mankind he continues to be the man of feeling he was
formerly, furtively exercising benevolence to every
needy soul his servant Francis brings to light. Francis provides the defining character sketch of the
Stranger:

> A good master, though one almost loses the use of
> speech by living with him. A man kind and clear—
> though I cannot understand him. He rails against
> the whole world, and yet no beggar leaves his door
> unsatisfied. I have now lived three years with
> him, and yet I know not who he is. A hater of so-
> ciety, no doubt; but not by Providence intended to
> be so. Misanthropy in his head, not in his heart.
>
> (I.i.p. 9)

The Stranger's wounded pride at first makes him reluctant to take back his repentant wife, when such an
action is suggested: "Oh! what a feast would it be for
the painted dolls and vermin of the world, when I appeared among them with my runaway wife upon my arm!
What mocking, whispering, pointing!" (V.ii.p. 67). But
in the final analysis,and to the scandal of Kotzebue's
contemporaries, benevolence prevents the Stranger from
invoking his "insulted pride" and "injured honor" (V.ii.
p. 68).

The body of writing expounding the nature of benevolent
misanthropy is completed, as far as I can tell, with
William Godwin's *Fleetwood* (1805),which is significantly
subtitled "The New Man of Feeling."[26] Fleetwood spends
his boyhood in the romantic wilds of Merionethshire in
an educational situation reminiscent of Rousseau's *Émile.*
But when he leaves this "natural" setting for the civi-

lized and artificial setting of Oxford and later the
"*grand monde*," he leaves also his natural innocence,
entering upon a career of dissipation obviously evoked
by the corruption of society. Innate virtue finally
reclaims this wayward man of feeling, but worldly experience has completely transformed him: "My education
and travels had left me a confirmed misanthrope" (p.162).
But Fleetwood is a benevolent, not a malevolent, misanthrope:

> I was a misanthrope. Not a misanthrope of the
> sterner and more rugged class, who,while they con-
> demn and despise everything around them, have a
> perverted sort of pleasure in the office,whose brow
> for ever frowns, whose voice has the true cynical
> snarl, and who never feel so triumphant a compla
> cency, as when they detect the worthlessness and
> baseness of whoever comes into contact with them....
> my misanthropy was a conclusion, however errone-
> ous,that I unwillingly entertained.... I felt what
> man ought to be, and I could not prevent the model
> of what he ought to be from being for over present
> to my mind. (pp. 63-64)

Fleetwood carefully relates his type of misanthropy to
Swift's, thus returning us to our point of departure:
"Perhaps that is the most incorrigible species of mis-
anthropy, which, as Swift expresses it, loves John,
Matthew, and Alexander, but hates mankind" (p. 163).

3

From Benevolent Misanthrope to Benevolent Satirist

Benevolism and the Defensive Satirist

Several discussions of benevolent misanthropy examined in the preceding chapter rather casually attribute satiric abilities to the benevolent misanthrope, indicating that he was expected to retain the satirist's functions assumed by the traditional misanthrope. In contrast, however, the benevolent misanthrope offered the possibility of a literary character type who could serve as an undisputedly benevolent satirist. By mid-eighteenth century, satire needed all the proof of benevolence it could find, for Benevolism was extremely insensitive to the ironic values of the satirist satirized convention, and with its rise the formal satire that had flourished during the Restoration and first half of the eighteenth century declined.[1] More positively, by distinguishing between "true" and "malevolent" satire, Benevolism did not seek the end of satire but of the maliciously inclined satiric spokesman. It demanded, in effect, that the satirist demonstrate his benevolence. In *Clarissa*, for example, Samuel Richardson argues that "True Satire must be founded in good nature, and directed by a right heart." Satire that merely exposes evil and corruption, like that delivered by the traditional misanthrope and the malicious spokesman of formal satire, lacks moral purpose: "When Satire is personal, and aims to expose rather than to amend the subject of it; how, tho' it were to be *just*, can it be useful?" In Richardson's view, "Friendly Satire may be

48

compared to a fine lancet,which gently breathes a vein
for health sake; the malevolent Satire to a broad sword
which lets, into the gashes it makes,the air of public
ridicule."[2] Thomas Warton, referring to John Marston,
argues that "The satirist who too freely indulges himself in the display of that licentiousness which he
means to proscribe, absolutely defeats his own design.
He inflames those passions which he professes to sup-
press, gratifies the depravations of a prurient curiosity, and seduces innocent minds to an acquaintance
with ideas which they might never have known."[3] Steele's
Tatler, No. 242, pretty well encapsulates the benevolist attitude: "I concluded, however unaccountable the
assertion might appear at first sight,that good-nature
was an essential quality in a satirist...."[4]
Benevolism, in effect, deflects attention away from
satire as an artistic form and returns to the Renaissance interest in the personality of the satiric spokesman. The focus, however, now falls on the problem of
producing a vigorous, effective attack and simultaneously showing that the satiric spokesman is really benevolent, a problem Ben Jonson earlier wrestled with in
dramatic terms when,after the ecclesiastical interdict
on formal satire,he sought to carry his "comical satyre"
onto the stage. He first attempted to resolve the problem by using multiple satirists.[5] In *Every Man Out of
His Humour*, Macilente is the railing satirist full of
malice and ill-will,while Asper is the benevolent satirist out to reform vice. The use of multiple satirists,
however, is rather cumbersome, and Jonson dropped the
device in *Cynthia's Revels* and *Poetaster*. But, unfortunately, the individual benevolent satirists he
created lack the energy and spirit to make their attacks on vice very powerful. Ironically, the very
values sought by benevolent satire tend to weaken its
delivery. Where the satirist satirized mode of attack
points to evil in all men, benevolent satire, like
Alcibiades, tries to distinguish between the universality of human evil and the inequality of human guilt.
All may be guilty of evil, but some are more guilty
than others. Reinhold Neibhur points out that at the
final "religious level of judgment" all moral discrimination disappears, but in all historic judgments it is

necessary to discriminate "between the oppressor and
his victim, between the congenital liar and the moderately truthful man, between the debauched sensualist
and the self-disciplined worker,and between the egoist
who drives egocentricity to the point of sickness and
the moderately 'unselfish' devotee of the general welfare."[6] In contrast with the convention of the satirist satirized, benevolent satire's desire to emphasize
the inequality of human guilt focuses on every individual's capacity for good and tends to project evil
primarily as the collective vices of society threatening the moral and physical welfare of the individual.
As the *vir bonus* and public defender spokesmen suggest,
the ultimate voice of benevolent satire is not that of
"ideal society" castigating its aberrant individuals,
but that of a "moderately truthful man" castigating an
aberrant society.

  William Whitehead's short poem, "On Ridicule," rather
concisely expresses the difficulties of presentation
that benevolent satire posed. At first Whitehead grants
that society tends to misconstrue the satirist's purpose, but then he retreats by saying that the satirist's
zeal often invites misconstruction:

  We oft, 'tis true, mistake the sat'rist's aim,
  Not arts themselves, but their abuses they blame.
  Yet if, crusader like, their zeal be rage,
  They hurt the cause in which their arms engage....
  Readers are few, who nice distinctions form,
  Supinely cool, or credulously warm.

Even when the satirist is not "crusader like," however, the question of motivation nags. Whitehead argues that as satirists "our motives should be known:
/Rail we to check his spleen, or ease our own?/Does
injur'd virtue ev'ry shaft supply,/Arm the keen tongue,
and flush th'erected eye?/Or do we from ourselves ourselves disguise?/And act, perhaps, the villains we
chastise."[7] William Boscawen points out in his *Progress
of Satire*, "True Candour pardons where it cannot praise."
The conclusion was inevitable: satire is not "a very
amiable...species of composition"; the "Muse of Satire"
is the "least attractive of the Nine."[8]

  In the face of such concentrated suspicion, satire

was forced to retrench. Ronald Paulson has demonstrated in his excellent study *Satire and the Novel in
Eighteenth-Century England* that it managed to survive
during the Age of Sensibility largely by accommodating
itself to other literary genres, particularly to the
emerging genre of the novel. The novel did not cause
the decline of satire, but rather "the best satirists
came to terms with the novel, adjusting its conventions,
sometimes modifying their severity, and usually sacri-
ficing either satire's or the novel's autonomy."[9] Benevolent misanthropy figured greatly in this accommoda-
tion, for paradoxically, if the satiric spokesman of
formal satire was suspected of being a malicious misanthrope, the benevolent misanthrope was a *bona fide*
man of feeling; he could readily and naturally assume
the role of satirist and deliver the "true" satire
Benevolism demanded. Moreover, the benevolent misanthrope in the role of satirist creates a complex
irony to counter the irony of the satirist satirized.
With the addition of railing, the benevolent misanthrope
ironically combines the satiric power of the traditional misanthrope with the qualities of moderation and
discrimination urged by the traditional misanthrope's
various adversaries——Hermes, Asper, Alcibiades, Freeman, Philinte. Further, his personality, itself an
ironic fusion of benevolent feeling with hatred, leads
to another ironic fusion of affectionate sympathy for
the benevolent misanthrope with scorn and ridicule for
the objects of his attack. While the concept of benevolent misanthropy was receiving discursive and imaginative exposition, the character type of a benevolent
misanthrope with satiric abilities was concurrently
emerging in literature, a character type that lasted
until the end of the century and reached perfection in
Matthew Bramble, the central figure in Tobias Smollett's
Humphry Clinker.

The Benevolent Misanthrope as Satirist

One of the major difficulties in presenting the benevolent misanthrope as satirist is suppressing all suggestions of the malicious and antisocial qualities associated with the traditional misanthrope. The nature of

the difficulty is indicated in *Tom Jones* (1749), where
Henry Fielding provides in the Man of the Hill a misanthropic satirist who shares qualities of both the
Timon archetype and the benevolent misanthrope.[10] The
Man of the Hill episode is usually thought to be somewhat extraneous to the novel, but it is, in fact, very
intimately connected with one of the novel's main
themes—Tom's quest for prudence. Fielding reserves
the term *prudence* itself mainly for characters like
Blifil who calculatingly promote only their own self-
interest. By this tactic he removes the "carnal" association from the kind of prudence that balances
benevolence. In Book III, Chapter Seven, the narrator
interrupts the action to tell "well disposed youths"
that from Tom Jones they should learn, "goodness of
heart and openness of temper, though these may give
them greater comfort within and administer to an honest
pride in their own minds, will by no means, alas! do
their business in the world. Prudence and circum-
spection are necessary even to the best of men. They
are, indeed, as it were, a guard to Virtue, without
which she can never be safe" (III, 131). When All-
worthy thinks he is dying, he advises Tom: "I am convinced, my child, that you have much goodness, generosity, and honour in your temper; if you will add prudence and religion to these, you must be happy,for the
three former qualities, I admit, make you worthy of
happiness, but they are the latter only which will put
you in possession of it" (III, 243).

The Man of the Hill episode expands the theme of prudence by focusing on a character whose own lack of prudence has driven him to misanthropy. The Man of the
Hill's theory of misanthropy sounds very much like
benevolent misanthropy:

> ...however it may seem a paradox, or even a con-
> tradiction, certain it is that great philanthropy
> chiefly inclines us to avoid and detest mankind;
> not on account so much of their private and selfish
> vices, but for those of a relative kind; such as
> envy, malice, treachery, cruelty, with every other
> species of malevolence. These are the vices which
> true philanthropy abhors, and which rather see and
> converse with, she avoids society itself. (IV,113)

The Man of the Hill's personal history and account of his world travels form satires on man, confirming his vision of evil and his disillusionment. And yet something is clearly wrong with his present position: if "true philanthropy abhors" the vices he listed, she is also outgoing to men and does not avoid "society itself." The Man of the Hill's lack of practical benevolence to accompany his speculative misanthropy suggests that his misanthropy is only remotely caused by disappointed benevolence. It is in fact immediately caused by injured pride—the betrayal by his former mistress and friend—and Tom rather shrewdly observes that he should have expected such a betrayal. "But you will pardon me," Tom comments, "...if I desire you to reflect who that mistress and who that friend were. What better, my good sir, could be expected in love derived from the stews, or in friendship first produced and nourished at the gaming table?" (IV, 152).

The Man of the Hill, by failing to exercise practical benevolence, thus becomes a satirist satirized; but he by no means becomes an actively malevolent misanthrope. Quite the contrary, his satiric account of his life is given to Tom as a warning. What he says about man is for the most part quite true for the world of the novel, and this is a fact Tom completely misses. London is indeed the sink of iniquity described by the Man of the Hill, and all of Tom's reflections on the old man's former mistress and friend return with double irony to castigate his own relationship with Lady Bellaston. His naive benevolence also prevents him from seeing the real character of Nightingale, nor does he ever understand the truth in the Man of the Hill's comment on those who praise mankind, a comment that ironically echoes Shaftesbury: "Knaves will no more endeavour to persuade us of the baseness of mankind than a highwayman will inform you that there are thieves on the road. This would, indeed, be a method to put you on your guard, and to defeat their own purposes. For which reason, though knaves, as I remember, are very apt to abuse particular persons, yet they never cast any reflection on human nature in general" (IV, 152-153).

At the end of the novel Fielding assures the reader that Tom has acquired the prudence he needs to survive in the world:

> Whatever in the nature of Jones had a tendency to
> vice, has been corrected by continual conversation
> with this good man [Allworthy], and by his union with
> the lovely and virtuous Sophia. He hath also, by
> reflection on his past follies, acquired a discre-
> tion and prudence very uncommon in one of his live-
> ly parts. (V, 373)

The hilarious pun in the last words of this quotation
reminds us that the world of *Tom Jones* is a world of
comedy in which a benevolent hero like Tom can escape
physically and psychologically unscathed while in the
process of learning prudence. "Good nature pays off,"
Alan McKillop points out, "yet it is not clear that this
result is grounded in 'the nature of things,'...or that
it follows the 'way of the world,' the normal course of
events in human society. In the long run, what chance
has candour in the London social scene of *Tom Jones* and
Amelia?"[11]
 Fielding's depiction of the Man of the Hill indicates,
however, that he was well aware that without prudence
the individual man of feeling stood little chance of
survival in the contemporary London social scene; but
in the light of a comic vision any individual failure
to survive would really be the "short run." Nevertheless, in realistic terms, we may agree with McKillop
that "there is something conventional about the way the
predicament of the comic character is eased or cleared
up,"[12] and we may even, perhaps, call this comic convention "luck," as does Sir George in Fielding's *The
Fathers; or, The Good-Natured Man*. Sir George is not at
all convinced that the individual man of feeling triumphs in this world. He tells his benevolent brother:
"You are a great deal too good for this world, indeed
you are; and really, considering how good you are, you
are tolerably lucky; for were I half so good, I should
expect, whenever I returned home, to catch my wife in an
intrigue; my servants robbing my house; my son married
to a chambermaid; and my daughter run away with a foot-
man" (XII, 160-161). In the real world luck may not hold
up, and, while Fielding is not suggesting the Man of
the Hill in *Tom Jones* as a model for the man of feeling,
he may be suggesting that with the addition of practical
benevolence he can become one.

The blueprint for this model had already appeared in the *Essay on Wit and Humour* published by Corbyn Morris in 1744.[13] Morris describes the benevolent misanthrope as a satirist but calls him a humorist. A humorist for Morris is not a blanket term covering all lovable eccentrics, as Stuart Tave's discussion of the *Essay* implies; lovable eccentrics in general Morris calls "characters," so that his humorist is only one of the many characters in the world.[14] Morris believes this particular character is worth dwelling upon, however, for, like Voltaire, he thinks that the English are "generally tinged, deeply or slightly, with the *Dye* of the Humourist" (p. 22). Morris's humorist is an abstract summary of Jack Roastbeef, Spatter, the misanthropic beau, and other characters to be examined later. The humorist (a) disdains all ostentation except that of his freedom and independence; (b) scorns all imitation of others and "condemns the rest of the World for being servilely obedient to Forms and Customs"; (c) is pleased to have his opinions slighted, for it proves to him that others are addicted to folly and weakness; (d) considers himself in the world as the only sober person among a company of drunken men (pp. 15-20). But such an irascible character serves an important purpose in society, for "It is He only, the Humourist, that has the Courage and Honesty to cry out, unmov'd by personal Resentment." The humorist is, then, a satirist exposing the frauds of every profession, all of which "feel the Lash of his Censure" (p. 20). Although he is a misanthrope and a satirist, he is still a man of feeling: "...no Person has certainly a quicker Feeling; and there are Instances frequent, of greater Generosity and human Warmth flowing from an Humourist, than are capable of proceeding from a weak Insipid, who labours under a continual Flux of Civility" (pp. 21-22).

Ironically, the first literary use of the benevolent misanthrope as satirist apparently occurs in the figure of the Englishman Jack Roastbeef, a minor character in the French playwright Louis de Boissy's *Le François à Londres* (1727). Roastbeef is more a surly man than a misanthrope, and his satiric abilities are rather limited. Yet he does deliver a pointed attack on the social pretentiousness of the Marquis de Polinville: "Fare ye well! I have given you Time to pour out all your Im-

pertinence. I had a Mind to see if you were so ridiculous as they say you are. I ought to do you Justice.
Your Fame is not sufficiently spread abroad. You are
in the wrong to shew yourself for nothing. You are an
excellent Buffoon. It's worth a Shilling a-piece to see
you."[15] The English, however, were credited with a desire for satire that far exceeded the mild attacks of
Roastbeef. When *Le François* was translated in 1755, the
anonymous translator dedicated the play to Samuel Foote
and clearly invited a comparison between Foote and Boissy. He was certain, moreover, that Foote would win the
applause, for the less voluble misanthropy depicted in
Boissy's caricature of the Englishman was clearly too
tame: "...the rough Briton, will, doubtless, give the
Palm to you; for he loves sound Sense and surly Satire."[16] Foote accepted the challenge of Boissy's translator, creating the benevolent misanthropic satirist
Giles Crab for his play *The Englishman Returned from
Paris* (1756), a play that was very favorably reviewed
in the first issue of Smollett's *Critical Review*.[17]

Giles Crab, like Morris's humorist earlier and Smollett's Matthew Bramble later, is a valetudinarian, "an
old fellow of sixty-six, who heartily hates business,
is tired of the world, and despises everything in it"
(I. pp. 137-138). Very early in the play the "Old Diogenes" (I. p. 151) announces to the audience his misanthropic nature and his railing ability: "Fresh instances, every moment, fortify my abhorence, my detestation of mankind. This turn may be termed misanthropy,
and imputed to chagrin and disappointment; but it can
only be by those fools who, through softness or ignorance, regard the faults of others, like their own, through
the wrong end of the perspective" (I. p. 145). As in
Bramble's case later, Crab is also the legal guardian
of a young man and woman, the son and the ward of a de-
ceased friend, however, rather than his nephew and niece.
Lucinda, his newly inherited charge, like Smollett's
Lydia, realizes that Crab's misanthropy and railing stem
only from his intellect, for his actions are benevolent
and his intentions towards individuals are generous.
To Lord John's comment that "Mr. Crab's manners are
rather too rough," Lucinda replies, "Not a jot; I am
familiarized to them. I know his integrity and can never

be disobliged by his sincerity" (I. p. 155). "Age and contempt" have long shut Crab's sensibilities to "flattery and dissimulation" (I. p. 146), so that the sincerity of his strictures against society cannot be questioned. In the style of Bramble, he rails against extravagance, luxury, and the lack of plain common sense, most of which he patriotically blames on the corrupting influence of France. The basic plot of Foote's play centers on the gulling of his friend's son, who has returned from France a Frenchified Englishman. The family circle consisting of a misanthropic valetudinarian and his two wards, however, forms the underlying motif of the play and clearly foreshadows the basic Bramble family unit and the troubles Matt has with his two wards.

The contest between French and English writers to embody in an Englishman the benevolent misanthrope as satirist continues with Voltaire and George Colman the elder. Voltaire dramatized his belief that London "est plein de Timons" in the character of Freeport, who appears in his comedy *L'Ecossaise*, published in 1760. Freeport lacks the voluble satiric railing of Giles Crab, but he is essentially a benevolent misanthrope who loves individuals. Although he continually makes satiric observations like "Men are not good for much; three quarters are knaves and fools; and the other fourth keep to themselves" (my translation), Freeport is known by everyone for his generous actions to individuals.[18] In 1767 the elder George Colman adapted Voltaire's play, preserving the same characters, but shifting the emphasis to Freeport, as indicated in his new title, *The English Merchant*.[19] Although Colman gave Freeport the lead and emphasized his benevolent misanthropy more, he did not greatly increase the satiric railing. Colman carefully stresses, however, that the particular attractiveness of his character results from the odd mixture of benevolence and misanthropy. Colman's Freeport is benevolence itself, but he is "grossness itself too.... He always cancels an obligation by the manner of conferring it; and does you a favour, as if he were going to knock you down" (I. p. 6). Freeport blames his misanthropy on the English malady, the spleen, and repudiates the external marks usually accompanying the man of feeling: "I have never cried in my life; and yet I can

feel too;...what signifies whimpering?" (II. p. 23).
Like Bramble later, Freeport is "always endeavouring to
do good actions in secret," but his benevolent feeling
cannot be hidden long, for "the world finds you out, you
see" (II. p.29). The affection felt for Freeport and
his type was becoming widespread, or at least Lessing
considered this the case when he reviewed both Voltaire
and Colman in the *Hamburgische Dramaturgie*. While the
audience must despise the truly malicious and venomous
misanthrope, represented in Voltaire's play by Frelon
and in Colman's by Spatter, it delights in the comic
mixture of surliness and benevolence exhibited in a Freeport: "We love his rude generosity and even the English
have considered themselves flattered by it" (my translation).[20]

Morris, Boissy, Foote, Voltaire, and Colman all treat
the benevolent misanthropic satirist as a valetudinarian, and this tendency predominates in the literary development. Both Sarah Fielding and Goldsmith, however,
sought to give the character type a youthful to middle
age appearance. Miss Fielding's most important benevolent misanthropic satirist appears as Mr. Spatter (whose
name Colman perhaps borrowed) in *The Adventures of David
Simple,* a novel published in the same year (1744) as
Morris's *Essay on Wit and Humour*.[21] Miss Fielding shares
the honor of giving the world one of the first two literary men of feeling in the character of David, but her
attitude toward the type is hardly one of clearcut admiration.[22] The standard view of this novel seems to
demand revision if her treatment of David within the
context of the entire novel and its sequel is emphasized, instead of stressing his type as a man of feeling. Rather than a sentimental novel advocating tender
feeling, *David Simple* is really an educational novel in
which the hero learns the ways of the world. David is
simple in the sense of *innocent*, and from this perspective he is quite admirable. As the novel progresses,
however, its purpose becomes clearer. David's adventures are contrived to remove his naive simplicity and
to demonstrate that the world is a place of fraud and
deceit calculated to destroy a man of feeling. A deep
pessimism about the general moral progress of man underlies the entire novel and its sequel. After a very

short stay in London, for example, David is tempted to
the misanthropy of Timon, but instead he retires to the
country with his wife and two friends. Country retirement, however, does not save this imprudent man of feeling, for in the sequel David and his companions all die
because of their inability to cope with the world. In
her characterization of the benevolent misanthropic
railer, Mr. Spatter, Miss Fielding offers a viable mode
of survival for the man of feeling.

Spatter's name indicates his railing abilities, which
his close association with the character tradition confirms. In the puff to his sister's novel, Henry Fielding writes that Spatter, Orgueil, and some of the other
characters "would have shined in the Pages of a Theophrastus, Horace or a La Bruyère" (I, xi-xii). Miss
Fielding's novel is conducive to the presentation of
detachable characters, for its structure essentially
follows the picaresque pattern with a man of feeling
substituted for the rogue as hero, a common technique
in novels dealing with the man of feeling. The satire
in the picaresque novel is usually implied in the picaro
himself, who mirrors the evils surrounding him and whose
participation in them eventually makes him as much an
object of satire as the world through which he travels.
Since David, unlike the picaro, does not mirror the evils
of the world and since his disgust with the world results only in moral lamentation, any direct satire must
come from another character. Miss Fielding transfers
the satirist's role to Spatter.23

Spatter takes on the job of the naive David's London
guide and tutor. He intends to show his pupil a sight
of man with "the Passions actuated," for then the "Mask
is thrown off, and Nature appears as she is" (I, 141).
Spatter's metaphor of removing the mask underscores his
satiric function in the novel. At the close of each
evening's entertainment he ran "through the Characters
of the whole Company, and at the finishing of every one,
uttered a Sentence with some Vehemence, (which was a
Manner peculiar to himself) calling them either *Fools*
or *Knaves*" (I, 144). Indeed, *fools* was the word Spatter "always chose to pronounce before he went to Bed"
(I, 170). Since David could not have tolerated Spatter's misanthropic railing if it was motivated by malev-

olence, he seeks an explanation and concludes that Spatter's misanthropy derives from benevolence. "Mr. Spatter seemed to take such Delight in abusing people; and
yet as [David] observed, no one was more willing to
oblige any Person, who stood in need of his Assistance:
he concluded that...perhaps it was only his *Love of Mankind*, which made him have such Hatred and Detestation
of their Vices, as caused him to be eager in reproach-
ing them..." (I, 148). David's estimation of Spatter
is later confirmed when he is told that "Mr. Spatter's
Ill-nature dwells no-where but in his Tongue; and the
very People who [sic] he so industriously endeavours to
abuse, he would do any thing in his Power to serve.   I
have known Instances of his doing the best-natured Actions in the World, and, at the same time, abusing the
very Person he was serving" (I, 179-180).   Spatter's
misanthropy protects his sensibility without hindering
his benevolence, and simultaneously his satiric railing
keeps an evil world in focus.

 Spatter's thematic importance in the novel is further
heightened by his relationship to Orgueil and Vernish,
like David, two extremes of human nature. Orgueil seems
to be a man of feeling, but according to Spatter he performs good deeds only from pride. He enjoys the evil
of other men because he can feel superior by comparison. Orgueil's hypocrisy is complemented by that of
Vernish, who perpetually speaks well of people, appearing to be the soul of benevolence; but for all his professed love of the species, no one has heard of anything
"remarkable he did to prove that Love" (I, 174).   The
balancing of Spatter between Orgueil and Vernish stresses the comic mixture of benevolence and misanthropy, for
the benevolent misanthrope is essentially a hypocrite
in reverse, ironically serving society as much by his
satire as by his benevolence.   Sarah Fielding was evidently fascinated by the type of the benevolent misanthrope as satirist, for she repeated him later in the
novel as one of the several suitors for the hand of the
lovely Corina. Everyone considered this particular beau
as ill-natured, morose, and misanthropic, "but he had
so much Tenderness in him, that he was continually *hurt*,
and consequently out of Humour. His Love of Mankind was
the Cause that he appeared to hate them..." (II, 234).

Corina's misanthropic beau serves very little structural purpose in the novel, but, since he enters the story after David has left Spatter, he vividly recalls the man of feeling who has succeeded in living in the midst of the evils of the world David soon abandons. Only with a rationally hearty hatred of man, like Spatter's, can a man of feeling seem to protect himself from deceit and imposition.

The tutor-pupil relationship established between David and Spatter recurs in what are probably the most care-fully wrought depictions of the benevolent misanthrope as satirist preceding Matthew Bramble, the Man in Black scenes from Oliver Goldsmith's *Citizen of the World*.[24] As a character sketch of a benevolent misanthrope, Dry-bone is justly famous; but he is much more than a mere amiable humorist, an eccentric man of feeling masquer-ading as a misanthrope. His misanthropy constitutes a protective armor for sensibilities easily open to im-position, but it also embodies a satiric vision of man and the world. Raised by a father who "loved all the world,and...fancied all the world loved him" (II,113), Drybone left home believing "that universal benevolence was what first cemented society" (II, 114). He soon discovered that at his entrance into "the busy and in-sidious world," he resembled "one of those gladiators who were exposed without armour in the ampitheatre at Rome" (II, 114). Drybone's disillusionment results in misanthropy, and he uses this misanthropy for satiric purposes. As a man of feeling, however, his private good deeds assure the moral earnestness of his public railing.

The central satirist of the *Citizen of the World* is un-doubtedly the Chinaman, Lien Chi Altangi. In terms of satiric spokesmen, however, Lien Chi is basically a naif who rarely employs the Juvenalian frontal attack.[25] His satire proceeds from the implications contained in his apparently simple questions and forthright reporting of events. The Chinaman approaches man and events from a rational standpoint and is confounded to find them ir-rational. Drybone's misanthropy usually evokes the blunter tactics of the railer, and Goldsmith brings the two satirists together in a kind of tutor-pupil rela-tionship that enhances both satiric methods. As a naif and a stranger to London life, the Chinaman finds himself in a situation closely resembling that of David Simple: he needs a mentor and guide. Like Spatter,Drybone fulfills this role and takes Lien Chi on his tour of London.

Because the *Citizen of the World* is rarely reprinted in its entirety, Drybone's particular satiric function has gone largely unnoticed, although in his first appearance in Letter XIII Goldsmith establishes his role. The Chinaman writes that as he was reflecting on the various occurrences in Westminster Abbey, "a gentleman dressed in black, perceiving me to be a stranger, came up, entered into conversation, and politely offered to be my instructor and guide through the Temple" (II, 57). With Drybone's offer, Lien Chi's education in English folly begins in earnest, for as Goldsmith takes pains to remind the reader throughout the Letters Drybone remains Lien Chi's guide throughout the entire London visit.   Letter XXVIII opens,"Lately, in company with my friend in black, whose conversation is now both my amusement and instruction..." (II, 120).   Letter LVIII also opens by drawing attention to Drybone's tutorial role: "...the man in black takes every opportunity of introducing me to such company as may serve to indulge my speculative temper, or gratify my curiosity" (II, 239). When Drybone does not come to conduct the China-man, the latter goes to him: "I had some intentions lately of going to visit Bedlam.... I went to wait upon the man in black to be my conductor..." (II, 390). When Lien Chi contemplates leaving London, he writes that he "shall have no small pain in leaving my usual companion, guide, and instructor" (II, 405).

The satiric nature of Drybone's office as both "amuser and instructor" and his blunt method of satiric attack become apparent during his first job as the China-man's guide through the Abbey. In the famous discussion of Pope's right to a tomb in the Abbey, Drybone reveals his satiric abilities: "I have been told of one Pope— is he there?—It is time enough, replied my guide, these hundred years; he is not long dead; people have not done hating him yet.—Strange, cried I; can any be found to hate a man whose life was wholly spent in entertaining and instructing his fellow-creatures?—Yes, says my

guide, they hate him for that very reason" (II,59-60).
Some of the most celebrated episodes in the Letters depend upon Drybone as either a direct satiric commentator or as a satiric "presenter" of a scene. It is Drybone who takes the Chinaman to his first London play and
attacks the cheap theatrics of the London Stage (Letter
XXI), and it is Drybone who presents Lien Chi to the
famous Club of Authors (Letters XXIX-XXX). The celebrated attacks on unmarried English women (Letter
XXVIII), the flatterers of the nobility (Letter XXXII),
the blasphemous services in St. Paul's (Letter XLI),
the stupidity and indolence of the clergy (Letter LVIII),
and the corruption of the courts (Letter XCVIII) are
only some of the many episodes in which Drybone either
presents the scene to the Chinaman or utters the satiric
attack himself. The close association of the two satirists concludes with the marriage of Drybone's niece
to the Chinaman's son (Letter CXXIII). Their satiric
roles do not end with the marriage, however, for the two
satirists plan to continue their observance of man and
his folly on a world tour together (Letter CXXIII).

Goldsmith has made misanthropy a vital structural device, for the Man in Black's satiric vision of man stems
directly from his misanthropy, while his heart over-
flows with compassion for individual men. As Lien Chi
writes, "I have known him profess himself a man-hater,
while his cheek was glowing with compassion; and, while
his looks were softened into pity, I have heard him use
the language of the most unbounded ill-nature" (II,109).
Drybone is indeed "a humourist in a nation of humour-
ists," but, like Spatter, he is a hypocrite in reverse:
"He takes as much pains to hide his feelings, as any
hypocrite would to conceal his indifference" (II,109).
The depth of this reverse hypocrite's misanthropy is
highlighted when the Chinaman one day discovers Drybone
thrown almost into the dregs of melancholy despair from
contemplating the wickedness daily performed by men (II,
365-368).

Goldsmith returned to the benevolent misanthrope as
satirist, although to a more limited extent, in Burchell,
one of the central characters of his now most famous
work, *The Vicar of Wakefield* (1766). In thematic terms
the novel moves from an emphasis on Parson Primrose's

benevolence to an emphasis on his need for prudence.[26]
The parson, however, is a complex and ambivalent character. As the relater of his experiences, Parson Primrose is a naif, like the Chinaman, unable to distinguish
appearances from reality, constantly confusing one for
the other. But as a character in the story, he is also
the object of satire as the vanity underlying his na-
iveté is revealed. His vanity constitutes a lack of
prudence that evokes more than sympathetic laughter, for
it causes physical and moral harm to others. Moreover,
Parson Primrose is also capable of satiric attack, especially against his wife and daughter, so that he becomes in effect a benevolent satirist who is himself
satirized not for his vices but for his lack of a necessary virtue.[27]

Direct satire of the parson, however, comes from Burchell, the disguised Sir William Thornhill, who is essentially the character of the benevolent misanthrope,
a toned-down Man in Black. His misanthropy is certainly
not developed at the length it is in the earlier work,
but there is enough of it to understand Thornhill's function as a satirist of Parson Primrose in particular and
of imprudent benevolence in general. Sir William, in
the disguise of the beggar Burchell, tells Parson Primrose that Sir William may be "a man of consummate benevolence," but he is now more prudent than when a young
man (IV, 29). Sir William "carried benevolence to excess when young; for his passions were then strong, and
as they all were upon the side of virtue, they led it
up to a romantic extreme" (IV, 29). Surrounded by others who displayed only one side of their character, "He
loved all mankind; for fortune prevented him from knowing that they were rascals" (IV, 29). Convinced now of
mankind's rascality, Sir William dispenses his benevolence under the guise of a misanthrope: "At present,
his bounties are more rational and moderate than before;
but still he preserves the character of a humourist, and
finds most pleasure in eccentric virtue" (IV, 30). His
eccentric virtue assumes on the surface the disguise of
a poor beggar; more deeply, as his name in disguise,
Burchell, implies, he is a satirist, a metaphoric lasher
of vice. In the words of the *Critical Review* for 1766,
"Sir William Thornhill in disguise is a very original

picture, and out of it a very amiable one."[28]

Throughout the novel Burchell attempts to warn and save Parson Primrose from impending disaster. The methods he uses are the typical satirist's devices of metaphorical lashing. Burchell sees that Primrose's benevolence is leading to the same path of destruction that he had traveled; Primrose was losing regard for private interest in universal sympathy. Burchell attempts to awaken the parson to his situation by appearing as a villain, making fun of and castigating the values the parson seems to accept. Burchell's warnings prove true; the parson never sees the meaning of Burchell's lash until it is too late. Burchell's wisdom is never disputed by Primrose, although his vanity refuses to let him accept it as valuable for himself. Primrose is extremely wary of Burchell's intellectual capabilities because he cannot reconcile poverty and wisdom in Burchell, ironically the very things he values in himself: "But what surprised me most was, that though he was a money borrower, he defended his opinions with as much obstinacy as if he had been my patron" (IV, 28). The parson, against his will, must admit that "he every day seemed to become more amiable, his wit to improve, and his simplicity to assume the superior airs of wisdom" (IV, 45).

All pretense at friendly intercourse begins to drop when Burchell assumes the satiric role in good earnest in the famous "Fudge" scene, where he deflates all the pretentiousness of Lady Blarney and Miss Skeggs. Primrose, however, misses the meaning of Burchell's satire and interprets it as rudeness: "I should have mentioned the very unpolite behaviour of Mr. Burchell, who during this discourse sate with his face turned to the fire, and at the conclusion of every sentence would cry out *fudge,* an expression which displeased us all, and in some manner damped the rising spirit of the conversation" (IV, 62). Burchell continues to grow in rudeness and belligerence until he has the audacity to argue with Mrs. Primrose herself, thus appearing to the family, for all intents and purposes, as an enemy to their happiness (IV, 70ff.). When he is finally banished from the house, all reason seems to have symbolically departed with him:

> Our breach of hospitality went to my conscience a little; but I quickly silenced that monitor by two

or three specious reasons, which served to satisfy
and reconcile me to myself. The pain which conscience
gives the man who has already done wrong, is soon
got over. Conscience is a coward; and those faults
it has not strength enough to prevent, it seldom has
justice enough to accuse. (IV, 71)

With Burchell departed, the family turns for help more
and more to the infamous Squire Thornhill, who the parson had already determined was an ignorant fop: "Mr.
Thornhill, notwithstanding his real ignorance, talked
with ease, and could expatiate upon the common topics of
conversation with fluency" (IV, 43). Completely aware
that the Squire is dangerous, the parson allows himself
to be taken in by his wiles.

 Burchell's second stroke of apparent hatred, his letter to the two London "ladies," causes one of the finest scenes in the novel, a flyting scene in the Renaissance fashion, which confirms all of the Primroses in
their suspicions that he is a misanthrope of the first
order: "...we are not to be surprised that bad men want
shame; they only blush at being detected in doing good,
but glory in their vices" (IV, 80). Yet Burchell's letter is one of the subtlest ironies in the novel and a
sharp satire of the parson, for it represents an active
attempt to preserve virtue. Primrose had never really
trusted Squire Thornhill, nor had he much use for the
Squire's fluent tongue; but the parson lacks all initiative to do anything about his fears; he trusts to discretion, he says, but never acts discreetly at all: "I
would have proceeded, but for the interruption of a servant from the Squire, who with his compliments sent us
a side of venison, and a promise to dine with us some
days after. This well-timed present pleaded more pow-
erfully in his favour than anything I had to say could
obviate. I therefore continued silent, satisfied with
just having pointed out danger, and leaving it to their
own discretion to avoid it. That virtue which requires
to be ever guarded, is scarce worth the centinel" (IV,
38). The absurdity of Primrose's theory of virtue recalls Sir William's youthful lack of prudence, which the
parson in his maturity has forgotten.

 Burchell thus moves through the novel disguised as a
man-hater doing all in his power to harm people. As a

character in the plot he stands in obvious contrast to
his nephew, the evil Squire, but he is more clearly a
scourge for Parson Primrose, as he attempts to prac-
tically lash prudence into the Primrose family. Both
his real name and his assumed name, Burchell, like the
Crabs, Drybones, and Brambles tagging the benevolent
misanthropes, indicate a disguised man of feeling, as
Parson Primrose finally realizes: "You were ever our
friend; we have long discovered our errors with regard
to you, and repented of our ingratitude. After the vile
usage you then received at my hands, I am almost ashamed
to behold your face; yet I hope you'll forgive me, as I
was deceived by a base ungenerous wretch, who, under the
mask of friendship, has undone me" (IV, 164). Primrose's metaphor of the mask of friendship implies the
opposite mask worn by Burchell, the mask of misanthropy
or hatred. The metaphor also highlights the movement
of appearance and reality in the novel. The parson is
not the wise man he appears to himself, and Burchell is
not the malicious misanthrope he appears to others.

The Man in Black, Burchell, and the other benevolent
misanthropic satirists are all related to the main character in Henry Mackenzie's *Man of Feeling* (1771). As
was seen in the first chapter, however, Mackenzie re-
fused to let Harley or his friend become misanthropes,
but he did see the possibility of a benevolent misanthrope and his function as a satirist.[29] In London Harley is taken to a dinner specifically to meet a "Misanthropist" who is animated by the "spirit of Diogenes"
(p. 23). The "Misanthropist" suffers from injured pride
in that his fiancee has run off with his friend, but he
has, like the Stranger, retained his benevolence—at
least, in the sense that he still loves little children
(p. 25). The "Misanthropist" delivers a long, Hobbesian
satire on the selfish nature of man, yet Harley is shrewd
enough to see that he is really a man of feeling still
and that his satire may be very useful:

> "This is a strange creature," said his friend to
> Harley. "I cannot say," answered he, "that his re-
> marks are of the pleasant kind: it is curious to
> observe how the nature of truth may be changed by
> the garb it wears; softened to the admonition of
> friendship, or soured into the severity of reproof:

yet this severity may be useful to some tempers; it
somewhat resembles a file: disagreeable in its op-
eration, but hard metals may be the brighter for
it." (p. 29)

One of these "hard metals" was undoubtedly Tobias George
Smollett, whose Matthew Bramble made his literary debut
in the same year as Mackenzie's Harley.

4

Tobias Smollett—
A Risible Misanthrope

Smollett's reputation as a novelist and satirist remained exceedingly high through the early nineteenth
century, but his fame continued to be over-shadowed by
Fielding and Sterne, particularly by Fielding, who is
inevitably compared with him.[1] Lewis Knapp observes,
"In the frequent critical comparisons of Smollett and
Fielding as men and writers Smollett's claim to be a
serious and moral satirist has been looked upon with
skepticism or even denied on grounds that are largely
subjective."[2] Recent critical studies have begun to make
clear that Smollett was, indeed, a "serious and moral
satirist." He was also, however, a comic novelist and
one who was very much concerned with the man of feeling
living in an unfeeling world. In all of his novels
Smollett sought to harmonize a satiric vision of the
world with a comic story of the man of feeling—a harmony that eluded him until his last novel, *Humphry Clinker*.[3] Through the concept of benevolent misanthropy
dramatized in Matt Bramble, Smollett finally achieved
his artistic goal, producing one of the most brilliant
satirists in the benevolent misanthrope tradition. This
chapter will attempt to place in perspective the artistic search that ended only with Smollett's last novel—
and with his death.
  Smollett's novels, particularly the early ones, are
usually described rather vaguely as picaresque, with a
modification of the picaro or rogue-hero into a "young
man of good family who has set out on his wanderings."[4]
To a certain extent, the picaresque formula applies, but

the label is far too limiting to provide any very in-
sightful analysis of Smollett's fictional world.   If
Smollett wrote within the picaresque tradition, he carefully subordinated it to his own idea that the novel
was a vehicle for satire.   In the Preface to *Roderick
Random*, for example, the Greek and Roman mythologies are
denominated "a collection of extravagant romances" in
verse (I, xl); the prose romances of the middle ages
are scorned as performances filled "with the most mon-
strous hyperboles" (I, xl). True romance originated
only with Cervantes, who "by an inimitable piece of
ridicule, reformed the taste of mankind, representing
chivalry in the right point of view, and converting romance to purposes far more useful and entertaining, by
making it assume the sock, and point out the follies of
ordinary life" (I, xli).

The importance of the novel lies then in its assumption of the sock, in its conversion into a mode of comic
satire.   Cervantes's "method," unlike that of his imitator Le Sage, evokes "that generous indignation which
ought to animate the reader against the sordid and vicious disposition of the world" (I, xli). This concept
of the novel as an important satiric form underlies the
famous paragraph opening the Preface: "Of all kinds of
satire, there is none so entertaining and universally
improving, as that which is introduced, as it were, occasionally, in the course of an interesting story, which
brings every incident home to life; and, by representing familiar scenes in an uncommon and amusing point of
view, invests them with all the graces of novelty, while
nature is appealed to in every particular" (I, xxxix).
While the novel is the proper satiric form, the satire
emerges from the story, and, as might be expected, the
story also had a specific meaning for Smollett—the history of one particular person:

> The reader gratifies his curiosity in pursuing the
> adventures of a person in whose favour he is pre-
> possessed; he espouses his cause, he sympathizes
> with him in distress; his indignation is heated
> against the authors of his calamity; the humane pas-
> sions are inflamed; the contrast between dejected
> virtue and insulting vice appears with greater ag-
> gravation; and every impression having a double
> force on the imagination, the memory retains the

circumstance, and the heart improves by the example. (I, xxxix)

Smollett reduces this rather diffuse discussion of the principal person to one celebrated paragraph in the Prefatory Address to *Ferdinand Count Fathom:*

> A novel is a large diffused picture, comprehending the characters of life, disposed in different groups, and exhibited in various attitudes, for the purpose of an uniform plan, and general occurrence, to which every individual figure is subservient. But this plan cannot be executed with propriety, probability, or success, without a principal personage to attract the attention, unite the incidents, unwind the clue of the labyrinth, and at last close the scene, by virtue of his own importance. (VIII, 3)

The novel, then, performed for Smollett two simultaneous functions: it related the adventures of one principal personage and rendered a satirical vision of the world in which these adventures took place. In externals, his own novels retain the rambling structure of the picaresque tradition: there is always room for one more adventure. But travel seemed to obsess Smollett; he converted it into the radical metaphor informing each of his novels, transforming the desultory travels of the picaro into a serious quest for secular and spiritual happiness in a world fraught with evil and corruption. The secular and spiritual ends evoke two parallel planes of travel that finally converge at the conclusions of the novels—usually in marriage, but always in rural retirement. This convergence occurs through the medium of satire and follows, on a purely literal level, from two contrasting movements of action. The secular quest draws the hero into elaborately portrayed urban scenes —the *beau monde*; the spiritual quest, on the other hand, initiates a counter movement in the direction of the country. All of the novels are generated by a cyclical pattern moving from the country to a large, complex urban society and then back to the country. Smollett's concept of rural retirement does not, however, imply an attempt to escape from the evils of the world. Country life requires as alert an engagement with evil as city life. The early career of Roderick Random in Scotland,

the evil Mrs. Pickle in *Peregrine Pickle,* and the unhappy Baynards in *Humphry Clinker* are sufficient evidence of this fact. But for Smollett the country does
offer more sanguine hopes for spiritual tranquility,
mainly because in rural retirement the density and complexity of the world's mask of appearances are reduced
to a more manageable scale.[5]

 Smollett's rather rigid insistence on a "principal
personage" is usually taken with a grain of salt, for
his practice in the novels seems to place the heaviest
emphasis on the incidents or scenes of action the hero-
traveler experiences. He has been accused, with some
justice, of writing to the incident or scene, so that
action controls the hero and not the reverse. At any
rate, the massive, graphic details of Smollett's scenes
have elicited more elaborate commentary than the heroes.
But the heroes have been neglected also because they appear, especially in the first two novels, to be rather
unpleasant, harsh characters, infused at times with
doses of feeling. Smollett's heroes, however, are often
more than they appear to be, and a consideration of
them, not in isolation, but in relation to the total
metaphoric structures in which they act, will reveal, I
think, that they are essentially holistic creations,
carefully wrought men of feeling infused at times with
doses of harshness. This is not intended as clever word
juggling, nor is it intended as an attempt to sneak the
"learned Smelfungus" into the sentimental camp through
the back entrance. Smollett never believed that the
benevolence of man could be aroused on a large scale;
but, like Swift, he did believe that it could be aroused
to a limited extent in individuals, and, again like
Swift, he believed that literature, especially satire,
contributed significantly to such arousal. Smollett's
view of literature is rigidly classical. In his Preface
to *A Compendium of Authentic Voyages,* for example, he
writes, "We live in an age of levity and caprice, that
can relish little besides works of fancy; nor do we lis-
ten to instruction unless it be conveyed to us under
the pleasing form of entertainment. But to mix profit
with delight should be the aim of all writers, and the
business of every book...."[6]

 Smollett also recognized that satire would have to be

accommodated to the Age of Sensibility's suspicion of the satirist. In his early verse satires, modelled on Juvenal, he evidences a testy awareness that the satirist in more on the defensive than ever before. In *Advice* (1746), the satiric spokesman's supposed friend (who is giving the advice) finally cries out, "Heav'ns how you rail! the man's consum'd by spite!" When the satirist publishes the dialogue with the friend, the friend returns in *Reproof* (1747) to remonstrate for making his advice seem meanspirited and hypocritical. The spokesman's defense consists of the traditional assertion that he merely reported the truth, exactly what the friend had said. The friend bitterly replies, "Yes, season'd with your own remarks between,/Inflam'd with so much virulence of spleen." The friend concludes triumphantly, "There needs no magic to divine your scope,/Mark'd as you are a flagrant misanthrope."[7] The arguments of the friend are, of course, partly traditional, but the specific accusation of misanthropy, obviously meaning that of a Timon, suggests the intensified distrust of the satirist inspired by Benevolism. Smollett tried to counter this distrust in his novels by introducing satire "as it were, occasionally, in the course of an interesting story" (I, xxxix), and by associating it with the Age's ideal of the virtuous man—the man of feeling.[8]

The Man of Feeling Indignant: RODERICK RANDOM (1748)

It may seem somewhat strange to discuss Roderick Random in terms of the man of feeling, for readers seem generally agreed that he is a harsh and even brutal character. He is the major satirist in the novel, and a satirist satirized too, for he displays endless rage, anger, and pride. Yet Smollett insists that he is basically a man of feeling. In the Preface he is described as having "modest merit" (I, xli-xlii). His heart is "naturally prone to every tender passion" (I, 157), and the "appearance of distress never failed to attract... [his] regard and compassion" (II, 156-157). Indeed, the tears of compassion and benevolence flow as bounteously in *Roderick Random* as in Mackenzie's *Man of Feeling*.

Roderick's natural tenderness also exerts itself in active benevolence, the sign of the true man of feeling. Even after Mrs. Gawky's base treatment of him, for example, Roderick generously assists her and reconciles her with her father. Roderick can even send the barbarous Dr. Mackshane, when reduced to poverty and prison, a gift of ten pistoles (III, 157, 193). But, perhaps, he displays his natural goodness most significantly when, indigent himself, he charitably gives protection to Miss Williams, the prostitute who had only recently attempted to trap him into marriage.

The "History of Miss Williams," generally considered a tedious interruption of the main action, serves rather as a revealing commentary on the problems of a man of feeling in the world and represents, to some extent, the conceptual movement of the novel in miniature. Rejecting the rigid Presbyterian doctrines of her guardian-aunt, Miss Williams avidly read "Shaftesbury, Tindal, Hobbes, and all the books that are remarkable for their deviation from the old way of thinking," until she became a "professed Freethinker" (II, 2), and, forgetting her Hobbes in favor of Shaftesbury, she became a refined woman of feeling. Her feelings eventually betrayed her into a seduction followed by her lover's desertion, so that, with honor lost, she was forced into prostitution to survive. Reduced to poverty and suffering from disease, she can only curse: "Cursed be the day on which I gave away my innocence and peace for a momentary gratification, which has entailed upon me such misery and horror! cursed be my beauty, that first attracted the attention of my seducer! cursed be my education, that, by refining my sentiments, made my heart the more susceptible!" (II, 6). Miss Williams's story is intended as a warning for Roderick, who has just entered the complex society of the *beau monde*; her attack is not leveled at feeling itself, but at unprotected feeling and the perfidy of the world, which destroys those who practice the virtues it preaches.

Roderick Random represents, then, the story of a man of feeling's initiation into the ways of the world. From the young Roderick's point of view, however, his travels are conceived primarily as a quest for material security. Early in his career he sets independence from the "caresses" of the world as his goal: "...my misfortunes had taught me how little the caresses of the world, during a man's prosperity, are to be valued by him; and how seriously and expeditiously he ought to set about making himself independent of them" (I, 39). Roderick's desire for material security is so intense that it often overshadows his quest for spiritual happiness. But early in the travels Strap, in one of his typical comic harangues, reveals the underlying spiritual goal: "What signifies all the riches and honours of this life, if one enjoys not content? And, in the next, there is no respect of persons.... What signify riches, my dear friend? do not they make unto themselves wings? as the wise man saith; and does not Horace observe, *Non domus et fundus, non aeris acervus et auri, Aegroto domini deduxit corpore febres, Non animo curas?*" (I, 108).

But little of the spiritual quest is evident, especially in the earlier portions of the novel, primarily because the narrator focuses on the travels as a form of satiric revelation; the young Roderick's view of his travels is subordinated to the larger, retrospective point of view taken by the older Roderick writing his memoirs. The older and wiser Roderick, from this distancing, sees his travels chiefly as his education in the ways of the world. In the discovery scene near the end of the novel, for example, Roderick's long lost father, Don Rodrigo, specifically calls our attention to the older Roderick's controlling point of view. Don Rodrigo "blessed God for the adversity I had undergone, which, he said, enlarged the understanding, improved the heart, steeled the constitution, and qualified a young man for all the duties and enjoyments of life, much better than any education which affluence could bestow" (III, 188).

The imagery of the tennis ball and the devil-midwife that opens the memoir brilliantly introduces the satanic phantasmagoria the young Roderick must endure in the process of his education. During her pregnancy, his mother "dreamed she was delivered of a tennis-ball, which the devil (who, to her great surprise, acted the part of mid-wife) struck so forcibly with a racket, that it disappeared in an instant" (I, 1-2). In "primitive" Scotland (and later on the sea) evil is so undisguised an affair, so openly brutal in its operations, that a

man of feeling requires little more than a robust constitution to survive. But beyond the restricted sphere
of the Judge Randoms and Captain Oakums, he faces Smollett's vision of a society enmeshed in a complex web of
appearances, a terrifying masquerade in which perception
and moral courage of an almost superhuman kind are required for survival. Strap's frequent descriptions of
London as the "devil's drawing-room" (I,128) repeat the
satanic imagery of the opening and establish Smollett's
whole Hobbesian conception of civilization: "Strap,
lifting up his eyes and hands to heaven, prayed that
God would deliver him from such scenes of iniquity; for
surely the devil had set up his throne in London" (I,
99).

To project his vision of the world of appearances Smollett adopts the traditional metaphor of clothes. Man's
treatment of man depends on external appearances rather than on internal worth. In Scotland, for example,
Roderick, though the best scholar in the village school,
becomes the whipping post because his beggarly appearance betokens to the schoolmaster his lack of worth.
On the road to London the clothes imagery expands, revealing the growing complexity of the world of appearances. Roderick and Strap, for example, have little
trouble discerning the real coward hiding behind the
military dress and stentorian voice of Captain Weazle,
but they are more readily duped (Roderick less so than
Strap) by the long white hair and humble dress of the
"venerable" innkeeper, who treats them on "ambrosia"
and Horace and then presents them an "unconscionable
bill" (I, 61). By the time Roderick and Strap reach
London the clothes imagery has achieved symbolic status.
In London Roderick is immediately told to change his
style of dress, if he hopes to make his way in the cap-
ital. At various times lengthy catalogues of wearing
apparel are presented, such as the descriptions of Beau
Jackson's elegant clothes (I,102), of Captain Whiffle's
dress (II, 106-107), and of the wardrobe Roderick acquires in France from Strap (II, 188-189). But the
clothes imagery reaches its peak of symbolic intensity
when Lieutenant Crampley and his crew beat Roderick
senseless, steal his clothes (which he had just described
in detail), and leave him naked on the coast of Sussex.

In his naked and forlorn condition, Roderick becomes every man stripped of his appearances, and, with grim irony, Smollett shows that so stripped the world at large will forsake him: Roderick receives no aid from the nearby villagers, is even taken for the devil by some simple farmers, and is bandied from door to door throughout the whole village, until he is finally rescued by an old woman suspected of witchcraft by the neighborhood (II, 128ff.).[9]

In terms of his education in the ways of the world, Roderick is never completely successful; but then Smollett implies that perfect penetration of the world's appearances may really be a humanly impossible feat. Near the end of the novel, for example, Mr. Concordance apologizes for earlier believing Mrs. Gawky's evidence that Roderick was a thief. He also argues, however, that appearances at the time left him little choice: "...if the plot had been unravelled to us by any supernatural intelligence, if it had been whispered by a genie, communicated by a dream, or revealed by an angel from on high, we should have been to blame in crediting ocular demonstration: but, as we are left in the midst of mortality, it cannot be expected we should be incapable of imposition" (III, 59).

When Roderick's youth in relationship to the total world of appearances in which Smollett places him is considered, the passions of rage and indignation he exhibits again and again seem less harsh and exaggerated. Roderick's frequent assertions that he is "boiling with indignation" (II, 171) may display uncontrolled passion, but at the same time they may also be the only reactions to Smollett's satanic world that are available to a young man of feeling. Alan McKillop points out that "spontaneous indignation" represents for Smollett a kind of ethical shortcut,[10] but it is also consistent with Roderick's position in the world. Undoubtedly M.A. Goldberg is correct when he argues that Roderick's travels also serve as a mode of self-revelation, that they are designed to teach him the need for controlling his passions and using his indignation more discriminately if he hopes to achieve the spiritual tranquility he seeks.[11] He is continually told throughout his travels that his "passions are too impetuous"

and that he "must learn to govern them better" (I, 96).
But until the achievement of maturity and of independence from the world's "caresses," spontaneous indignation remains almost the sole protection a young man of
feeling has, if he intends, as Roderick does, to actively pursue his goals in the world: "It was happy for me
that I had a good deal of resentment in my constitution,
which animated me on such occasions against the villainy
of mankind, and enabled me to bear misfortunes other-
wise intolerable" (II,171). It is precisely this spontaneous indignation that prevents Roderick from yielding to the Timonian misanthropy that often tempts him:
"A thousand times I wished myself a bear, that I might
retreat to woods and deserts, far from the hospitable
haunts of man, where I could live by my own talents,
independent of treacherous friends, and supercilious
scorn" (II, 172).

The Man of Feeling as "Practical Satirist":
PEREGRINE PICKLE (1751)

In *Peregrine Pickle,* Smollett adopted the omniscient
third person narrator, perhaps, as has been often suggested, in imitation of Fielding. As in *Roderick Random,* the hero's travels are conceived as a secular and
spiritual quest. But, unlike Roderick, Perry seeks a
secular goal that is basically incompatible with his
spiritual one. Where Roderick sought independence from
the "caresses" of the world through wealth, Perry seeks
wealth through a dependency on those very "caresses."
While Perry's travels reveal to him the evils and vice
of the world, they are more particularly structured as
a course in self-knowledge and in the folly of his secular choice. In prison, near the close of his adventures, Perry finally grasps the incongruity of his two
goals: "'If I must be a prisoner for life,' said he to
himself, 'if I must relinquish all my gay expectations,
let me at least have the satisfaction of clanking my
chains so as to interrupt the repose of my adversary;
and let me search in my own breast for that peace and
contentment, which I have not been able to find in all
the scenes of my success'" (VII, 133).

Like Roderick, Perry possesses an excessive amount of
rage and indignation at the vices of the world, but
these passions do not form an armor for his feelings;
moreover, they are far overshadowed by more vicious
passions. The narrator often comments, "In a word,van-
ity and pride were the ruling foibles of our adventurer..." (VI, 23), and to these must be added a completely
shameless indulgence in sexual crimes. In such cases
as the adulterous amour with Mrs. Hornbeck, the attempted rape of his beloved Emilia, and the attack on Pipe's
life, Perry's vices reach almost nauseating peaks. But
despite his misguided secular goal and his vices, Perry
is mainly a man of feeling gone astray. He possesses a
"fund of good-nature and generosity in his composition"
(IV, 79); he has "natural benevolence" (IV, 184), and
he is "naturally compassionate" (V, 13). Since, however, his hopes for secular happiness rest on the "caresses" of the *beau monde,* he considers the passions of
pride, vanity, and even sexual promiscuity best adapted to success. He thus suppresses his natural benevolence because he feels it will jeopardize his career.
Ultimately, of course, Perry never does thrive on the
"caresses" of the *beau monde,* but his opinion that feeling will hinder his chances is ironically correct, as
Lady Vane's celebrated "Memoirs" only too well demonstrate.[12]

These "Memoirs of a Lady of Quality" have been a source
of continual embarrassment to Smollett's readers, for
they seem to have little connection with the novel's
thematic development. A complete defense of their relationship to the total ideational pattern of the novel
would be out of place here, but, surely, on one level
at least, they are intended to illuminate Perry's consistent attempt to keep his benevolence hidden. The
"Memoirs," considered by themselves, pretend to offer,
if not a justification, at least an explanation of Lady
Vane's marital infidelity to her second husband. But,
in terms of the novel, the explanation, though sympathetic to Lady Vane, serves to expose the incompatibil-
ity of feeling with the ways of the world and, at the
same time, to indict the world for its refusal to live
up to the benevolence it claims is natural to man. The
introductory letter to the "Memoirs" sets the basic tone:

"Your natural sensibility had been, by this extraordinary care, tenderness, and attention, cherished and improved to such a degree of delicacy, as could not possibly relish the attachment of the common run of hus-
bands" (VI, 72). Despite her sexual crimes, which she
frankly confesses, Lady Vane describes herself as a
woman of feeling with a heart always "uncorrupted" (VI,
14). As a young girl with an "unbounded benevolence of
heart" (VI, 202), she believed every one's heart was as
sincere as her own (VI, 75). Quite significantly, Lady
Vane does not expect the world's sympathy or understanding for her infidelity to a gross and unfeeling second
husband; rather, she writes only to those who can *feel*
(VI, 78) and who, like herself, reject marriages of convenience like the one her father persuaded her to enter.
  The world, of course, has completely ignored Lady Vane's
feelings and benevolence and reproached her for her infidelity. But on closer examination it has not really
censured her for her infidelity as much as for her lack
of carnal prudence in scorning wealth and material security. It is in reality her benevolence that has incurred the world's ill will. One of Lady Vane's most
telling points occurs in the description of her decision to abandon her second husband should her adulterous union result in pregnancy. She claims that "had
our mutual passion produced any visible effects, I
would immediately have renounced and abandoned my husband for ever, that the fruit of my love for Mr. S——
might not have inherited, to the detriment of the right
heir" (VI, 108). In the eyes of the world, however,
such a decision was folly:

> This was my determination, which I thought just, if
> not prudent; and for which I have incurred the im-
> putation of folly, in the opinion of this wise and
> honest generation, by whose example and advice I
> have, since that time, been a little reformed in
> point of prudentials, though I still retain a strong
> tendency to return to my primitive way of thinking.
> (VI, 108)

Perry's approval of Lady Vane's benevolence and feeling does not obscure his realization that such passions
have been the cause of her ruin and if displayed open-

Smollett—A Risible Misanthrope 81

ly by him will ruin his hopes for the "caresses" of the
world. Lady Vane "was *all for love, or the world well
lost*" (VI, 109), but Perry is not—not even with Emilia. Thus, he takes pains to hide his tender heart.
When he returns to see the dying Trunnion, for example,
"He endeavoured to conceal his tenderness,which, in the
wildness of his youth, and the pride of his disposition,
he considered as a derogation from his manhood..." (VI,
16). Perry continually performs benevolent deeds in
secret. He procures Emilia's brother, Godfrey, a com-
mission in the army (IV, 214ff.) and later obtains his
promotion to a lieutenancy (V, 233). While in London,
during his own attempts at financial reformation, he
continues his secret benevolence, while appearing hard-
hearted in public·

> Numberless were the objects to which he extended
> his charity in private. Indeed, he exerted this
> virtue in secret, not only on account of avoiding
> the charge of ostentation, but also because he was
> ashamed of being detected in such an awkward un-
> fashionable practice, by the censurious observers
> of this humane generation. In this particular, he
> seemed to confound the ideas of virtue and vice;
> for he did good, as others do evil, by stealth; and
> was so capricious in point of behaviour, that fre-
> quently, in public, he wagged his tongue in satir-
> ical animadversions upon that poverty which his hand
> had in private relieved. (VII, 48)

Perry's secret philanthropy and public satire suggest
a tendency towards benevolent misanthropy, recalling
especially Mr. Spatter and the Man in Black. But Smollett does not make the transformation, although he does
use Perry to experiment further with the depiction of
the satirist as a character in the novel. Perry has in
addition to his feeling a natural disposition for satire: "Peregrine's satirical disposition was never more
gratified than when he had an opportunity of exposing
grave characters in ridiculous attitudes..." (IV,146)
Smollett calls this exposure of grave people "practical
satire" (VI, 228), and by this phrase he seems to mean
a physical, even brutal, castigation and exposure of
the foolish and vicious. Ronald Paulson has persua-

sively argued that much of the physical harshness running through Smollett's novels stems from efforts to
translate the conventions of formal verse satire into
prose fiction.[13] This undoubtedly explains Smollett's
fondness for broken shins and heads—"practical satire"
—but, unfortunately, it does not very well explain the
malicious or at least amoral purpose that prompts a
great deal of Perry's satire. Sometimes, to be sure,
it appears to proceed from his suppressed feelings of
benevolence, to reveal the virtuous indignation of the
good man; too often, however, it seems to arise from
the libertine, revealing envy, spite, personal pique,
or plain malice. As Paulson notes, his satire may be
just, but it is also inhumane and lacks moral respon-
sibility, so Perry becomes a satirist satirized.[14]

Perry's gradual realization that the happiness he seeks
will not be derived from either the reckless indulgence
of his selfish passions or from the "caresses" of the
beau monde is accompanied by a corresponding awareness
that satire can become a morally responsible instrument
of reform only when it proceeds from the very benevolence he considers a "derogation from his manhood."
Nearly all of Perry's satire in the first half of the
novel—from his early youth at the Garrison through the
Grand Tour—forms little more than a series of grotesque
practical jokes. At the Garrison, for example, Perry's
"practical satires" are usually at the expense of Commodore Trunnion's superstitious fear of ghosts or his
humorous hatred of lawyers and kinsfolk. All of them
range somewhere between the high spiritedness of youth
and downright cruelty. On the Grand Tour this same
spirit of cruel practical jokes continues. Pallett the
painter and the Doctor are sort of burlesque contenders
in Smollett's version of the controversy between the
ancients and the moderns and undoubtedly deserve Perry's
ridicule. But again, little more than cruelty and malice underlie scenes like the masquerade to which Perry
escorts Pallett in the guise of a woman or the "mock"
duel he foments between the two pedants. And Perry's
chastisement of the wronged Hornbeck reduces his "practical satire" to a vicious form of personal revenge.

The return to England, however, marks a definite advance in the moral significance of the satire. With

Godfrey's assistance Perry exposes and punishes the
cardsharpers and corrupt physicians of Bath. But at
Bath Perry also meets Cadwallader Crabtree, a Timonian
misanthrope, who offers Perry a new insight into the
satirist's role in society. Crabtree represents Smollett's version of the misanthrope-satirist of the Renaissance character books and drama. He is "altogether
misanthropical" (VI, 6) and acts as a self-appointed
public satirist who is detached from the vice he ridicules: "I now appear in the world, not as a member of
any community, or what is called a social creature, but
merely as a spectator, who entertains himself with the
grimaces of a Jack-pudding, and banquets his spleen in
beholding his enemies at loggerheads" (VI, 13-14).
Crabtree's detachment from mankind strikes Perry as the
ideal moral position from which a satirist can best expose and castigate man's vices. The two satirists join
forces in a thoroughly Jonsonian scheme of necromancy
in which Crabtree sets up as a seer while Perry plays
the role of shill. This new exercise in "practical satire," however, has a benevolent side, for the scheme
was devised in such a way that "the expense of this ministry should be defrayed from the profits of their professions; and the remainder be distributed to poor families in distress" (VI, 237). Smollett associates the
role of public satirist with the traditional concept
that satire is the extraordinary arm of the law: "Had
the executive power of the legislature been vested in
him, he would have doubtless devised strange species of
punishment for all offenders against humanity and decorum..." (VII, 3).

Ultimately Perry sees that Crabtree's detachment is
only a feigned objectivity concealing a Timonian lack
of compassion: "...our young gentleman began to be disgusted, at certain intervals, with the character of this
old man, whom he now thought a morose cynic, not so much
incensed against the follies and vices of mankind as
delighted with the distresses of his fellow-creatures"
(VII, 66). An even closer view of Crabtree reveals that
the misanthrope cannot bear the misfortunes of the world
any more stoically than Perry himself; his detachment
is really an arrogant aloofness, and the satire resulting from it is malicious and sterile, ultimately re-
coiling on the satirist himself:

"These are the comfortable fruits of your misanthropy," answered the youth; "your laudable scheme
of detaching yourself from the bonds of society,and
of moving in a superior sphere of your own. Had
you not been so peculiarly sage, and intent upon
laughing at mankind, you could never have been disconcerted by such a pityful inconvenience.... But
now the world retorts the laugh...." (VII, 75)

Crabtree is here the Renaissance humorous misanthrope
mocked, the satirist satirized.

Misanthropy, however, seems to dog the man of feeling,
and Perry himself at one time comes dangerously close
to Crabtree's malicious rejection of man. With all
hopes of preferment from the *beau monde* blasted, Perry
is arrested for debt at the instigation of the very man
for whom he incurred it, Sir Steady Steerwell. Lan-
guishing in the Fleet prison, "He was gradually irri-
tated by his misfortunes into a rancorous resentment
against mankind in general, and his heart so alienated
from the enjoyments of life, that he did not care how
soon he quitted his miserable existence.... He was even
more cautious than ever of incurring obligations....
and at length secluded himself from all society" (VII,
231-232). Perry even rejects the kind offices of his
friends, whom he tries to repulse by declaring "that he
had broke off all connexion with mankind, and that he
impatiently longed for the hour of dissolution, which,
if it should not soon arrive by the course of nature,
he was resolved to hasten with his own hands, rather
than be exposed to the contempt, and more intolerable
pity of a rascally world" (VII, 238). The reader never
fears, of course, that Perry will persist in his Timonian misanthropy, but the final decision in favor of
society rather significantly turns not on the reformation of society, but on the honest individual who some-
how redeems the species. The letter containing the re-
payment of a debt with interest that Perry receives from
the honest sailor Benjamin Chintz, long given up as dead
or absconded, is in Perry's estimation "a more convincing argument... [for rejoining society] than all the
casuists in the universe can advance" (VII, 239).

This Swiftian argument that the honest individual renders mankind at least tolerable is not as arbitrarily

introduced as might at first appear. Perry's public satire of those he aids in secret has suggested the concept
of benevolent misanthropy, but as early in the novel as
the Grand Tour Smollett had treated the Swiftian paradox of loving the individual and hating mankind. The
Doctor, apart from his pedantry, is satirized for his
complete lack of feeling: "Indeed, the ties of private
affection were too weak to engage the heart of this re-
publican, whose zeal for the community had entirely swal-
lowed up his concern for individuals" (V, 95-96). Smollett dramatizes the conflict between "zeal for the community" and "concern for individuals" when he gives the
Doctor the opportunity to assist Pallett. Thinking that
Pallett is mad, both Jolter and the Doctor fear to enter the room to aid him; Jolter intimates that this
duty really belongs to the Doctor, since he and Pallett
had been friends for some time:

> This insinuation introduced a dispute upon the na-
> ture of benevolence, and the moral sense, which,
> the republican argued, existed independent of any
> private consideration, and could never be affected
> by any contingent circumstance of time and fortune;
> while the other [Jolter], who abhorred his princi-
> ples, asserted the duties and excellence of private
> friendship, with infinite rancour of altercation.
> (V, 157-158)

The irony of the fact that neither of these benevolists
has rendered assistance to Pallett is heightened when
Perry, the actual cause of Pallett's predicament, is
moved to compassion for him (V, 159). Throughout *Peregrine Pickle*, then, Smollett skirts the concept of benevolent misanthropy. Only after he held the man of
feeling up to more penetrating light, however, did it
develop into the informing principle of *Humphry Clinker*.

The Man of Feeling Disenchanted:
FERDINAND COUNT FATHOM (1753)

The disillusionment at mankind experienced by Smollett's first two heroes is somewhat unusual in the treatment of men of feeling. In the first place, it par-

tially involves wounded pride and vanity as well as disappointed benevolence. More importantly, however, since
both heroes learn while very young that man is more
often vicious than benevolent, their disillusionment
does not stem from this discovery but rather from the
discovery that the forms of vice are countless.   In
Ferdinand Count Fathom, Smollett turns instead to the
man of feeling's disenchantment with the world and sets
forth one of the Age of Sensibility's most comprehen-
sive fictional cases for the man of feeling's need to
arm himself "against malignity." His virulent opposition to any belief that without protection a man of
feeling will find happiness in the world is revealed in
the narrator's savagely ironic assurances that his biography of Fathom will exclude satire, which, since the
age is so morally refined, could be construed only as
malicious libel.   Instead he will depict a hero of
"splendid connexions," who confirms the steady moral
progress of mankind:

> Our hero shall, with all convenient dispatch, be
> gradually sublimed into all those splendid connex-
> ions of which you are enamoured; and God forbid,
> that, in the meantime, the nature of his extraction
> should turn to his prejudice in a land of freedom
> like this, where individuals are every day enobled
> in consequence of their own qualifications.... Yes,
> refined reader, we are hastening to that goal of
> perfection, where satire dares not show her face;
> where nature is castigated, almost even to still
> life; where humour turns changeling, and slavers in
> an insipid grin; where wit is volatilized into a
> mere vapour; where decency, divested of all sub-
> stance, hovers about like a fantastic shadow; where
> the salt of genius, escaping, leaves nothing but
> pure and simple phlegm; and the inoffensive pen for
> ever drops the mild manna of soul-sweetening praise.
> (VIII, 9)

Smollett is here attacking the sentimental use of exemplary characters in moral discourses and literature
and suggesting that his intent in *Fathom* is to invert

the whole exemplary formula. Smollett set little trust in arousing the latent natural goodness in evil men, and he believed even less in man's moral progress. As he wrote to Dr. John Moore in 1758, "I really believe on my conscience that mankind grows every day more and more malicious."[15]

The dominant critical view of *Ferdinand Count Fathom* is fairly well summarized in George Saintsbury's assertion that it "may be considered Smollett's least good novel."[16] This low opinion of *Fathom* derives in part from the assumption that it seeks to imitate Fielding's *Jonathan Wild*.[17] If such is the case, the novel is indeed a miserable failure, and only the patriotic Sir Walter Scott could prefer it to *Wild*.[18] Smollett, however, nowhere suggests he intended to follow Fielding's precedent of an ironically admirable antihero. As Saintsbury himself observes, Smollett's presentation of Fathom completely lacks the sustained ironical admiration that so characterizes *Wild*.[19] To the contrary, Smollett rather self-consciously represents his novel as the biography of a rogue treated as a rogue. In the Preface, Smollett almost overemphasizes Fathom's villainy, and in the opening chapter the narrator goes out of his way to disagree with Cardinal de Retz's theory that histories should be autobiographical on the very grounds that autobiographers "are naturally partial to their own causes" (VIII, 6). Fathom would certainly not project himself in the lurid and true light that the objective narrator does. Indeed, the narrator is so sensitive to Fathom's villainy that he often comments on it, even breaking into the narrative once, with great rhetorical flourish, to repent his writing the biography of such a miscreant (IX, 87).

Except for using the villain as hero, a practice that Smollett carefully traces in the Preface to the English stage villains of the Renaissance and not to Fielding, Smollett's presentation of Fathom contrasts with Fielding's presentation of Wild, and the repeated assertions of Fathom's villainy constitute direct rather than ironic satiric attacks. Smollett's overt insistence on this villainy suggests that the novel will come into clearer focus if approached with its other main character in view, the benevolent Renaldo. On the surface, as Saintsbury argues, Smollett uses Renaldo as "a virtuous character in opposition to the adventurer." Renaldo is doubtless opposed to Fathom, as Heartfree is to Wild, and his benevolence receives high praise from the narrator. But the purpose of this opposition is not to demonstrate that virtue ultimately triumphs, as it does in the allegorical terms of *Wild*, but that to survive in the world virtue needs protection against the wiles of the Fathoms and of society, which both tolerates and encourages the Fathoms.[20] *Fathom* is, in the manner of *David Simple*, an educational novel in which the virtuous man learns from the villain that the world is out to destroy virtuous men.

In the Preface Smollett totally inverts the sentimental exemplary formula by appealing not to the alluring powers of virtue to deter vice but to fear: "The impulses of fear, which is the most violent and interesting of all the passions, remain longer than any upon the memory; and for one that is allured to virtue, by the contemplation of that peace and happiness which it bestows, a hundred are deterred from the practice of vice, by that infamy and punishment to which it is liable, from the laws and regulations of mankind" (VIII, 3-4). The villain thus replaces the man of feeling as an exemplary character—and in Smollett's new formula he is exemplary for the man of feeling as well. "I declare," Smollett claims, "my purpose is to set him [Fathom] up as a beacon for the benefit of the unexperienced and unwary, who, from the perusal of these memoirs, may learn to avoid the manifold snares with which they are continually surrounded in the paths of life" (VIII, 4). Ironically, Smollett's inversion of the exemplary formula to include the man of feeling reintroduces Fielding again, for in carrying out this formula Smollett seems to have borrowed his structural pattern, some dominant imagery, and the various modes of deception Fathom employs from Fielding's most important nonfictional contribution to the prudent benevolence theme, *An Essay on the Knowledge of the Characters of Men*.[21]

Smollett's intended use of Fathom as a warning to men of feeling echoes Fielding's claim that in the *Essay* he seeks to expose hypocrisy and to "arm as well as I can, the honest, undesigning, open-hearted man, who is generally the prey of this monster, against it" (XII, 238). In the first paragraph of the *Essay* he reiterates this intention, lamenting the fact that many writers have expended their talents on works that assist the hypocrite, while few or none have helped to arm the innocent (XIV, 281). Smollett's first allusion to Fielding's *Essay*, however, probably occurs in his title page epigraph:

> _____ Materiam risus, invenit ad omnes
> Occursus hominum. _____
> Ridebat curas, nec nor et gaudia vulgi;
> Interdum et lachrymas fundebat. _____

Lewis Knapp translates the epigraph as "Food for laughter he found in all his meetings with men. He laughed at the worries and even at the joy of the rabble; at the same time he shed tears." The first part of the epigraph comes from the tenth satire of Juvenal, but Knapp can find no source for the concluding line.[22] That source is probably the *Essay*: "For admitting, that laughing at the vices and follies of mankind is entirely innocent (which is more, perhaps, than we ought to admit), yet, surely, their miseries and misfortunes are no subject of mirth;...the world is so full of them, that scarce a day passes without inclining a truly good-natured man rather to tears than merriment" (XIV, 286).

Borrowing Fielding's major comments on the evils and frauds of the world, Smollett translates them into dramatic action. Fielding claims that a determining principle for good or evil exists in everyone from childhood, even "in persons, who from the same education, etc., might be thought to have directed nature in the same way" (XIV, 282). Fielding, of course, displayed this belief in his contrasting portraits of Blifil and Tom Jones, and it turns up significantly in the early chapters of *Fathom* as the basic distinction between Ferdinand and Renaldo. While Renaldo was fated from infancy to benevolence, Ferdinand was "determined, ere he was yet twelve days old" to villainy (VIII, 10). This natural villainy is enhanced by the fact that before

Fathom was thirteen months old, he had been taught to
"suck brandy impregnated with gunpowder, through the
touch-hole of a pistol" (VIII, 12).

Fielding also warns that "while the crafty and design-
ing part of mankind, consulting only their own separate
advantage, endeavour to maintain one constant imposition on others, the whole world becomes a vast masquerade, where the greatest part appear disguised under
false vizors and habits" (XIV, 283). Smollett seizes
the masquerade metaphor for Ratchcali's rhapsody on
England. London, Ratchcali exclaims to Ferdinand, "is
a vast masquerade, in which a man of stratagem may wear
a thousand different disguises, without danger of detection" (VIII, 203). Ratchcali's confidence that the
two villains can impose upon the town without danger of
detection probably alludes to Fielding's efforts to form
an efficient police force. Ratchcali comes to his conclusion, based on an earlier statement that England is
a paradise for frauds, because "so jealous are the na-
tives of their liberties, that they will not bear the
restraint of necessary *police*, and an able artist may
enrich himself with their spoils, without running any
risk of attracting the magistrate" (VIII, 202-203).
Fielding had been appointed Justice of the Peace for
Westminster in 1748 and was diligently organizing the
London police force. The outbreak of crime in 1750 produced his essay *An Enquiry into the Causes of the Late
Increase of Robbers*, which appeared in 1751, two years
before the publication of *Fathom*.

In Don Diego's first encounter with Fathom, Smollett
dramatizes Fielding's comment on physiognomy as a re-
vealer of character. Fielding believes that "the passions of men do commonly imprint sufficient marks on
the countenance" to discern character, and "it is owing
chiefly to want of skill in the observer that physiognomy
is of so little use and credit in the world" (XIV, 284).
Echoing the first part of Fielding's statement, Don
Diego tells Fathom: "Indeed, I was at first sight prepossessed in your favour, for, notwithstanding the mistakes which men daily commit in judging from appearances, there is something in the physiognomy of a stranger from which one cannot help forming an opinion of his
character and disposition" (VIII, 174-175). Don Diego

confides to Fathom that "We live in such a world of wickedness and fraud, that a man cannot be too vigilant in his own defence" (VIII, 166), and then illustrates a "want of skill in the observer" by concluding, "For once, my penetration hath not failed me; your behaviour justifies my decision; you have treated me with that sympathy and respect which none but the generous will pay to the unfortunate" (VIII, 175). Don Diego is betrayed by Fathom precisely because of a failure of penetration, just as earlier he had failed to penetrate Renaldo beneath the disguise of a tutor.

Since "a more subtile hypocrisy will sometimes escape undiscovered from the highest discernment," Fielding offers a more "infallible guide" (XIV, 289), which is the judgment of men's actions instead of their words or their public reputation. Smollett capitalizes on Fielding's advice, for Fathom deceives the benevolent and innocent precisely because they accept either his word or his public reputation. Mademoiselle de Melvil's maid, Teresa, for example, enters into a collusion with Fathom to steal from her mistress, but she allows Fathom to seduce her only after he has made several pious oaths that he will be true to her (VIII, 39-40). Wilhelmina surrenders to Fathom, in the narrator's ironical words, "Without any other assurance, than his solemn profession of sincerity and truth" (VIII, 66). And since Fathom's public character is one of virtue, he goes unscathed most of the time, even when he is clearly guilty, as when Renaldo is blamed by his teacher and his father for Fathom's cheating (VIII, 25ff.). Renaldo, however, finds it difficult to learn from experience, for his benevolence overcomes his reason; he accepts the blame for cheating and then puts more confidence in Fathom than ever. Even late in the story, when Renaldo finds Fathom in prison, he "implicitly believed the story and protestations of Fathom" (IX, 23). Smollett underscores the irony of this naive faith by revealing that Fathom himself expected a violent rebuke (IX, 22) and that Renaldo had been summoned to the prison by a trick—once again the victim of "fraud and imposition" (IX, 25).

Fielding next lists the various characters whom the man of feeling should consider as potential hypocrites

(XIV, 292ff.). A summary of the list with references to Fathom should sufficiently demonstrate Smollett's borrowings. The flatterer appears first, followed by the professor of friendship, the promiser, the pryer into secrets, the slanderer, and the saint. Fathom's use of the art of flattery needs little comment, for it is the basis of his ability, to use Fielding's words, of "obtaining our good opinion" (XIV, 291). Fathom is, of course, adept at professing friendship and promising his help, as is illustrated in his "sincere" determination to help Renaldo obtain money to return to Hungary (IX, 61-70). As a slanderer, Fathom successfully separates Renaldo and Monimia (IX, 42ff.), and as a "saint" he is constantly offered to Renaldo "as a pattern and reproach" (VIII, 25). Count de Melvil sends Fathom with Renaldo into the world both as a companion and as a "preceptor and pattern" (VIII, 53). In effect, with this gallery of deceptive portraits, both Fielding and Smollett seek to disenchant the man of feeling with the world's false appearances and instill in him the perceptiveness that comes from prudence. Perhaps the most recurring words in the *Essay* are *perceive, discern,* and other synonyms for perceptiveness, and the pattern is repeated in *Fathom*. So pervasive is the pattern that the faculty of perception is raised, on both the physical and spiritual levels, to symbolic status.[23]

Ironically, however, in *Fathom* all the men and women of feeling—Monimia, Don Diego, Count de Melvil, and Renaldo—are conspicuous for their lack of perception. Only the villains see the significance of perception, for it is they who "always keep the faculty of discerning in full exertion" (VIII, 56). Fathom takes Fielding's advice and studies the characters of men: "He dived into the characters of mankind, with a penetration peculiar to himself..." (VIII, 36). Fathom "seldom or never erred in his observations on the human heart" (VIII, 125), for "He had studied mankind with incredible diligence, and knew perfectly well how far he could depend on the passions and foibles of human nature" (VIII, 180). Smollett never implies that completely accurate perception is always possible; Fathom after all "was calculated by nature to dupe even the most cautious" (VIII, 25). The narrator comments on the seduction of Elenor to this same point: "Had she been well seasoned with knowledge and experience, and completely armed with caution against the artifice and villainy of man, her virtue might not have been able to withstand the engines of such an assailant..." (VIII, 194). At the same time, however, men of feeling have an inherent tendency to blind themselves with appearances of virtue.

Count Melvil, Renaldo's father, establishes the pattern of blindness Smollett sees in the man of feeling. He is completely deceived by the young Fathom's professions of filial devotion, for "being himself a man of extraordinary benevolence, [he] looked upon the boy as a prodigy of natural affection" (VIII, 21). The blindness, however, is communicated from one man of feeling to another. The Count advises Renaldo "to encourage every sentiment of candour and benevolence, and to behave with moderation and affability to all his fellow-creatures" (VIII, 28). Renaldo's benevolence needs little encouragement, but, ironically, his good deeds are soon misinterpreted. The narrator shrewdly comments, "Nothing is more liable to misconstruction than an act of uncommon generosity; one half the world mistake the motive...and the rest suspect it of something sinister or selfish..." (VIII, 29). Not only is the man of feeling's vision blind, it often fails to gain sight even from experience, as the scenes with Don Diego and Renaldo cited above suggest. Of all the men and women of feeling in the novel, only Madam Clement is enlightened, for she perceives Fathom's duplicity and saves Monimia from his clutches.

Against the background of Fielding's *Essay, Ferdinand Count Fathom* becomes, in effect, a problem or thesis novel, and the extremely black and white characters, the overcharged scenes of sensibility, and the elaborately formal, even stilted, style—all points usually held against it—suggest that Smollett is imposing something like a morality play structure on his familiar fictional world. His vision of the man of feeling's need for disenchantment seems to be cast in a quasi-allegorical and symbolic mold that instantiates character and sometimes action. Highly stylized, anaglyphic characters enact, in terms of the man of feeling, an

almost archetypal struggle between good and evil against
the grim background of a satirically heightened and intensified world.

 Much of this symbolic intellectual drama arises from
the religious imagery used in describing the principal
characters and several of the notorious sentimental
scenes. Renaldo, the man of feeling, for example, possesses "more than mortal goodness" (IX,255), and Monimia, whose real name is significantly Serafina, stands
out as an essentially redemptive figure; she is continually described as divine, celestial, and angelic.
While still separated from her, Renaldo thinks he sees
Monimia in a heavenly vision and trembles with "the in-
firmity of human nature, oppressed by the presence of a
superior being" (IX, 203). The chapter relating Fathom's frustrated attempt to ravish Monimia is pointedly
titled "Monimia's Honour Protected by the Interposition
of Heaven" (IX, 77). Faced with her drawn sword, Fathom "was not so much affected by his bodily danger, as
awestruck at the manner of her address, and the appearance of her aspect, which seemed to shine with something supernatural" (IX, 79). Fathom himself is usually
depicted by both the narrator and the other characters
in satanic imagery. His birth is even somewhat dia-
bolic, for his mother, a camp-follower, was thought to
have "some supernatural quality inherent in her person"
(VIII, 17), and, "though he first saw the light in Holland, he was not born till after the carriage arrived
in Flanders" (VIII, 7). Wilhelmina, one of the first
women he seduces, once mistakes him for satan "in *pro-
pria persona*" (VIII, 71). He is continually described
as the "devil incarnate"(VIII, 218), a serpent nourished in Renaldo's bosom (IX, 165), a "fiend in reality" (IX,171), and a "venomous serpent" (IX, 199). The
religious imagery and instantial representation carry
over to the secondary characters also, particularly to
the benevolent ones. Madam Clement, as her name indicates, personifies "clemency," while the Jew's benevolence is "more than human" (IX, 68).

 The characters are instantial throughout the novel,
but the scenes are not instantiated until roughly the
last quarter of the narration, which traces the progression of Renaldo's disenchantment. The preceding action

is no less symbolic, but the symbolism is rendered primarily through the more usual Smollettean form of satirical intensification. Smollett again frames his novel with the familiar travels, and in the first sections they serve to reveal a world that is little more than a Hobbesian battlefield. The celebrated opening battlefield scene, in which Fathom's mother robs the dead and wounded, may be cynical, but it also serves as a brilliant symbolic introduction to the Hobbesian world presented in most of the novel. In the time sequence of the novel, it precedes the idyllic paradise of Count de Melvil's home, where Fathom, the snake in the garden, grows up with Renaldo. Fathom's entrance into society immediately follows this pastoral interlude. Smollett's society is a metaphoric battlefield that is just as cruel and destructive as the battlefield of a literal war.

Fathom's "aim was to dwell among the tents of civil life, undisturbed by quarrels and the din of war" (VIII, 105). As Smollett's image suggests, Fathom wishes to exchange one kind of war for another. All his activities are described in military terms: he "reconnoitres" the ground, sets up "operations," "takes to" or "retreats from" the field. Even his seductions are viewed as military operations. Elenor, for example, "submitted to his desire; not with the reluctance of a vanquished people, but with the transports of a joyful city, that opens its gates to receive a darling prince returned from conquest" (VIII, 198). Moreover, society justifies Fathom's satiric view that it is a civil battlefield: "He had formerly imagined, but was now fully persuaded, that the sons of men preyed upon one another, and such was the end and condition of their being. Among the principal figures of life, he observed few or no characters that did not bear a strong analogy to the savage tyrants of the wood" (VIII, 54). This Swiftian vision is not limited to Fathom, who often functions as a satirist even while being satirized,[24] for the narrator editorializes often enough to indicate that he shares it. When, for example, Fathom achieves fame as a doctor through malpractice instead of ability, the narrator intrudes:

> Success raised upon such a foundation would, by a
> disciple of Plato, and some modern moralists, be

ascribed to the innate virtue and generosity of the
human heart,which naturally espouses the cause that
needs protection. But I, whose notions of human
excellence are not quite so sublime, am apt to believe it is owing to that spirit of self-conceit
and contradiction, which is, at least, as universal, if not as natural, as the moral sense so warmly contended for by those ideal philosophers. (IX,
116-117)

This very Christian society, which exalts benevolence
and admires men of feeling, refuses to aid the "benevolent" Renaldo, forcing him to resort to a Jew (IX, 62
ff.), while it adds plumes to Fathom's character when
he is brought to court by the Trapwells; it even receives him back as an equal member, consciously pre-
tending he had been abroad, when he procures more money
(VIII, 239-240; IX, 88).

The remarkable "Gothic" scenes in the storm-lashed
forest and at the hut of the murderous peasant woman
structurally reinforce the Hobbesian world in which Fathom thrives. The gloomy forest and the midnight terrors
of the storm may foreshadow the trappings of the Gothic novel, but for Smollett they are more than mere decoration or intensification of the *surnaturel expliqué*.
First of all, the scenes occur just after Ratchcali's
robbery and desertion of Fathom and immediately precede
Fathom's entrance into Hobbesian society. They thus
unite the evil of Fathom's personal world to the evil
of the larger world of man. Secondly, the terrors of
the forest and of the old woman's hut are accurate fore-
shadowings of future evils, not merely the exploita-
tions of emotional situations for their own sake; nor
is there any question of supernatural involvement, for
the old woman is not a witch or ethereal being, but a
real murderess in collusion with a real band of robbers
who plan to murder and rob Fathom. These two scenes,
then, symbolize in miniature the world Fathom will encounter and simultaneously recall the opening battlefield scene.

The last quarter of the novel drops Fathom and the satiric scenes into the background and focuses on Renaldo's progressive disenchantment with the world. The
process of disenchantment occurs in a rapid succession
of what can best be described as symbolic tableaux in

which religious imagery rises to almost unparalleled
heights in Smollett. The disenchantment begins when
Renaldo's sister "removes the Film which had long ob-
structed his Penetration, with regard to Count Fathom"
(IX, 158). Immediately following this revelation, Renaldo receives the letter informing him of Monimia's
supposed death, and, like her, he falls into a fever,
dies, and then revives—climaxing a pattern of deaths
and resurrections initiated by Monimia (who does not
"arise" until the last pages of the book),continued by
Renaldo's step-father, Count Trebasi, re-echoed in Don
Diego's flashback relation of his supposed murder of
his wife, daughter, and Orlando (Renaldo in disguise),
and concluded by Fathom himself. Renaldo, however, is
"reborn" with a hatred of Fathom as excessive as his
former love. But finally alerted to the reality of
evil, he gradually learns to transfer his hatred from
the individual to mankind. After hearing Ratchcali's
tale, he is "inspired...with great contempt for human
nature. And next day he proceeded on his journey with
a heavy heart, ruminating on the perfidy of mankind..."
(IX, 182). Almost immediately this hatred is countered by Don Diego's reference to the honest individual:
"'Praised be God,' said he, 'that virtue and generosity
are still to be found among the sons of men'" (IX, 184).
Monimia's "resurrection" in the tomb scene marks the
redemption of the man of feeling from blindness. Renaldo's return to England was originally conceived as
"a pilgrimage to the dear hallowed" tomb of Monimia and
as an opportunity to take "vengeance on the perfidious
Fathom" (IX, 177), to sacrifice him, in Major Farrel's
words, "to the manes of the beauteous Monimia" (IX,
175-176). But it is the "reborn" Monimia, the "divine"
Serafina, who completes Renaldo's enlightenment by
teaching him to transform vengeance into justice and
then to temper justice with mercy: always to keep the
individual in view. In Monimia's eyes, Fathom has already received both the vengeance and justice of Heav-
en: "His fraud, ingratitude, and villainy are, I believe, unrivalled; yet his base designs have been defeated; and heaven perhaps hath made him the involun-
tary instrument for bringing our constancy and virtue
to the test.... The doctor, who has traced him in all

his conduct and vicissitudes of fortune, will draw a
picture of his present wretchedness,which,I doubt not,
will move your compassion..." (IX, 227-228). Renaldo
finally agrees to see Fathom who,suddenly revived from
a feverish delirium, thinks that he is "now arrived at
the land of departed souls,and that the shades of those
whom he had so grievously injured were come to see him
tormented according to his demerits" (IX, 252). The
whole scene in which Fathom repents and converts, like
that in Monimia's tomb, is obviously theatrical and
probably based on current theatrical practice.[25] But
Fathom's plea for mercy, set speech that it is, completes the imagery of fear initiated in the Preface,
translating fear of secular justice into fear of divine
justice: "Is there no mercy then for penitence? Is
there no pity due to the miseries I suffered upon earth?
Save me, O bountiful Heaven! from the terrors of everlasting woe; hide me from these dreadful executioners,
whose looks are torture" (IX, 252). Fathom's Pauline
decision to "work out...[his] salvation with fear and
trembling" (IX, 256) seems valid in Smollett's world
for villain and man of feeling alike—but for different
reasons.
  Fathom's conversion and repentance conclude the death-
rebirth symbolism and clarify Smollett's attitude towards the man of feeling's uselessness as an exemplary
character. In Smollett's world virtue,with perception,
can and must combat and restrain evil, but rarely will
it deter those hesitating on "the brink of iniquity"
(VIII,4) or convert those who have already made the
plunge. As Smollett argues in the Preface, fear of
secular and ultimately of divine justice is a more as-
sured moral persuader than an exemplary character. Moreover, in the narrator's terms, Fathom might never have
repented had he successfully evaded the law and "remained without the verge of misfortune" (IX, 156). At
the same time, the man of feeling's blindness makes him
unfit for the struggle with evil. Indeed, benevolent
feeling can be one of the principal causes for the success of hypocrisy in the world. Renaldo's sister finally tells him, "Nothing is more easy...than to impose
upon a person, who, being himself unconscious of guile,
suspects no deceit. You have been a dupe,dear brother,

not to the finesse of Fathom, but to the sincerity of your own heart" (IX, 162). In the narrator's words, "All that can be done by virtue, unassisted with experience, is to avoid every trial with such a formidable foe, by declining and discouraging the first advances towards a particular correspondence with perfidious man, however agreeable it may seem to be. For there is no security but in conscious weakness" (VIII, 228).

Renaldo's triumph in the final section of the novel stands in ironic contrast to the opening scene of the battlefield and constitutes a "tonal bifurcation," as M.A. Goldberg contends,[26] only if Renaldo is accepted as a serious combatant against evil. Renaldo becomes disenchanted with Fathom and the pleasing appearances of the world, but it is too late to defeat Fathom. Nor are any of the other men of feeling ever responsible for Fathom's various downfalls. Ronald Paulson notes that Fathom is often gulled,[27] and he certainly ends miserably, but it is extremely important to observe that he is always gulled and finally defeated by other sharpers—criminals whose faculty of discerning is keener than his own. He falls a victim to the machinations of the jeweller's wife (VIII, 95), Ratchcali (VIII, 114), Sir Stentor Stiles and Sir Giles (VIII, 149-150), Trapwell (VIII, 236ff.), Maurice and the lawyer (VIII, 248 ff.), and finally Dr. Buafflo (IX, 138ff.). Fathom is usually superior to his fellow criminals "in point of genius and invention," but, as the narrator comments when Ratchcali deceives Fathom, they have "the advantage of him in the articles of age and experience" (VIII, 114). The irony of Fathom's various downfalls and of his final defeat, however, does not reside merely in the complete ineffectuality of the men of feeling; much of its pungency arises from the paradoxical legal injustice of his imprisonments. Fathom's crimes undoubtedly deserve legal action, but strikingly enough, whenever he is brought to trial or imprisoned, he is being punished for crimes he never committed. He is usually imprisoned for debt or because of the false accusations of people like the Muddys and Dr. Buafflo (IX, 128ff.). Fathom suffers for his crimes, but he suffers at the hands of villains greater than himself, not at the hands

of justice. Indeed, in Smollett's Hobbesian world justice seems always to be at the mercy of fraud and deceit, although with grim irony it is served.

The novel, in a sense, ends where it began—on the battlefield. Renaldo and his friends have been disenchanted and Fathom has repented, but Smollett's Hobbesian
society remains intact.   Renaldo must even suspect
Fathom's repentance. Fielding advises in his *Essay*:

> I shall not here dispute the doctrine of repentance,
> any more than its tendency to the good of society;
> but as the actions of men are the best index to
> their thoughts, as they do, if well attended to and
> understood, with the utmost certainty demonstrate
> the character; and as we are not so certain of the
> sincerity of repentance, I think we may with justice
> suspect, at least so far as to deny him our confi-
> dence, that a man whom we once knew to be a villain,
> remains a villain still.   (XIV, 302)

Renaldo and the other men of feeling retain their benevolence, even for Fathom: "Though not one of them
would say that such a miscreant ought to live, yet all
concurred in approving the offices of humanity which
had been performed" (IX, 253). At the same time, however, the now disenchanted Renaldo refuses Fathom any
"office requiring integrity" and a resumption of personal friendship until there is "undoubted proof of
amendment" (IX, 256). In the society Smollett depicts
it is almost certain that a villain remains a villain
still, and men of feeling enter that society at their
peril if they lack the security of "conscious weakness."

The Man of Feeling as Administrator of Justice:
SIR LAUNCELOT GREAVES (1760-61)

Ferdinand Count Fathom upholds the orthodox belief in
the salutary effects of the fear of justice, and in so
doing it strikes at the sentimental tendency Benevolism
fostered—the tendency to rely on the alluring power
of benevolence. Shaftesbury had insisted again and
again that virtue should not be pursued either for re-
wards, temporal or eternal, or from a fear of justice,

but "for its own sake, as good and amiable *in itself*."[28] As was shown in the first chapter, this proposition was inculcated primarily by insisting that benevolence was natural to man and by pointing to the worldly happiness —even pleasure—that supposedly accompanied benevolent acts. Smollett, of course, had no quarrel with the "pleasures" of virtue—these are, after all, what Renaldo retains after his disenchantment; his argument was rather with the sentimental conclusion that they were powerful enough to attract evil men.

From a more positive viewpoint, however, *Fathom* makes justice a virtue equal in importance to benevolence. Justice, of all the virtues subsidiary to benevolence, was the most difficult for Benevolism to accommodate. In the first place, its traditional association with the deterring power of fear obviously made it an uncomfortable ally of the notion that virtue should be sought for its own sake as something desirable in itself. Furthermore, it jeopardized the sentimental concept of candor, for it implied that the man of feeling must take continual notice of man's actual depravity rather than of his potential for good. Finally, the prosecution of evil doers that justice encourages, perhaps in opposition to benevolent feelings, could easily lead to the enjoyment of punishment. For all of these reasons, justice was played down in Benevolism, receiving only cursory notice.

In *Sir Launcelot Greaves*, Smollett treated the positive side of justice extensively, trying to fuse it with benevolence in a man of feeling who could expose and chastise the evils of the world. Sir Launcelot's benevolence requires little demonstration. He is a typical man of feeling, who personally goes from door to door distributing alms and even repairing the homes of his poor tenants (X, 28ff.). His father is proud of Sir Launcelot's "feeling heart" (X, 30), while the whole countryside turns out to greet the young man of feeling whenever he appears in public; indeed, "one would have thought the golden age was revived in Yorkshire" (X, 31). Like all Smollett's heroes, however, even Sir Launcelot must learn to moderate his feelings. While visiting the inevitable Smollettean prison, his "miniature republic," the benevolent prisoner, Felton, takes

the opportunity to teach Sir Launcelot the need for the
restraining reins of prudence:

> God forbid...that I should attempt to thwart your
> charitable intention; but this, my good sir, is no
> object—she has many resources. Neither should we
> number the clamorous beggar among those who really
> feel distress; he is generally gorged with bounty
> misapplied. The liberal hand of charity should be
> extended to modest want that pines in silence, en-
> countering cold, nakedness, and hunger and every spe-
> cies of distress. (X, 236).

As a man of feeling administering justice, however,
Sir Launcelot is a more complicated creation. In many
respects, Smollett has merely converted the many ironic
encomiums of Fathom as a soldier into a straightforward
presentation of knight-errantry. Smollett literally
arms Sir Launcelot and treats his travels in terms of
the traditional chivalric quest: "It was his opinion
that chivalry was an useful institution while confined
to its original purposes of protecting the innocent,
assisting the friendless, and bringing the guilty to
condign punishment" (X, 203). The precedent for this
treatment of chivalry obviously derives from *Don Quixote*, but, at the same time, Sir Launcelot is not merely
a slavish imitation of the famous Don. He is not mad,
nor does he joust with windmills; he tells the Timonian
misanthrope Ferret, who accuses him of imitating Don
Quixote, "I see and distinguish objects as they are
discerned and described by others. I reason without
prejudice..." (X, 16). Nor is there any irony in his
attack on vice: he has full possession of his faculties and the vice he castigates is real vice; he does
not, like Don Quixote, seek imaginary evils while ironically exposing real evils all around him. Sir Launcelot is not even feigning madness to gain acceptance for
his strange dress and behavior: "He that counterfeits
madness, unless he dissembles, like the elder Brutus,
for some virtuous purpose, not only debases his own
soul, but acts as a traitor to Heaven, by denying the
divinity that is within him" (X, 16).
The complete lack of irony in Sir Launcelot's presentation suggests that Smollett is treating chivalry as

a symbolic mode of administering justice more in the manner of Spenser's moral allegory of justice in Book V of the *Faerie Queene*. The absence of ironic ambiguity and Quixotic insanity in Sir Launcelot's attempts to eradicate vice render him a more modern version of Sir Artegall than of Don Quixote. Sir Launcelot's riding "in preservation of peace"(X,18), his quarreling "with none but the foes of virtue and decorum,...the natural enemies of mankind" (X,16), and his paradoxical use of violence to enforce justice recall Spenser's Knight of Justice.[29] The election scene in *Greaves*, for example, seems to owe a great deal to the famous attack of Sir Artegall on the giant with the scales. The election scene hinges on Launcelot's attempts to counsel moderation and reconciliation of opposing views; but "The doctrine of moderation was a very unpopular subject in such an assembly; and accordingly they rejected it as one man.... They hissed, they hooted, and they halooed; they annoyed him [Sir Launcelot] with missiles of dirt, sticks, and stones; they cursed...till, at length, his patience was exhausted" (X, 104). Sir Artegall's argument with the giant and the crowd is very similar in theme; the giant, like Smollett's assembly, refuses to hear a doctrine of moderation because "it was not right which he did seeke;/But rather strove extremities to way" (V.ii.49.2-3). When Sir Artegall's squire, Talus, overthrows the giant, the crowd becomes a mob, and Talus must use his "flaile" to disperse it:

> But soone as they him nigh approaching spide,
> They gan with all their weapons him assay,
> And rudely stroke at him on every side:
> Yet nought they could him hurt, ne ought dismay.
> But when at them he with his flaile gan lay,
> He like a swarme of flyes them overthrew;
> Ne any of them durst come in his way,
> But here and there before his presence flew....
> (V.ii.53.1-8)

In like manner, Sir Launcelot finally "brandished his lance, and riding into the thickest of the concourse, laid about him with such dexterity and effect, that the multitude was immediately dispersed" (X, 104).

The administration of justice, however, was also close-

ly associated in Smollett's mind with the activity of
the satirist, as was seen in *Peregrine Pickle*. In his
Letters on Several Subjects (1776), William Melmoth,
writing under the pseudonym of Thomas Fitzosborne, illustrates how traditional such an association was: "He
[the satirist] may be considered as a sort of supplement to the legislative authority of his country; as
assisting the unavoidable defects of all legal institu-
tions for the regulating of manners, and striking terror even where the divine prohibitions themselves are
held in contempt."[30] Sir Launcelot's knight-errantry
seems also to be connected with this conception of the
satirist. Sir Launcelot has much the same tempera-
mental reactions to evil as Roderick and Perry: "indignation" flashes from his eyes (X, 17); he is as "has-
ty as gunpowder" (X, 37), and he boils with indignation
(X, 105). Moreover, his belief that knight-errantry is
a mode of chastising vice beyond the reach of the law
has the ring of the satirist's typical claim: "I do
purpose...to act as coadjutator to the law,and even to
remedy evils which the law cannot reach; to detect fraud
and treason, abase insolence, mortify pride,discourage
slander, disgrace immodesty, and stigmatise ingratitude
..." (X, 18). Such a desire merges the satirist and the
knight-errant into the conscious administrator of justice described by Samuel Butler: "A Satyr is a kinde of
Knight Errant that goes upon Adventures, to Relieve the
Distressed Damsel Virtue, and Redeme Honor.... And op-
prest Truth, and Reason out of the Captivity of Giants
and Magitians."[31]
Both the satirist and the knight-errant are extraordinary enforcers of the law,an idea Sir Launcelot suggests in his speech before the evil Justice Gobble:

> ...if such a contemptible miscreant shall have it
> in his power to do such deeds of inhumanity and op-
> pression, what avails the law? Where is our admired
> constitution, the freedom, the security of the sub-
> ject, the boasted humanity of the British nation!
> Sacred Heaven! if there was no human institution
> to take cognisance of such atrocious crimes, I would
> listen to the dictates of eternal justice, and,arm-
> ing myself with the right of nature, exterminate
> such villains from the face of the earth! (X, 132)

This is not Don Quixote speaking, but the conscious
satirist pronouncing his archetypal formula in the face
of the collapse of law.

Although Sir Launcelot is not himself mad, the theme
of madness plays an important role in developing the
concept of the "just" satirist-knight. Nearly all of
the characters in the novel, of course, think that Sir
Launcelot is mad, despite all the evidence to the contrary; "madness" and "lunacy" are probably the most repeated words in the book, and the concluding scenes occur in the madhouse where both Sir Launcelot and his
beloved Aurelia Darnel are confined. Smollett's pre-
occupation with the madness theme indicates his determined effort to satirize society in the novel. While
the world thinks Sir Launcelot is mad, Smollett implies
that it is the world that should look to its own sanity.
Captain Crowe, captivated by Sir Launcelot's courage
and benevolence and planning to follow him in chivalry,
insinuates this aspect of the madness theme: "Mad!
what then? I think for my part one half of the nation
is mad—and the other not very sound—I don't see why
I han't as good a right to be mad as another man..."
(X, 70). Launcelot's confinement in an actual madhouse
confirms his opinion that innocent and sane people are
often put away as mad when it is their confiners, perhaps, who should be, if not in the madhouse, at least
in prison: "A judicial writ *ad inquirendum* being ex-
ecuted, the prisons of his inquisition were laid open,
and several innocent captives enlarged" (X, 273).

In terms of satire, the madness theme indicates the
satirist's need for justice; if he is to promote justice, his own administration of the law must be equally
just. As the satiric spokesman of *Advice* claims, "Two
things I dread, my conscience and the law."[32] In the
madhouse Sir Launcelot meets Dick Distich, a satirist
who has abused his trust and who is confined lest he be
prosecuted for libel. Launcelot's comments to this vicious satirist are revealing: "...your character must
stand as that of a man who hath some small share of
genius, without an atom of integrity. Of all those whom
Pope lashed in his Dunciad, there was not one who did
not richly deserve the imputation of dulness..." (X,
256). Distich's refusal to be liberated from the mad-

house indicates that that is precisely where the malevolent satirist belongs.   Distich's final words to Sir
Launcelot confirm this: "If you see Ben Bullock, tell
him I wish he would not dedicate any more of his works
to me.——D——n the fellow, he has changed his note, and
begins to snivel.—For my part, I stick to my former
maxim, defy all the world, and will die hard, even if
death should be preceded by damnation" (X, 270).

Sir Launcelot's final appeal to the ordinary forms of
the law to rescue Aurelia from the madhouse climaxes
the madness theme and reveals the need for the satirist-
knight to refrain from physical interference with the
ordinary processes of the law. As a knight in armor
Sir Launcelot failed to obtain Aurelia's release, and,
although illegally confined in the madhouse himself,his
dress and behavior only convinced his keepers that he
was truly mad.   The traditional satirist, as scourger,
surgeon, or even knight-errant, attacks and chastizes
corruption through the medium of verbal discourse. Sir
Launcelot's exploits reveal again Smollett's translation of satiric conventions into "practical satire,"
physical attack.   The traditional satirist claims to
promote justice by effecting a moral and spiritual administration of the law; Sir Launcelot, on the other
hand, effects only a corporal administration that often
places him in the position of merely taking the law into his own hands.   Such is, indeed, the case with many
of his exploits. When he forces lecherous farmers to
marry the girls they have seduced and horsewhips hus-
bands who have maltreated their wives, for example,Sir
Launcelot may be morally in the right, but, at the same
time, he oversteps the bounds of a private citizen (X,
53-58).   In such cases the satirist, benevolent as he
may be, is as subversive of public order as Ferret, the
Timonian misanthrope, and his kind.   In the words of
Crowe's nephew, the attorney Tom Clarke, "Sir Launcelot's generosity seemed to overleap the bounds of discretion, and even in cases might be thought tending to
a breach of the King's peace" (X, 53).

The Man of Feeling as Benevolent Misanthrope:
HUMPHRY CLINKER (1771)

Humphry Clinker is doubtless Smollett's finest novel, and in it he finally harmonizes his satire of society with a comic treatment of the man of feeling. In the character of Matt Bramble, Smollett is able to convey the benevolent satire he strove for in his earlier novels and still confine it artistically within the framework of a comic story. Matt Bramble may be an extension of the peevish traveler in Smollett's *Travels through France and Italy*; he may even be an idealization of Smollett's own personality.[33] Essentially, however, he derives from the tradition of benevolent misanthropy with which Smollett was certainly familiar, since, as indicated before, the first issue of the *Critical Review* had praised Samuel Foote's *The Gentleman Returned from Paris,* a play that stars a benevolent misanthrope as satirist, Giles Crab, and that has a family situation closely resembling the one Smollett creates in *Clinker*.

Jery, Matt's nephew, establishes Matt's misanthropy and cynicism early in the novel: "My uncle is an odd kind of humourist, always on the fret, and so unpleasant in his manner, that, rather than be obliged to keep him company, I'd resign all claim to the inheritance of his estate. Indeed, his being tortured by the gout may have soured his temper, and, perhaps, I may like him better on farther acquaintance" (XI, 9). Soon Jery discovers that Matt's humor is an odd mixture of extreme feeling and misanthropy. "I was once apt to believe him a complete Cynic, and that nothing but the necessity of his occasions could compel him to get within the pale of society. I am now of another opinion; I think his peevishness arises partly from bodily pain, and partly from a natural excess of mental sensibility; for, I suppose, the mind as well as the body, is, in some cases, endowed with a morbid excess of sensation" (XI, 20).

Jery's diagnosis strikes to the core of benevolent misanthropy; mental sensibility is appalled at what it encounters in a corrupted world and resorts to misanthropy as a defense against it; the result is a benevolent satirist and an amiable humorist:

His singularities afford a rich mine of entertain-

> ment; his understanding...is well cultivated; his
> observations on life are equally just, pertinent,
> and uncommon. He affects misanthropy, in order to
> conceal the sensibility of a heart which is tender
> even to a degree of weakness.... Respectable as he
> is, upon the whole, I can't help being sometimes
> diverted by his little distresses, which provoke him
> to let fly the shafts of his satire, keen and pene-
> trating as the arrows of Teucer. (XI, 35)

Aware that feeling is a weakness as well as a strength,
Matt has gained a knowledge of the characters of men
and has guarded against imposition.

Jery discovers Matt's true generosity and feeling when
he overhears Matt's secret attempts to help a poor widow (XI, 25-26). The reader, however, has seen Bramble's
peculiar personality at work long before this. Matt's
first letter to Dr. Lewis, the first letter of the novel reveals the misanthrope, in the midst of his cynicism, ordering his corn to be sold to the poor "at a
shilling under market-price" (XI, 5).   He settles his
domestic affairs in an equally nonmisanthropic manner:
"Let him give five pounds to the poor of the parish,
and I'll withdraw my action.... Let Morgan's widow
have the Alderney cow, and forty shillings to clothe
her children. But don't say a syllable of the matter
to any living soul—I'll make her pay when she is able"
(XI, 6). Jery notes elsewhere, "Indeed I never knew a
hypochondriac so apt to be infected with good-humour.
He is the most risible misanthrope I ever met with" (XI,
63). Jery's later discoveries are further revealing:
"Mr. Bramble is extravagantly delicate in all his sensations, both of soul and body.... His blood rises at
every instance of insolence and cruelty.... On the other hand, the recital of a generous, humane, or grateful
action, never fails to draw from him the tears of ap-
probation, which he is often greatly distressed to conceal" (XI, 86-87).

Matt's misanthropy also derives from the body, as Jery
notes, for, like many benevolent misanthropes, Matt suffers from the spleen. He is thus in part a humorist
whose satire can also be diagnosed as a cathartic, a
release from physical suffering. Matt often blames his
invective on the spleen: "We have been at court and

'change, and everywhere; and everywhere we find food
for spleen, and subject for ridicule" (XI, 139-140).
The continuity of the humor tradition is revealed in the
rather conventional discovery scene in which Clinker
learns that Matt is his natural father.[34] As a youth,
like Shakespeare's Jaques, Matt had been a libertine:
"In short, the rogue proves to be a crab of my own plant-
ing, in the days of hot blood and unrestrained liber-
tinism" (XII, 18). Matt's change of name also has significance for his misanthropy; the sins of youth were
committed under his maternal name Lloyd, which he later
abandoned for his paternal name, Bramble—symbolizing
his moral reformation and his new satiric disposition
(XII, 186-188): "I took my mother's name, which was
Lloyd, as heir to her lands in Glamorganshire; but, when
I came of age, I sold that property, in order to clear
my parental estate, and resumed my real name; so that
I am now Matthew Bramble of Brambleton Hall, in Mon-
mouthshire..." (XII, 187-188).

Unlike the Renaissance splenetic humorists, however,
Matt does not become a misanthrope because of personal
misfortune, pride, envy, or vanity. Smollett pointedly contrasts him with a group of his old friends, who
disgust Matt precisely because they resemble the Renaissance malcontent: "Each of them apart, in succeeding
conferences, expatiated upon his own particular griev-
ances; and they were all malcontents at bottom. Over
and above their personal disasters, they thought themselves unfortunate in the lottery of life" (XI, 72).
Matt is thus cleared of any of the vices that would subject him to the same ridicule he hurls at the world.
Nor as a man of feeling is he given to sentimental fits
of indiscriminate benevolence. In the character of Mr.
Serle, Smollett in fact condemns such sentimentality.
"My uncle," writes Jery, "says that he is a man of uncommon parts and unquestioned probity; that his fortune, which was originally small, has been greatly hurt
by a romantic spirit of generosity, which he has often
displayed, even at the expense of his discretion, in
favour of worthless individuals" (XI, 89). Serle does
not even possess the sense to learn from his mistakes
or to arouse a just sense of indignation at those who
have imposed maliciously on him (XI, 88-89).

Matt's union of misanthropy and benevolence lends his satire exceptionally ironic force. His vision of the world carries over the madness metaphor from *Launcelot Greaves*: "In a word," Matt writes triumphantly, "the whole nation seems to be running out of their wits" (XI, 115). Perhaps the world is even madder than those confined in asylums. When he observes the citizens of London in vain pursuit of luxury and folly, madness he feels must motivate them: "...how can I help supposing they are actually possessed by a spirit more absurd and pernicious than anything we meet with in the precincts of Bedlam?" (XI, 116). Jery often indicates that Matt's misanthropic observations and castigations usually fall into the Cynic tradition. Like the Cynics, and especially Diogenes, his railings can be divided rather clearly into attacks on man in general and on the luxuries of overrefined civilization. Over and over Matt cries that "we live in a vile world of fraud and sophistication" (XI, 48). In horror he sees men as "all a pack of venal and corrupted rascals; so lost to all sense of honesty, and all tenderness of character, that, in a little time...nothing will be infamous but virtue and public spirit" (XI, 99-100). London and Bath display the human species in every aspect of its depravity, so that Matt concludes: "But what have I to do with the human species? except for a very few friends, I care not if the whole was—Hark ye, Lewis, my misanthropy increases every day.—The longer I live, I find the folly and the fraud of mankind grow more and more intolerable" (XI, 60).

Benevolence and men of feeling only demonstrate to Matt that he has a just view of man and society, for there are so few men of feeling that they prove exceptions to the rule. The famous "sentimental" scene depicting Captain Brown's homecoming is completely ironic, for Smollett offers it as validation of Matt's misanthropic position. To Matt he "had in some measure redeemed human nature from the reproach of pride, selfishness, and ingratitude" (XI, 116). But Captain Brown's feeling sheds further light on Matt's own benevolent misanthropy as a solution for a man of feeling in this world. While the captain may redeem human nature, he is still to Matt "one of those few men of worth...that serve only as exceptions; which, in the grammarian's phrase, confirm and prove a general canon" (XI, 100). The "general canon" calls forth Matt's satirical letters, the overflowing of spleen,or, as Matt, echoing the prophet Jeremiah, tells Dr. Lewis, *"the lamentations of Matthew Bramble"* (XI, 42).

The stage forms one of the central metaphors of the novel and is closely associated with Jery. The stage metaphor offers Jery a comic way of viewing the world, for the sights he sees while traveling constitute continuing acts of a comedy in the theatre of life. "I cannot account for my being pleased with these incidents any other way," claims Jery, "than by saying they are truly ridiculous in their own nature, and serve to heighten the humour in the farce of life, which I am determined to enjoy as long as I can" (XI, 63). The theatre imagery runs through the entire novel and structures the subplot involving Matt's niece, Lydia, and Wilson. Young Dennison's assumption of the name Wilson and his disguise as an actor imply the complicated problem of appearance and reality that the theatre expresses. Lydia's certainty that Wilson (Dennison) "is not what he appears to be" and that "time will discover" (XI, 10) reflects light on the whole Bramble family. Matt is not the misanthrope he appears to be; Jery is not the pert young jack-a-napes Matt thinks he is; in fact, no one is quite what he appears to be, particularly Humphry Clinker, who turns out to be a gentleman born.

But the theatre imagery most properly belongs to Jery, for he speaks and thinks in terms of the theatre more than any of the other travelers.[35] It is significant, however, that Jery's theatre always has a comedy on the boards. Jery stands, of course, in contrast to Matt's gloomy and more tragic vision of the world; he is a Democritus laughing at the world's vice and follies: "Those follies which move my uncle's spleen excite my laughter" (XI, 63). Jery represents the opposite side of the cynical attitude. If Matt derives from Diogenes, Jery traces his ancestry to the gayer Cynics,Crates and Menippus.[36] Most obviously, of course, Jery represents youth opposed to Matt's age, but Jery's youthful comic view of life strengthens the comic undertone of

the novel and, supporting Matt's underlying benevolence,
anticipates the comic conclusion. Jery's comic insights
are also significant for our understanding of the real
characters of the Bramble family.   Tabby, Lydia, and
Winifred Jenkins all write letters that rebound on their
characters, letters that are ironically self-revealing,
but their comments on each other and on the other members of the family are for the most part superficial.
Only Jery takes it upon himself to dissect philosophi-
cally each member of the family and to write incisive
comments on their characters. Jery, for example, is the
sole member of the group who reaches a philosophical
understanding of Matt's apparently contradictory nature.

Jery's stage metaphor readily complements   the humor
elements in Matt, Lismahago, and Tabby; the final mellowing of all three recalls the Jonsonian method of ex-
hibiting a humorist on the stage for ridicule with the
intention of curing the humor.   This dehumoring intention of Jery's stage metaphor can most readily be seen
in the famous Lismahago. Lismahago appears to be a humorist of what McKillop calls the "incorrigible" type,[37]
but his relationship to the Bramble family often makes
him a touchstone for views of Matt and Jery. As a humorist, he most clearly contrasts with Matt and by implication points up Matt's benevolence. The humors of
both characters, of course, derive from the traditional
English view of the Welshman as proud and peppery and
the Scotsman as dour and pragmatical.[38]

Smollett elaborates Lismahago's humor into a peevish
contentiousness that delights in maintaining paradoxes:

His manner is as harsh as his countenance; but his
peculiar turn of thinking, and his pack of knowledge,
made up of the remnants of rarities, rendered his
conversation desirable, in spite of his pedantry
and ungracious address. I have often met with a
crab-apple in a hedge, which I have been tempted to
eat for its flavour, even while I was disgusted by
its austerity. The spirit of contradiction is so
strong in Lismahago, that I believe in my conscience
he has rummaged, and read, and studied with inde-
fatigable attention, in order to qualify himself to
refute established maxims, and thus raise trophies

for the gratification of polemical pride. (XII, 32-33)

Matt thus points out that Lismahago can be entertaining because of his sourness, but, at the same time, he is not an amiable humorist. He belongs rather clearly to that Jonsonian type of humorist who descends in a direct line from Theophrastus' "Grumbler," through the Renaissance "surly man," to Samuel Johnson's "contentious man." He bears in fact a rather close resemblance to Samuel Johnson's "contentious man":

> ...from the first exertion of reason I was bred a disputant, trained up in all the arts of domestic sophistry, initiated in a thousand low stratagems, viable shifts, and sly concealment; versed in all the turns of altercation, and acquainted with the whole discipline of fending and proving.... I never spoke but to contradict, nor declaimed but in the defense of a position universally acknowledged to be false, and therefore worthy, in my opinion, to be adorned with all the colours of false representation.[39]

This type of character would have been associated in the eighteenth-century mind with the philosophical position of the detested Stoics. One eighteenth-century historian of philosophy writes, "The logic of the Stoics was perfectly embarrassing; it was rather the art of endless disputation, and of maintaining contradictions, than of investigating truth."[40] Lismahago was then an excellent object of ridicule.

Lismahago is not quite incorrigible, however, for his slight mellowing at the end indicates that Jonson's belief in cure through ridicule has worked somewhat. Since Matt most often disputes with Lismahago, drawing out both his good and bad traits, Matt can perhaps be compared to Asper in Jonson's *Every Man Out of His Humour*, while Lismahago resembles Macilente. But Jery's stage metaphor most clearly provides the Jonsonian dehumoring, at least of Lismahago. He thinks of himself almost as a stage manager: "In my last two you had so much of Lismahago, that I suppose you are glad he is gone off the stage for the present" (XII, 39). Even Matt, however, can conceive of his own railings in the stage met-

aphor and view the follies that pass before his eyes as
various acts and scenes of a drama, which his satire
exposes to ridicule. The excited activity of Bath, for
example, he sees as merely "a tiresome repetition of the
same languid frivolous scene, performed by actors that
seemed to sleep in all their motions" (XI, 84).

Matt definitely dominates the travels, and, although
Jery's laughing satire contributes to the comic tone,
Matt's more tragic view of vice and folly outweighs it.
Jery's rather happy estimate of the human scene easily
falls prey to Matt's misanthropy. Matt and the actor
Quin confirm each other's view of man: "My uncle and
he are perfectly agreed in their estimate of life,which
Quin says, would stink in his nostrils, if he did not
steep it in claret.... I must entertain you with an incident that seems to confirm the judgment of the two
cynic philosophers. I took the liberty to differ in
opinion from Mr. Bramble, when he observed, that the
mixture of people in the entertainments of this place
was destructive of all order and urbanity...and vulgar-
ised the deportment and sentiments of those who moved
in the upper spheres of life"(XI, 65). The complete
breakdown of decorum that ensues in the dessert contest
proves Jery wrong and even makes Matt unhappy, for "He
hung his head in manifest chagrin, and seemed to repine
at the triumph of his judgment" (XI, 67).

The root metaphor of the novel, however, is not the
stage, but travel, and reveals man's search for physical and mental well-being. Unlike Roderick and Perry,
Matt possesses from the outset wealth and independence,
and yet he is not happy. Wealth and independence may
be necessary for happiness, as Smollett always implies,
but they do not guarantee it. What Matt learns from his
travels is, in Dr. Johnson's phrase, that man needs a
celestial wisdom that "calms the mind,/And makes the
happiness she does not find."[41] Matt also learns that
the individual can best make this happiness in the country. The novel is in fact structured on the opposition
between the city and the country, an opposition that informs Matt's satire.[42] His denunciations arise from
the sight of man debauched by the density of population,
the breakdown of social order, the extravagance, the
luxury, and the corruption found in cities. Bath, al-

though the Square is "pretty well laid out, spacious, open, and airy" (XI, 43), is in the final analysis a mere sink of profligacy and extortion, luxury and extravagance (XI, 73). London is nothing but "a reservoir of folly, knavery, and sophistication" (XI, 140). In his June 8 letter to Dr. Lewis, Matt sets up a detailed opposition between the defects of London life and the excellencies of his own country life in Wales. His argument covers an extensive variety of areas (housing, air, food, drink, recreation, rest, social intercourse) and includes such minute particulars as the difference between the quality of beer available in London and in rural Wales (XI,153-162). Matt's diatribes against the city complement his Cynic philosophy, for they can be traced to Diogenes' celebrated invectives. Diogenes "said that men first came together in cities that they might not suffer wrong from the outside; but there they turned about and did all manner of wrong to one another and committed the most atrocious deeds, as though this had been the purpose of their coming together."[43]

Unlike the Cynics, however, Matt does not oppose progress when it excludes luxury and extravagance; Matt hardly favors the hard primitivism of early Cynicism. In his tour of Scotland, for example, Matt cannot praise highly enough the commercial progress of towns like Leith and Glasgow (XII, 74; XII, 79ff.). Scotland represents progress without the corruption and decadence that Smollett saw in England's commercial successes. Smollett's praises of Scotland undoubtedly derive from his patriotic fervor; but at the same time they are artistically consistent with Matt's character. Even when Matt rhapsodizes, for example, in Edinburgh, he does not dismiss the blemishes (XII, 75). His comments on the district surrounding Stirling Castle are certainly as caustic as his satire on the architecture at Bath,centering characteristically on the lack of convenience, upkeep, and commercial productivity (XII, 88-89).

Opposed to the city are the peace and tranquility of the country, which are continually on Matt's tongue. Only in the country does Matt hope to find the sanity and friendship lacking in the great cities, and it is to the country that the weary travelers eventually return. All of Smollett's novels, as noted earlier, end

with a migration to the country as a place of felicity
and ultimate salvation from the wiles of the world. Roderick moves back to Scotland and his country estate;
Perry, in prison, dreams of pastoral scenes enjoyed with
his beloved Emilia, which he achieves at his father's
death and after his discharge from prison; Fathom retires to a country town to carry out his reformation;
and Sir Launcelot returns to his country estate with
his new wife, Aurelia. In the earlier novels, however,
the return to the country tends to be only a formula to
end the story. But in *Humphry Clinker* the myth of the
country continually underlies the structure of the novel
itself, for the travels of the Bramble family are only
temporary; a return to Wales is anticipated by all. Unlike Roderick, Perry, Fathom, and even Sir Launcelot,
none of the Bramble family intends to use the city either
for making his way in the world or for personal profit.

In the light of Matt's satire, the country becomes a
standard against which he can measure the evils he sees
on the journey. As noted above, Matt's famous satiric
description of London gains its bitter asperity from
the debit and credit comparison of country virtues and
London vices (XI,150ff.). Even before reaching London,
Matt concludes his diatribe against Bath with a dream
of home: "...such is the atmosphere I have exchanged
for the pure, elastic, animating air of the Welsh mountains. *O Rus, quando te aspiciam*!" (XI, 85). After his
London visit, Matt's desire to return to the country is
stronger than ever, and his attack on the city becomes
even more bitter:

> My letter would swell into a treatise were I to par-
> ticularise every cause of offence that fills up the
> measure of my aversion to this and every other crowd-
> ed city. Thank Heaven! I am not so far sucked into
> the vortex, but that I can disengage myself without
> any great effort of philosophy. From the wild up-
> roar of knavery, folly, and impertinence, I shall
> fly with double relish to the serenity of retire-
> ment, the cordial effusions of unreserved friend-
> ship, the hospitality and protection of the rural
> gods; in a word, the *jucunda oblivia vitae*, which
> Horace himself had not taste enough to enjoy. (XI,
> 160-161)

Both Jery and Matt are pleased with Scotland because its customs, language, people, and progress without moral degeneration remind them of the simplicity of their country life in Wales.[44]

In terms of the plot, the country provides the matrix out of which the satire can be overcome by the transcendental vision of comedy. As the story moves from the Baynard episode into the extended visit with the Dennisons, whom Matt considers living the perfect life, the satire of the novel easily recedes into the comic happy ending. Even the romantic Lydia seeks the country. After her raptures over Bath and London, for example, she is finally forced to admit that she would rather retire to a less dissipated country life. "I wish my weak head may not grow giddy in the midst of all this gallantry and dissipation; though as yet I can safely declare I could gladly give up all these tumultuous pleasures for country solitude, and a happy retreat with those we love..." (XI, 123). Even the satiric implications of Lydia's "romantic" rhetoric do not undermine the seriousness of her final conversion to Matt's view of the world.

> Nature never intended me for the busy world; I long for repose and solitude, where I can enjoy that disinterested friendship which is not to be found among crowds.... Unexperienced as I am in the commerce of life, I have seen enough to give me a disgust to the generality of those who carry it out; there is such malice, treachery, and dissimulation...and when vice quits the stage for a moment, her place is immediately occupied by folly, which is often too serious to excite anything but compassion. (XII, 173)

The comic vision of the country myth also contains the resolution of the antithesis between Scotland and England. The lives of the Baynards and Dennisons are essentially the thesis of the novel in miniature. The extravagance and luxury of the Baynard household epitomize Matt's denunciations of Bath and London, while the Dennison's mode of rural life reflects his praises of Scottish industry and thrift. Mrs. Baynard's extravagance has destroyed Baynard's magnificent country es-

tate and has flung Baynard himself into financial ruin
(XII, 143-158). She has tried to imitate in the country the vices of the city that Matt so bitterly denounced.
In contrast, the Dennisons have achieved economical and
financial security through the proper cultivation of
their small farm.

 As the Baynard episode indicates, however, Smollett
does not offer the country as an absolute means of salvation nor as merely an escape from the wickedness of
the world; the country represents simply one of the few
places where evil expresses itself in a less complex
manner and where extravagance can be avoided if man
humbly and actively pursues a harmonious spiritual and
physical life. The objections that Dennison's friends
raised to a country life, for example, were based on a
theory that expenses would be higher in the country.
These objections were proved wrong "because they were
chiefly founded upon the supposition that he would be
obliged to lead a life of extravagance and dissipation,
which he and his consort equally detested, despised, and
determined to avoid. The objects he had in view were
health of body, peace of mind, and the private satisfaction of domestic quiet, unallayed by actual want,
and uninterrupted by the fears of indigence.... He required nothing but wholesome air, pure water, plain
diet, convenient lodging, and decent apparel" (XII, 192).
The Dennisons have turned to the *Beatus Ille* tradition
in its peculiar eighteenth-century interpretation, for
to them the country is not an escapist rejection of society, but a personal fulfillment that is exceptionally
social in its consequences.[45]

 The virtues that the Dennisons have cultivated in the
country offer the sanity of mind and body that Matt
sought on his journey. Ironically, he finds his cure
in the very place his travels began—the country.[46]
What Matt had lacked in his earlier country life was the
proper attitude of humility and activity—the realization that happiness must come from within, a creation
of each individual. Thus, the travels represent Matt's
own symbolic search for happiness, and when he finds it
he can transcend the world of his satire to achieve a
comic equilibrium.[47]   This equilibrium does not mean
that the satirized world has dissolved. On the con-

trary, the viciousness of that world is even more real because of Bramble's exposé; but salvation is, as the Dennisons have demonstrated, a personal matter, and it can be worked out only by each individual. The satirist, by revealing the evil of the world, has done all he can do. Each individual, including the satirist, must take over from there, and if he strives he may imitate Dennison, who, in Matt's estimation, "has really attained to that pitch of rural felicity at which I have been aspiring these twenty years in vain" (XII, 90).

Matt's final letter indicates that he will cease to be a satirist, and, like Pope in the "Epistle to Dr. Arbuthnot," will instead actively strive for the personal salvation that the Dennisons have achieved: "As I have laid in a considerable stock of health, it is to be hoped you will not have much trouble with me in the way of physic, but I intend to work you on the side of exercise.... That this scheme of life may be prosecuted the more effectually, I intend to renounce all sedentary amusements, particularly that of writing long letters..." (XII, 231). Matt returns to the rural life convinced that the material advantages of the country outweigh those of the city and that each individual can, with hard labor, cure his own body and spirit. The intense physical and moral struggle that Baynard requires for his redemption brings the laborious aspect of the cure dramatically home to Matt. But the excursion into the world of vice and folly contributes extensively to each man's judgment of the need for and the means to the cure. Jery writes, "Without all doubt, the greatest advantages acquired in travelling and pursuing mankind in the original, is that of dispelling those shameful clouds that darken the faculties of the mind, preventing it from judging with candour and precision" (XII, 206).

With these clouds dispersed for the Bramble family, the comic vision of life towards which the novel was moving can finally triumph over the satiric. Jery's concluding stage metaphor symbolizes this harmonious reconciliation of comedy and satire: "The comedy is near a close, and the curtain is ready to drop..." (XII, 224). But the comic vision is realized only by the few who actively seek it—Baynard, Matt, the Dennisons—and it demands that men of feeling squarely face the evils that

the satiric vision of man brings into the foreground.
Through the benevolent misanthropy of Matt Bramble,
Smollett fused satire and comedy into a single vision—
a vision of "tragic optimism"[48]—one that reveals man's
potential for virtue and for happiness, but insists,at
the same time, that this potential will probably never
be realized by man at large. Those men of feeling who
seek to realize the potential may, however, have to become benevolent misanthropes. Like Kierkegaard's religious man, they may have to wear the incognito of a
humorist and assume the role of a comic character. Such
was the case with the living embodiment of benevolent
misanthropy in eighteenth-century England, that celebrated literary figure known as Mr. Oddity, Dr. Samuel
Johnson.

5

Samuel Johnson—
A Religious Misanthrope

Johnson and Human Depravity

Samuel Johnson exhorts men in "Sermon IV" to "meditate
on the excellence of charity, and improve those seeds
of benevolence, which are implanted in every mind, but
which will not produce fruit, without care and cultivation."[1] If Johnson believes with St. Basil that the
"germ" of charity is present in all men, he also believes with St. Augustine that few actually cultivate
that germ. Johnson writes in *Rambler*, No. 172, "The
greater part of mankind are corrupt in every condition,
and differ in high and low stations, only as they have
more or fewer opportunities of gratifying their desires,
or as they are more or less restrained by human cen-
sures."[2] *Rambler*, No. 175, reasserts Johnson's position:

   The depravity of mankind is so easily discover-
   able, that nothing but the desert or the cell can
   exclude it from notice. The knowledge of crimes
   intrudes uncalled and undesired. They whom their
   abstraction from common occurrences hinders from
   seeing iniquity, will quickly have their attention
   awakened by feeling it. Even he who ventures not
   into the world, may learn its corruption in his clos-
   et.[3]

As the sister of Sir Joshua Reynolds noted, Johnson was
well known for his "common assertions that Man was by

121

Nature much more inclined to evil than to good,"[4] and
this view extended even to children, who, he claimed,
"are always cruel."[5] When on his famous tour through
the Hebrides Lady McLeod asked, "if no man was naturally good," Johnson replied, "No, madam, no more than a
wolf." Lady McLeod was prompted to say, "in a low voice,
'This is worse than Swift.'"[6]

The paradox to those that read Johnson's works and
heard such sentiments from him in person was that Johnson himself was an active benevolist. Hester Chapone
writes:

> I had the assurance to dispute with him on the sub-
> ject of human malignity, and wondered to hear a man
> who by his actions shews so much benevolence, main-
> tain that the human heart is naturally malevolent,
> and that all the benevolence we see in the few who
> are good, is acquired by reason and religion.[7]

The stories of Johnson placing pennies in the hands of
destitute children, of maintaining the menagerie of in-
grates in his home, of assisting a prostitute, of ex-
horting men in his sermons to perform benevolent acts
without making the recipient humiliated confirm Johnson's life of charity.[8] In the words of Sir John Hawkins, Johnson may have been terrifying and ferocious at
times, but he also "had a natural imbecility about him,
arising from humanity and pity to the sufferings of his
fellow-creatures, that was prejudicial to his interests; and also, that he neither sought nor expected
praise for those acts of beneficence which he was daily
performing, nor looked for any retribution from those
who were nourished by his bounty."[9]

In effect, Mr. Oddity was a living embodiment of benevolent misanthropy, and like his literary counter-
parts his benevolence was disappointed at man's ingratitude and lack of benevolence. He knew, in turn, that
men often failed to perceive his paradoxical nature.
Late in life he said:

> I look upon myself to be a man very much misunder-
> stood. I am not an uncandid, nor am I a severe man.
> I sometimes say more than I mean in jest; and peo-
> ple are apt to believe me serious: however, I am
> more candid than I was when I was younger. As I

know more of mankind, I expect less of them, and
am ready now to call a man *a good man*, upon easier
terms than I was formerly.[10]

Moreover,Johnson understood the need for a man of feeling to have protection. In *Rambler*, No. 175,he writes,
"He that endeavours to live for the good of others,must
always be exposed to the arts of them who live only for
themselves, unless he is taught by timely precepts the
caution required in common transactions, and shewn at a
distance the pitfalls of treachery."[11]

Like many literary benevolent misanthropes, Johnson
was also a satirist. Johnson does not create fully developed benevolent misanthropes but is rather himself
the benevolent misanthropic satirist behind such sketchy
characters as the satiric spokesman in the "Vanity of
Human Wishes" and the narrator in *Rasselas*. Johnson's
satire, however, has a different bent from that examined thus far. He shares the moral intent of the literary benevolent misanthropic satirist, for as he says
in *Rambler*, No. 8, "my purpose...[is] to consider the
moral discipline of the mind, and to promote the increase of virtue rather than of learning."[12] But Johnson's purpose is also religious, in that he intends by
satirizing the evils and miseries of man to raise the
reader's hopes to a better and more perfect state of existence beyond this life. Johnson brings to fruition
the religious resources Percival Stockdale saw in benevolent misanthropy. Johnson falls into the category
of men described in his "Sermon V":

Some have endeavoured to engage us in the contemplation of the evils of life for a very wise and
good end. They have proposed, by laying before us
the uncertainty of prosperity, the vanity of pleasure, and the inquietudes of power, the difficult attainment of most earthly blessings, and the short
duration of them all, to divert our thoughts from
the glittering follies and tempting delusions that
surround us to an inquiry after more certain and
permanent felicity not subject to be interrupted by
sudden vicissitudes, or impaired by the malice of
the revengeful, the caprice of the inconstant, or
the envy of the ambitious. They have endeavoured
to demonstrate, and have in reality demonstrated to

all those who will steal a few moments from noise
and show, and luxury, to attend to reason and to
truth, that nothing is worthy of our ardent wishes,
or intense solicitude, that terminates in this state
of existence, and that those only make the true use
of life that employ it in obtaining the favour of
God, and securing everlasting happiness.[13]

As Johnson writes in *Adventurer*, No. 120, "The miseries of life may, perhaps afford some proof of a future
state...."[14]

But if Johnson's misanthropic vision of the world is
intended to "increase virtue" and to set our minds on
a future state, it is not intended to make us despair
of enjoying the good things of this life, to drive us
to the cloister, or even worse, to drive us into a Timonian rejection of mankind. Johnson writes in "Sermon
III":

He is happy that carries about with him in the
world the temper of the cloister; and preserves the
fear of doing evil, while he suffers himself to be
impelled by the zeal of doing good; who uses the
comforts and the conveniences of his condition as
though he used them not, with that constant desire
of a better state, which sinks the value of earthly
things; who can be rich or poor, without pride in
riches, or discontent in poverty; who can manage
the business of this life with such indifference as
may shut out from his heart all incitements to fraud
or injustice: who can partake the pleasures of sense
with temperance, and enjoy the distinctions of honour with moderation; who can pass undefiled through
a polluted world; and, among all the vicissitudes
of good and evil, have his heart fixed only where
true joys are to be found.[15]

The religious dimension of Johnson's life, conversation,
and writings, which has received much comment in recent
years, cannot be divorced from his deep "pessimism," what
I am here calling from an historical perspective his
benevolently misanthropic vision of man. The religious
depths of this vision can be found in nearly all of his
works, but it is revealed most completely, I think, in
his famous satiric apologue, *Rasselas*.

The Happy Valley and Normal Society

Even the most casual reading of *Rasselas* will show that the plot of the apologue follows the basic pattern of an inexperienced man of feeling's entrance into the ordinary world of men, the world of experience.[16] It is precisely the pattern followed in Sarah Fielding's *David Simple,* Smollett's *Ferdinand Count Fathom,* and Goldsmith's later *Citizen of the World*—the pattern of "Man of Feeling" novels. To some readers the Happy Valley that Rasselas leaves for the world of experience represents an earthly paradise and Rasselas' departure from it a fall from innocence.[17] Such a view, however, ignores Johnson's ironic presentation of the Happy Valley. The physical setting of the Happy Valley is undoubtedly intended to appear paradisaical, and much of the imagery describing it evidently comes from Father Lobo's *Voyage to Abyssinia* and other sixteenth- and seventeenth-century writers who visited or wrote about Ethiopia.[18] But the Happy Valley is a false paradise. For Rasselas and the other Abyssinian princes it is a place of seclusion that prevents them from knowing the real workings of men. For those, like Imlac, who are allowed to enter it after experience in the world, it becomes a place of retreat from the duties and responsibilities of life. This dark view of the Happy Valley Johnson suggests through the imagery of imprisonment:

> Such was the appearance of security and delight which this retirement afforded, that they to whom it was new always desired that it might be perpetual; and as those, on whom the iron gate had once closed, were never suffered to return, the effect of longer experience could not be known. Thus every year produced new schemes of delight, and new competitors for imprisonment. (p. 10)

The prison imagery is picked up later in the apologue by Imlac, who tells Rasselas that after his weary life in the world he "resigned...[himself] with joy to perpetual confinement" (p. 61). The irony, however, is that he now knows "not one of all...[Rasselas'] attendants who does not lament the hour when he entered this retreat" (p. 62). Moreover, Imlac tells Rasselas that "they are weary of themselves, and of each other, and

expect to find relief in new companions. They envy the
liberty which their folly has forfeited,and would gladly see all mankind imprisoned like themselves" (p.63).
Imlac himself wishes he could prevent new admissions to
the Happy Valley: "I look with pity on the crowds who
are annually soliciting admission to captivity, and wish
that it were lawful for me to warn them of their danger" (p. 63).[19]

The unhappiness with the Happy Valley that Imlac finds
in Rasselas' attendants is, of course,reflected in Rasselas himself. At the age of twenty-six Rasselas finally discovers that he is totally bored with his existence. "I am hungry and thirsty..., but when thirst
and hunger cease I am not at rest; I am...pained with
want, but am not...satisfied with fulness. The intermediate hours are tedious and gloomy; I long again to
be hungry that I may again quicken my attention.... I
can discover within me no power of perception which is
not glutted with its proper pleasure, yet I do not feel
myself delighted" (pp. 14-15). Rasselas, from the time
he discovers his boredom, seeks to escape from the Happy Valley, but it seems that the languor encouraged by
this "earthly paradise" prevents him from taking effective action. Rasselas laments that for twenty months
nature has continued to change and act, but he has been
idle: "I only have made no advances, but am still help-
less and ignorant. The moon by more than twenty changes,
admonished me of the flux of life; the stream that
rolled before my feet upbraided my inactivity. I sat
feasting on intellectual luxury, regardless alike of
the examples of the earth, and the instructions of the
planets" (p.24). Earlier Rasselas had told his tutor,
"I shall long to see the miseries of the world, since
the sight of them is necessary to happiness" (p. 19).
Despite his inactivity during the twenty-month span of
time, Rasselas' "original curiosity was not yet abated;
he resolved to obtain some knowledge of the ways of men"
(p. 26).

Rasselas' desire to escape from the prison of the Happy Valley is based on the assumption that when he obtains "some knowledge of the ways of men" he will be
able to make a "choice of life" that will bring him perfect happiness. He understands that the ordinary world

has evil and misery, but he thinks that wisdom can help the individual man of feeling avoid them. Such indeed is the belief he harbors during his period of inactivity:

> His chief amusement was to picture to himself that world which he had never seen; to place himself in various conditions; to be entangled in imaginary difficulties: But his benevolence always terminated his projects in the relief of distress, the detection of fraud, the defeat of oppression, and the diffusion of happiness. (p. 21)

Rasselas' benevolent intentions accompanied by his actual inactivity in the Happy Valley foreshadow the situation of Matthew Bramble in *Humphry Clinker*. Like Matt, Rasselas must learn that, whether he is living in the false paradise of the Happy Valley (Bramble's rural retreat in Wales) or in the ordinary world, perfect happiness is not *found* but *made* by a "celestial wisdom" working in each individual. And this "celestial wisdom" emerges from humility and benevolent activity. Again like Matt Bramble, Rasselas does not need a journey into the world to make this discovery. Imlac makes this fact only too clear to Rasselas:

> Long journies in search of truth are not commanded. Truth, such as is necessary to the regulation of life, is always found where it is honestly sought. Change of place is no natural cause of the increase of piety.... (pp. 54-55)

Journies in search of truth may not be *necessary*, but journeys into the world of experience definitely assist in the discovery of truth, as Matt Bramble learns. Matt, of course, is already convinced that the world is a place of fraud and deceit calculated to destroy men of feeling. Since this is a fact Rasselas must learn, his journey from seclusion to the world of experience more closely resembles that of Sarah Fielding's David Simple or Smollett's Renaldo in *Ferdinand Count Fathom*. Rasselas learns about the unfeeling world in two different ways—at second hand from the discourse of Imlac, who relates his experiences in the world, and at first hand from his own experiences after he leaves the Happy Valley with Imlac as his guide. Imlac thus plays the same

role to Rasselas that Spatter plays to David Simple and
the Man in Black to the Chinaman. Rasselas emphasizes
this tutorial role when he says to Imlac, "thou shalt
be the companion of my flight, the guide of my rambles,
the partner of my fortune, and my sole director in the
choice of life" (p. 64). Agostino Lombardo comments to
the point, "If *Rasselas...* is not so much the story of
the search for happiness as of the acquisition of experience, there is no doubt that the Prince of Abissinia
acquires such experience not only directly but above
all through the words of Imlac."[20] Imlac becomes Rasselas' tutor and guide, a role that also turns him into
a philosophic satirist exposing or "unmasking" the "ways
of men" and pointing the moral whenever Rasselas becomes disenchanted with the world.

Imlac is perhaps the most completely developed fictional representation of Johnson's own benevolent misanthropy. His discourse to Rasselas, which constitutes
a brief autobiography, is generally accepted as a miniature preview of Rasselas' own journey. In this discourse Imlac tries to teach Rasselas the "way of the
world." At one point, in fact, Rasselas cries, "Stop a
moment.... Is there such depravity in man, as that he
should injure another without benefit to himself?" (p.
43). Imlac's recital continues to discomfort Rasselas.
Rasselas, for example, is upset to learn that oppression exists in his father's kingdom, and Imlac delivers
a lecture on the inevitability of oppression in even
the best ruled kingdom:

> Oppression is, in the Abissinian dominions, neither
> frequent nor tolerated; but no form of government
> has been yet discovered, by which cruelty can be
> wholly prevented. Subordination supposes power on
> one part and subjection on the other; and if power
> be in the hands of men, it will sometimes be abused.
> The vigilance of the supreme magistrate may do much,
> but much will still remain undone. He can never
> know all the crimes that are committed, and can sel-
> dom punish all that he knows. (pp. 37-38)

Imlac also tries to warn Rasselas that in the ordinary
world a man cannot expect his accomplishments to be
recognized and applauded. When Imlac returned from his

travels, for example, he found that "of my companions
the greater part was in the grave, of the rest some
could with difficulty remember me, and some considered
me as one corrupted by foreign manners" (pp. 60-61).
Imlac, however,remained at first undaunted: "I forgot,
after a time, my disappointment, and endeavoured to
recommend myself to the nobles of the kingdom" (p.61).
But he discovered that in the end no one cared much about
the wisdom he had gained: the nobles "admitted me to
their tables,heard my story,and dismissed me. I opened
a school, and was prohibited to teach" (p. 61). The
essence of Imlac's instruction is contained in the now
famous line, "Human life is every where a state in which
much is to be endured, and little to be enjoyed" (p.
57). Imlac, however, agrees to become Rasselas' tutor
and guide in the world, but only after a final warning:
"The world, which you figure to yourself smooth and
quiet as the lake in the valley, you will find a sea
foaming with tempests, and boiling with whirlpools: you
will be sometimes overwhelmed by the waves of violence,
and sometimes dashed against the rocks of treachery"
(p. 64).

Rasselas' first initiation into "normal" society results in disillusionment. Rasselas complains, "I am
more unhappy than any of our friends. I see them perpetually and unalterably chearful, but feel my own mind
restless and uneasy. I am unsatisfied with those pleasures which I seem most to court; I live in the crowds
of jollity, not so much to enjoy company as to shun myself, and am loud and merry to conceal my sadness" (p.
78). Imlac, however, points the moral: "...when you
feel that your own gaiety is counterfeit, it may justly lead you to suspect that of your companions not to
be sincere" (p. 121). Rasselas remains long convinced,
however, that perfect happiness is somewhere to be
found, that "one condition is more happy than another,
and wisdom surely directs us to take the least evil in
the *choice of life*" (p. 79). But Imlac warns Rasselas
that to seek the most perfect conditions for everything
is dangerous: "The causes of good and evil, answered
Imlac, are so various and uncertain, so often entangled
with each other, so diversified by various relations,
and so much subject to accidents which cannot be fore-

seen, that he who would fix his condition upon incon-
testable reasons of preference, must live and die in-
quiring and deliberating" (p.79). Despite Imlac's warning, however, Rasselas remains hopeful that "happiness
is somewhere to be found" (p. 80), and he decides to
seek it among young people: "Youth, cried he, is the
time of gladness: I will join myself to the young men,
whose only business is to gratify their desires, and
whose time is spent in a succession of enjoyments" (p.
80). But Rasselas gives up the experiment, discover-
ing that the merriment of youth wearies and disgusts him:
"Their mirth was without images, their laughter without
motive; their pleasures were gross and sensual, in which
the mind had no part; their conduct was at once wild and
mean" (p. 81).

Rasselas hopes that the hermetic life will provide the
happiness he cannot find in society, but the hermit he
seeks out offers him no comfort: "I have been long com-
paring the evils with the advantages of society," the
hermit asserts, "and resolve to return to the world to
morrow. The life of a solitary man will be certainly
miserable, but not certainly devout" (p. 96). Almost
in desperation, Rasselas looks to political power as the
mode of life most conducive to happiness but concludes
that such a life can be enjoyed by too few men: "There
can be no pleasure, said he, equal to that of feeling
at once the joy of thousands all made happy by a wise
administration. Yet...this sublime delight can be in
one nation but the lot of one" (p. 103). In effect,
Rasselas arrives at Imlac's conclusion that even under
the wisest ruler evil will persist. As he tells his
sister, "Whoever has many to please or to govern, must
use the ministry of many agents, some of whom will be
wicked, and some ignorant; by some he will be misled,
and by others betrayed" (p. 120). At one point in his
long discussion with Nekayah, Rasselas suggests that
perfect happiness must reside in virtue. Nekayah argues, however, "that we do not always find visible happiness in proportion to visible virtue. All natural
and almost all political evils, are incident alike to
the bad and good: they are confounded in the misery of
a famine, and not much distinguished in the fury of a
faction; they sink together in a tempest, and are driv-

en together from their country by invaders" (p. 123). Nekayah concludes with a traditional Christian argument, "All that virtue can afford is quietness of conscience, a steady prospect of a happier state; this may enable us to endure calamity with patience; but remember that patience must suppose pain" (p. 123). Rasselas finally discovers the paradox that while perfect happiness "must be something solid and permanent" (p. 81), man nevertheless finds an illusory happiness in the prospect of continual change. "Such, said Nekayah, is the state of life, that none are happy but by the anticipation of change: the change itself is nothing, when we have made it, the next wish is to change again" (p. 208).

The Biblical Context of Religious Misanthropy

Rasselas' journey into the world of experience is, in effect, a satiric exposure of an unfeeling world where perfect happiness is impossible to find. At first glance the journey seems to confirm the opinion of Chapone:

I think the only maxim one can deduce from the story is, that human life is a scene of unmixt wretchedness, and that all states and conditions of it are equally miserable; a maxim which, if adopted, would extinguish hope, and consequently industry, make prudence ridiculous, and, in short dispose men to lie down in sloth and despondency.[21]

Neither Imlac's tutoring nor Rasselas' experiences, however, are intended to evoke Chapone's opinion. Chapone and those who agree with her are reading the apologue through the eyes of reason, whereas Johnson, I think, expects it to be read through the eyes of religion. The best preface to the apologue is probably Johnson's allegory *The Vision of Theodore* (1748), wherein the hermit Theodore receives a vision of men climbing the Mountain of Existence. The correct guide up the greater part of the Mountain is Reason, "of all subordinate Beings the noblest and the greatest."[22] But Reason's proper role, Theodore learns, is to hand him and others over to someone greater: "...if thou wilt receive my Laws, [I] will reward thee like the rest of my Votaries,

by conducting thee to *Religion*" (p.152). Religion alone
can lead Theodore to happiness: "Look upwards, and you
perceive a Mist before you..., a Mist by which my Prospect is terminated, and which is pierced only by the
Eyes of *Religion*. Beyond it are the Temples of *Happiness*, in which those who climb the Precipice by her Direction, after the Toil of their Pilgrimage repose for
ever. I know not the Way..." (p. 152). The "Road of
Happiness"is thus for Johnson discovered only by the
eyes of Religion. As Theodore learns, when the seekers
of happiness pass through the mist, "*Reason*...discerned
that they were safe, but *Religion* saw that they were
happy" (p. 156). In *Rasselas* the role of Reason is
filled by Rasselas' guide and tutor, Imlac, who eventually leads Rasselas to Religion in the catacombs of
Cairo. *Rasselas* is not designed to evoke Timonian misanthropy, but a benevolent misanthropy based on a religious vision of the Temples of Happiness. This vision
arises from the biblical context in which Johnson places
the apologue.

 Boswell, commenting in the *Life of Johnson,* suggests
that *Rasselas* echoes the *vanitas vanitatum* theme of Ecclesiastes: "This tale, with all the charms of oriental imagery, and all the force and beauty of which the
English language is capable, leads us through the most
important scenes of human life, and shows us that this
stage of our being is full of 'vanity and vexation of
spirit.'"[23] The Rev. Mr. Ralph Churton, however, writing to Boswell in 1792 about Johnson's works in general, attacks the validity of any relationships with Ecclesiastes, even if Johnson had intended them. Life,
he argues, is not "that state of constant wretchedness
which Johnson always insisted it was." Such an attitude, Churton continues, "appears not consistent with
fact and experience, so neither does it seem to be coun-
tenanced by Scripture. There is, perhaps, no part of
the sacred volume which at first sight promises so much
to lend its sanction to these dark and desponding notions as the book of Ecclesiastes, which so often, and
so emphatically, proclaims the vanity of things sub-
lunary. But 'the design of the whole book, (as it has
been justly observed,) is not to put us out of conceit
with life, but to cure our vain expectations of a com-

pleat and perfect happiness in this world....'"[24]

Two aspects of Churton's argument are especially significant. The first is its indication that Ecclesiastes provoked two Christian schools of interpretation. The older or "traditional" school, dating from patristic times, maintained that the Preacher's futile quest for happiness in Ecclesiastes teaches man that he should despise and reject this world to contemplate the world to come. To this school belong such eminent figures as St. Jerome, St. Ambrose, and St. Augustine. Beginning at about the time of the Reformation, however, a new "reformed" school of interpretation began to develop, and it argued that Ecclesiastes taught us not to despise the pleasures of this world but to enjoy them.[25] Perhaps the most eloquent expounder of this school was Luther, but in any event it included most of the English divines of the Restoration and eighteenth century, including Bishop Simon Patrick, whose *Paraphrase upon the Book of Ecclesiastes* and other scriptural writings, in conjunction with those of William Lowth, made up the "standard" Augustan commentary on the Old Testament. It was "Lowth and Patrick" that Johnson recommended to Boswell for his study of the Old Testament.[26]

The second noteworthy aspect of Churton's argument is that Johnson's view of life, even if he never consciously related it to Ecclesiastes, was in opposition to that book's "true" meaning, which is obviously for Churton the meaning advanced by the "reformed" school of interpretation. In this part of his argument, however, Churton is completely mistaken, at least in regard to *Rasselas*, for Johnson's apologue is, I think, actually designed to recall both the Preacher's futile quest for perfect happiness and the meaning of that quest as the "reformed" school interpreted it. In another place I have gathered together abundant evidence demonstrating that Bishop Patrick's *Paraphrase* is the source for many of the images, sentiments, and ideas that appear in *Rasselas*.[27] The apologue thus falls unequivocally into the context of Ecclesiastes. The very use of Bishop Patrick would indicate that Johnson is also recalling the "reformed" version of the Preacher's futile quest for perfect happiness. The remainder of this chapter attempts to show that the thematic structure of *Rasselas* is indeed adapted from the thematic structure attributed to Ecclesiastes by the "reformed" school and that this adaptation forms the religious basis of Johnson's benevolent misanthropy in the apologue.

According to the "reformed" school, the ultimate purpose of Ecclesiastes is to convince man that perfect happiness is reserved for the next world, so that in this world his only "true" happiness lies in a life of virtue, a life that prepares him for eternity. In his exegesis of Ecclesiastes (1639),Michael Jermin writes, "The greatest labour of Philosophers hath been to finde out the greatest good of man; wherein what hath their labour been, but a labyrinth, in which themselves being lost,they were far from finding that which they sought. But this being the scope of the Royal Philosopher...in this Booke, he shews where it is, by shewing it not to be in the things of this world."[28]   Echoing Jermin, Bishop Patrick argues:

> For the scope of this discourse is concerning the *chief good* or happiness of man: the *great end* he should propose to himself all his life long. Which is not that he shows which men generally follow, but that which is generally neglected.... [Men] after all their busy thoughts,designs,and labours, come to this conclusion, that to *fear God and keep his commandments* is the happiness of man: who ought therefore to use all the pleasures of this world (which is the only good it can afford us) with a constant respect to the future account we must all make to God.[29]

Thus the Preacher, "after all the experiments he could make, came to this resolution, which he had better have taken at first, that religion and virtue are the only things that can make a man happy."[30]   In like manner, but very briefly, Samuel Clarke writes, "The Scope of this Book is to direct us in the way to true Happiness," which is found finally in a virtuous life that "provide[s] for Death and Judgment."[31]

To demonstrate that the "fear of the Lord...and this alone," in Bishop Patrick's words, "can make a man's mind quiet, still, and calm, both in life and death,"[32] the Preacher follows the negative method of showing that no state or condition of human life is capable of providing perfect happiness. Bishop Patrick summarizes this "negative" method in a syllogism:

Whatsoever is vain and perishing cannot make men happy;
But all men's designs here in this world are vain and
  perishing;
Therefore, they cannot by prosecuting such designs make
  themselves happy.[33]

As Michael Jermin writes, "the *vanitie* then whereof the Preacher speaketh, is in the lying promise of contentment which worldly things make,and the no-profit which is made of them."[34] Thus, in Bishop Patrick's terms, "there are two principal parts of the whole sermon. The first of which contains a recital and confutation of men's false opinions about their chiefest good: the other teaches in what our genuine, true, and solid felicity lies, both in this life and in the next."[35]
 By pointing out that this world is incapable of giving perfect happiness, however, the Preacher nowhere suggests that man should therefore despise this world and its pleasures. On the contrary, his secondary purpose, argues the "reformed" school, is to show that once man realizes his inability to find perfect happiness in this world, he can and should enjoy to the fullest the limited joys it offers. As Bishop Patrick claims, the Preacher is paradoxically saying, "excite thyself, by the remembrance of death, to a cheerful enjoyment of those good things present."[36] In his "Preface," Bishop Patrick provides a fuller statement of the problem:

> Such, indeed, is the dulness of mankind, that, hearing all was but vanity, they might condemn everything as evil and hurtful; and declaim too bitterly against this world. Which was so far from Solomon's intention, that having explained the vanity of all our enjoyments here, and the vanity of human cares, solicitous desires, and endeavours, he persuades all men to be content with things present, to give God thanks for them, to use them freely with quiet minds: living as pleasantly, and taking as much liberty, as the remembrance of a future account will allow; void of anxious and troublesome thoughts, what will become of them hereafter in this life.[37]

The Preacher's intent, then, is not to make men despise and hate the world, but, as Bishop Patrick later notes, "to draw us from the desire and love of earthly things, and from the perverse use of them; and then to lead us unto the true and lawful use of them, without any offence to God, as well as without hurt to ourselves."[38] Echoing Bishop Patrick, William Sherlock, in the passage quoted by Churton, provides a concise summary of the "reformed" school's attitude toward the matter:

> We must observe then, that the Design of the whole Book of *Ecclesiastes* is not to put us out of Conceit with Life, but to cure our vain Expectations of a compleat and perfect Happiness in this World; to convince us that no such thing is to be found in mere external Enjoyments, which are nothing but *Vanity and Vexation of Spirit*. And the end of all this is, not to make us weary of Life, but to teach us to moderate our Love to present Things, and to seek for Happiness in the Practice of Virtue, in the Knowledge and Love of God, and in the Hopes of a better Life.[39]

The Religious Misanthropy of RASSELAS

Rasselas shares the same ultimate purpose or design that the "reformed" school found in Ecclesiastes. As Boswell claims, "Johnson meant, by showing the unsatisfactory nature of things temporal, to direct the hopes of man to things eternal."[40] The entire ideational movement of *Rasselas* is directed away from this life toward the next life. Johnson keeps this movement in the foreground of the apologue through the repeated terms "choice of life," terms that Rasselas uses again and again to describe his belief that some one condition or state of life offers perfect happiness. Like the Preacher, Rasselas is unwilling at first to agree with Imlac that "happiness is never to be found" (p. 78). Before leaving the Happy Valley Rasselas asserts, "I am not yet unwilling...to suppose that happiness is so parsimoniously distributed to mortals; nor can believe but that, if I had the choice of life, I should be able to fill every day with pleasure" (p. 58). Ras-

selas is resolved to test Imlac's experience, to see
for himself "the various conditions of men,and then to
make deliberately my *choice of life*" (pp. 64-65). Imlac
understands perfectly well that his role as tutor and
guide is to help Rasselas make the test of experience.
As soon as the group arrives in Cairo he tells Rasselas,
"you will see all the conditions of humanity, and enable your self at leisure to make your *choice of life*"
(p. 75). After two years in Cairo Rasselas "began to
accompany Imlac to places of resort, and to enter into
all assemblies, that he might make his *choice of life*"
(p. 77). Even after a series of initial failures Rasselas nevertheless remains convinced that he should continue to seek a condition or state of life that offers
perfect happiness, for "wisdom surely directs us to take
the least evil in the *choice of life*" (p. 79). Rasselas seeks the hermit's advice on his "choice of life"
(p. 94), and he even asks the astronomer for "his opinion on the choice of life" (p. 203).

At the climax of the apologue, however, the whole quest
for happiness through making a "choice of life" is completely reversed. Rasselas and his companions end their
search for perfect happiness in the catacombs of Cairo,
hoping that what they "can no longer procure from the
living may be given by the dead" (pp. 211-212). Imlac,
however, prepares for their "descent into Hades" with a
lecture on the true purpose of life and the value of
mortification: "Pleasure, in itself harmless, may become mischievous, by endearing to us a state which we
know to be transient and probatory, and withdrawing our
thoughts from that, of which every hour brings us near-
er to the beginning, and of which no length of time will
bring us to the end. Mortification is not virtuous in
itself, nor has any other use, but that it disengages
us from the allurements of sense" (p. 211). Imlac thus
argues that life is a preparation for eternity, which
is the state of permanence Rasselas had ascribed to happiness, and that since death is the entrance man can
keep his thoughts on death, preparing for eternity,
through acts of mortification. As Johnson says elsewhere, "All acknowledged...what hardly anybody prac-
tised, the obligation we are under of making the con-
cerns of eternity the governing principles of our

lives."[41] In the catacombs themselves, Imlac delivers
a discourse on the immortality of the soul, and at the
end Nekayah announces, "To me...the choice of life is
become less important; I hope hereafter to think only
on the choice of eternity" (p. 219). Johnson had earlier
prepared for this reversal of choices with the words
of the old man Rasselas and his companions met on the
banks of the Nile: "I...hope to possess in a better
state that happiness which here I could not find, and
that virtue which here I have not attained" (p. 196).

Like the "reformed" conception of Ecclesiastes, *Rasselas* also proceeds to its affirmation of eternity
through the negative method of showing that no state or
condition of human life can provide the perfect happiness man desires. As Agostino Lombardo comments, the
narrative is ironic, centering "on a constant process
of construction and destruction, affirmation and negation."[42] The number of states of life that Rasselas
experiences and rejects is, indeed, almost overwhelm-
ing: sensual pleasure in an "earthly paradise," the
mindless life of youth, the stoic life, the hard and
soft pastoral lives, the hermitic life, the monastic
life, life "according to nature," the wealthy life, the
poor life, the middle station of life, the married life,
the celibate life. But again, as in the "reformed" conception of Ecclesiastes, the purpose of *Rasselas* is not
to put us "out of Conceit with Life," to make us Timonian misanthropes, nor to drive us into the asceticism
of the monks of St. Anthony. On the contrary, like the
"reformed" version of Ecclesiastes, it is designed to
show that after choosing eternity, man can and should
then partake of the limited goods of this world. Man
cannot make a "choice of life" in the sense of choosing
a particular state or condition of life that is perfectly happy. He can, however, find relative happiness
in the goods of this world by making a "choice of life"
in the sense of choosing life itself.

This aspect of the theme is revealed most dramatically perhaps when Nekayah threatens to retire from the
world in grief over the apparent loss of Pekuah. Imlac,
however, reproaches her with the argument that "while
we glide along the stream of time, whatever we leave
behind us is always lessening, and that which we ap-

proach increasing in magnitude. Do not suffer life to
stagnate; it will grow muddy for want of motion: commit yourself again to the current of the world" (p.157).
Before attempting to retire from the world, Nekayah
should have recalled her own speech to Rasselas, a
speech that concludes her negative and pessimistic remarks on family life and marriage by explicitly setting
forth a positive attitude toward the goods of this world:

> Every hour...confirms my prejudice in favour of the
> position so often uttered by the mouth of Imlac, "That
> nature sets her gifts on the right hand and on the
> left." Those conditions, which flatter hope and
> attract desire, are so constituted, that, as we ap-
> proach one, we recede from another. There are goods
> so opposed that we cannot seize both, but, by too
> much prudence, may pass between them at too great a
> distance to reach either.... Of the blessings set
> before you make your choice, and be content. No
> man can taste the fruits of autumn while he is de-
> lighting his scent with the flowers of the spring:
> no man can, at the same time, fill his cup from the
> source and from the mouth of the Nile. (pp.133-134)

Johnson emphasizes the idea of commitment-to-life rather
than to the search for a perfectly happy state or condition of life in the final section of the apologue.
Rasselas, Nekayah, and Pekuah are "still dreaming of a
perfect state of happiness" (p. 261). They exemplify
two arguments Johnson sets forth in his own commentary
on Ecclesiastes, "Sermon XII." The first argument refers to the failure of learning from experience: "So
great is our interest, or so great we think it, to believe ourselves able to procure our own happiness, that
experience never convinces us of our impotence."[43] The
second refers to man's inability to limit his imagination: "When to enjoyments of sense are superadded the
delights of fancy, we form a scheme of happiness that
can never be complete, for we can always imagine more
than we can possess."[44]
In contrast, however, "Imlac and the astronomer were
contented to be driven along the stream of life without
directing their course to any particular port" (p.220).
The verb "were contented" recalls Nekayah's quotation

from Imlac, "of the blessings set before you make your
choice, and be content" (p. 134). The verb "driven," as
Donald Korte argues,[45] does connote "a lack of control
over one's destiny," but that, I think, is one of the
main points Johnson makes in his insistence that man
cannot make a "choice of life" in the sense of choosing
a specific state or condition of life. Imlac and the
astronomer seem to understand what Johnson argues in
"Sermon XII": "To live in a world where all is vanity,
has been decreed by our Creator to be the lot of man—
a lot which he cannot alter by murmuring, but may soft-
en by submission."[46] The phrase "without directing their
course to any particular port" suggests not "passivity,"
as Korte claims, but "submission" to the fact that "all
is vanity"; moreover, it also suggests a purposeful
commitment-to-life itself rather than to a specific or
"particular" way of life (a port).

 Man's problem then is that, like Rasselas, he thinks
that some state or condition of life offers perfect happiness. Continually seeking greener grass, he forgets,
in Imlac's terms, that "while you are making the choice
of life, you neglect to live" (p. 135). Johnson's suggestion, in fact, is that the choice of life itself and
the choice of eternity are really the same choice. This
suggestion is carried primarily by the water imagery in
the apologue. On the one hand, the water imagery symbolizes the transitoriness of goods in this life. While
contemplating his escape from the Happy Valley, for example, Rasselas remembers the "flux of life" and is upbraided by the "stream that rolled before...[his] feet"
(p. 24). Rasselas wonders once why life should not
"glide quietly away" (p. 58), and Imlac, who thinks of
the first time he left home as his entrance into the
"world of waters" (p.42), tells Rasselas that life outside the Happy Valley, unlike the quiet lake there, is
"a sea foaming with tempests, and boiling with whirlpools" (p. 64). The water imagery, with its connota-
tions of change and motion, emphasizes Johnson's thesis
that the goods and joys of this life are transitory and
therefore insufficient to produce perfect happiness.
Hence the folly of directing one's course "to any particular port." This very transitory nature of earthly
goods, however, should point man in the direction of

eternity, as Johnson makes explicit in Imlac's discourse on the immortality of the soul.

Rasselas' comments at the end of the discourse, however, make clear that, if the goods of this life are transitory, life itself is eternal: "How gloomy would be the mansions of the dead to him who did not know that he shall never die; that what now acts shall continue its agency, and what now thinks shall think on for ever" (p. 218). This passage receives further illumination from Johnson's "Sermon XII":

> When the present state of man is considered, when an estimate is made of his hopes, his pleasures, and his possessions; when his hopes appear to be deceitful, his labours ineffectual, his pleasures unsatisfactory, and his possessions fugitive, it is natural to wish for an abiding city, for a state more constant and permanent, of which the objects may be more proportioned to our wishes, and the enjoyments to our capacities; and from this wish it is reasonable to infer, that such a state is designed for us by that infinite Wisdom, which, as it does nothing in vain, has not created minds with comprehensions never to be filled.[47]

The water imagery supports the idea of the eternal life process, for just as it connotes the idea of transitory earthly goods, it also connotes the idea of a constant or eternal flux. This connotation is made all the more apparent when it is recalled that Johnson calls the Nile the "Father of Waters" (p. 7) and later has the astronomer say, "For us the Nile is sufficient" (p. 188). Moreover, the Nile, according to a classical legend noted by Father Lobo, had its source at the throne of Zeus.[48] The eternal flux of water suggests that in this world man sees only the temporal phase of the eternal process of life, and that this process is eternal Johnson makes clear when he has Imlac assert that the soul, the very principle of life, "will not perish by any inherent cause of decay, or principle of corruption" (p. 218). In effect, the "choice of eternity" is made by making the "choice of life." This double choice seems implicit in Imlac's charge that Nekayah commit herself again "to the current of the world" (p. 157) and in the

decision of Imlac and the astronomer to be driven "along
the stream of life" (p. 220). The choice of life/
choice of eternity theme also follows the circular structure of the work. This life, as the title of the final
chapter implies, is projected as a "Conclusion, in which
nothing is concluded," for this life is merely part of
a life cycle, the temporal phase that is concluded only
in eternity. The title of the last chapter, in fact,
recalls Nekayah's assertion of fear when leaving the
Happy Valley: "I am almost afraid...to begin a journey
of which I cannot perceive an end..." (p. 72).

Imlac's statement, however, that "Human life is everywhere a state in which much is to be endured, and little to be enjoyed" (p. 57) does not mean that the apologue enjoins man from enjoying that little that can be
enjoyed in this life. I think it does just the opposite. Again to quote Nekayah, who is quoting Imlac:
"There are goods so opposed that we cannot seize both,
but, by too much prudence, may pass between them at too
great a distance to reach either" (p. 134). A gloss of
this passage, perhaps of the whole apologue, can be
found in the conclusion to "Sermon XII," where Johnson
argues that the man who is persuaded "all earthly good
is uncertain in the attainment, and unstable in the
possession" will, along with becoming modest and benevolent, "not fix his fond hopes upon things which he
knows to be vanity, but will enjoy this world as one
who knows that he does not possess it."[49] The penulti-
mate sentence of the apologue, "Of these wishes that
they had formed they well knew that none could be ob-
tained" (p. 221), closes *Rasselas* on a positive note of
openness to life, whether the characters are returning
to the Happy Valley or merely to Abyssinia. The travelers, of course, may relapse, but as of the moment
their fond hopes are not fixed upon things they know to
be vanity, so that possibly they, particularly Imlac
and the astronomer, will enjoy the world as persons who
know they do not possess it. While in its temporal
phase, however, as Johnson wrote to Boswell in 1766,
"Life is not long, and too much of it must not pass in
idle deliberation, which those who begin it by prudence,
and continue it with subtilty, must after long expence
of thought, conclude by chance. To prefer one future

mode of life to another, upon just reasons, requires faculties which it has not please our Creator to give us."[50]   *Rasselas*, like Ecclesiastes, argues instead "that they who are studious to fear God, and do well, being secure of God's administration and of the event of things, should enjoy the present good things which his divine bounty bestows upon them with cheerful minds, and with thanksgiving to him."[51] In practical terms this religious vision means that Rasselas and his friends, now imbued with Imlac's benevolent misanthropy, should be able to carry out the benevolently misanthropic advice Rasselas himself had earlier given to Nekayah: "We will not endeavour to modify the motions of the elements, or to fix the destiny of kingdoms. It is our business to consider what beings like us may perform; each labouring for his own happiness, by promoting within his circle, however narrow, the happiness of others" (p. 125).

6

The Gloomy Fraternity and Its Demise

The literary benevolent misanthrope, except perhaps Matthew Bramble, never achieved the religious dimension Johnson developed in his own benevolent misanthropy and projected in his writing, especially in *Rasselas*. He did, however, succeed in transcending the general category of amiable humor to become an established comic character type in his own right. Many of the characters created in the atmosphere of amiable humor were merely a meaningless union of eccentricity and philanthropy; certainly most of them were only "characters for a day," amiable grotesques whose life and relevance were confined to the individual works for which they were created. The benevolent misanthrope in contrast recurs again and again in late eighteenth-century English literature. As a man of feeling, he demonstrates the good nature and moral purpose behind his public satire. As a satirist, he attempts to reform individuals, while at the same time his misanthropy protects his sensitive feelings. Most ironically, his continued literary development counters the fashionably sentimental beliefs in moral progress and a utopian future; for the very world that admires the man of feeling also forces him into the position of a misanthrope and a satirist to defend himself from it.

The *Perth Magazine* ran in its June 1772 issue the first installment of a tale entitled "The Misanthrope."[1] The tale was evidently never completed, but its hero, Friendly, bears a striking resemblance, the anonymous

author notes, to "old Bramble in *Humphry Clinker*" (I,
5). Friendly is known as an "old capricious cynic,...
[who] rails, they say, incessantly, and having an in-
exhaustible fund of sarcastical humour, pours it forth
in torrents of ill nature indiscriminately on all mankind" (I, 3). He befriends Mr. Heartily, however, who
is evidently suffering from the recent loss of his wife.
When Heartily visits the "Misanthrope, with a firm resolution to retaliate every part of his bad usage" (I,
3), he discovers that Friendly rails "at his fellow-
creatures, but every word he uttered to their disadvan-
tage, cost him a groan" (I, 5). Like Bramble, "he had
too much sensibility, a heart too open, and a temper
too soft to be happy, according to the common notions
of happiness in any situation whatever" (I, 5).

It is not clear from the existing fragment of the story
how the plot would have developed, but the overt association of Friendly with Matt Bramble suggests that
Smollett's creation firmly entrenched the benevolent
misanthrope as a satirist in literature. In 1782 the
London Magazine published a revealing imaginary dialogue between Walter Shandy and Matt Bramble, indicating the widespread recognition and acceptance of this
new satirist. The altercation between these famous
literary characters ultimately resolves into a question
of which of the two types of humorists offers the world
a greater amount of amusement and instruction. Shandy
admits that the "worthy Matthew Bramble...was generally
wont to speak worse than he thought, and [his] goodness
of heart belied the asperity of his tongue." But Shandy feels that his followers, the Shandean philosophers
or "system-builders," contribute more to the world than
the Cynics, however benevolent:

> The world is indebted for more amusement to them
> [Shandean philosophers] (and for ought I know as
> much instruction) than all the Cynic philosophers,
> from Diogenes to MATTHEW BRAMBLE inclusive. He, it
> is said, literally lived in a tub; his descendants,
> your gloomy fraternity, metaphorically in a subter-
> aneous dungeon of their own digging, where they dwell
> in a darkness and then complain for want of light.

The cynic philosophers do not much enhance the cheer of

society, for, Shandy argues, "to throw a veil over the
bright side of things, and exhibit only the shade, or
the most disgusting objects in it, is not very amiable
.... At any rate, they are pests to the chearfulness
of society, and ought to be excluded from it." But,
significantly, Matt has the last word in the dialogue;
he knows that the gloomy fraternity has both amused and
instructed mankind, and he ironically concludes, "[I]
heartily bid you farewell, with a better temper than
you may give me credit for."[2] This chapter focuses on
the rise and decline of the gloomy fraternity in the
literary period extending from Smollett to Sir Walter
Scott.

Members from the Drama

Except for Louis de Boissy, Samuel Foote, Voltaire,and
the elder George Colman, whose works were examined in
chapter three, the use in the drama of the benevolent
misanthrope as satirist seems to have been confined to
the notorious sentimental playwright Richard Cumberland. In the year following Smollett's publication of
Humphry Clinker Cumberland produced *The Fashionable Lover* (1772), which has as a main character the benevolent
misanthrope Mortimer.[3] By uniting satire and feeling
in the benevolent misanthrope, Cumberland achieved the
best of both worlds, a feat that other sentimental play-
wrights rarely learned. Mortimer serves both as *deus ex
machina* for the young lovers of the play and as moral
instructor to the dissipated Lord Aberville. As a satirist, he lashes the evil individuals of the play and
the wicked world in general. In his biography of David
Garrick, Thomas Davies recognizes Mortimer's type with
the casualness of familiarity,commenting that "Mortimer
is a good character; though not new; he pleases, because
he exhibits to us a generous mind, and is a warm lover
of justice and humanity."[4]

To the world, however, Mortimer appears as a cynic and
a misanthrope: "I'm a sour fellow; so the world thinks
of me; but it is against the proud, the rich I war..."
(I.i.p.30). Augusta, one of the young lovers whom Mortimer eventually saves, thinks he is a misanthrope (I.
ii.p.21), and Lord Aberville calls him a cynic who has

turned traitor to society (I.i.p.12). But Mortimer's misanthropy arises from a tender heart; it reflects his intellectual conviction of and his real hatred for the corruption of the world; at the same time it operates as a defense mechanism against the imposition of this very corruption. As he tells his servant Macleod,"Sheath a soft heart in a rough case, 'twill wear the longer; fineer [sic] thyself...as thy master does, and keep a marble outside to the world" (II.i.p.27). His sensibility, however, is so refined that Macleod's depiction of the objects of charity saved in one day by Mortimer's benevolence turns Mortimer to tears: he is "one of nature's children,and...[has not] yet left off the tricks of the nursery" (II.i.p.28).

As the satiric moralist, Mortimer lashes Lord Aberville, while he simultaneously does all in his power to save him from the certain destruction his dissipated ways foreshadow. To Lord Aberville, Mortimer's satiric invective and private good deeds are a constant reproach. Mortimer, he admits, "is the glass in which I see myself, and the reflection tortures me" (III.ii. p.51). From dissipated individuals Mortimer turns to attack the world in general, and his castigation gains in asperity, since his private life of virtue qualifies him for his public role as satirist. With impunity he can ask, "What is it our men of genius are about? Jarring and jangling with each other, whilst a vast army of vices overruns the whole country at discretion" (II. i.p. 27). In his eyes, the world is so evil that "no corrosive can eat deep enough to bottom the corruption" (IV.ii.p.76). In contrast to the corruption that he attacks with Juvenalian virulence stands his own benevolent heart, which actively seeks to remedy the evil his tongue lashes; he is "one who does a thousand noble acts without the credit of one; his tongue wounds and his heart makes whole" (IV.i.p.68). Perhaps his role in the play is best summed up in his own words to Augusta's father: "Let us do good, sir,and not talk about it..." (IV.ii.p.77).

Cumberland realized the satiric possibilities that such a character offered to sentimental drama, for he repeated him in the person of Ruefull in *The Natural Son* (1785).[5] As satirist, Ruefull ridicules both the

world and the affectations of individuals in it: "When
a miser or a manhater is mentioned, Ruefull's name is
in every body's mouth" (III.i.p.40). Mortimer and Ruefull are both fully developed benevolent misanthropes
whose intellectual conviction of the evil of the world
manifests itself in satire, while their benevolent
hearts seek to save as many individuals as possible.
As fully realized satirists and men of feeling, however,
they offer an interesting contrast to Penruddock of Cumberland's later play *The Wheel of Fortune* (1795). *The
Wheel of Fortune* is primarily a dramatic demonstration
that even traditional misanthropes may be converted to
men of feeling, and, moreover, that if this is the case
they can be profitably used as satirists.[6] Penruddock,
like Molière's Alceste and Shakespeare's Timon, becomes
a misanthrope because of his mistreatment by the world.
Cumberland carefully draws out the satiric possibilities of Penruddock by tracing his development from antisocial to benevolent misanthropy. Penruddock is one
of the characters Cumberland describes in his *Memoirs*
as usually "butts for ridicule and abuse," but which he
has "endeavoured to present...in such lights, as might
tend to reconcile the world to them, and them to the
world."[7] As a misanthropic railer with a benevolent
heart, Penruddock is much inferior to Mortimer and Ruefull, since most of the play concentrates on his antisocial, Timonian misanthropy and his internal struggle
to overcome it. As a character study in the evolution
of benevolent misanthropy after Smollett, however,
Penruddock possesses an interest beyond his railing
abilities.

In the early part of the play, Penruddock appears as a
typical Timonian misanthrope who resorts to bitter invective to satirize the follies and corruption of London (III.iii.p.41ff.). His early invective is shroud-
ed in malice, for his latent benevolence has not been
activated. The play concentrates on Penruddock's struggle to master his antisocial maliciousness and to bring
out his underlying benevolence. By the last act, Penruddock has succeeded and has abandoned his thoughts of
revenge against those who had wronged him. But if his
benevolence triumphs, it cannot destroy his misanthropy,
for the real evils of the world still exist. Instead,

he is transformed into a benevolent misanthrope and assumes the humor of Mortimer and Ruefull. His own description of himself to Emily signals his movement from malevolent to benevolent misanthropy: "I hope, madam, there is something here present more amusing to your sight than a crabbed old clown, who happens to have a little more kindness at his heart than he carries in his countenance" (V.i.p.66). The nature of Penruddock's new misanthropy can be discerned in the new direction of his satire. Before the emergence of his benevolence,Penruddock wished to retire again from the world: "I am weary, sick, discomfited. This world and I must part once more. That it has virtues, I will not deny; but they lie buried in a tide of vanities, like grains of gold in sand washed down by mountains of torrents: I cannot wait the sifting" (IV.ii.p.53). After the victory of benevolence, Penruddock sees that the world remains the same, as he tells Emily: "Certainly, madam, this world is a great polisher; it makes smooth faces and slippery friendships" (V.i.p.67). But Penruddock also says this to a new friend, and he plans to remain in the world to help individuals who need his benevolence.

Members from the Novel

The traditional misanthrope received his most extensive treatment in the drama, but the benevolent misanthrope, developing simultaneously with the rise of the novel, flourished in that genre, where both Courtney Melmoth (Samuel Jackson Pratt) and Robert Bage provided extensive range for his satiric railing. In *Liberal Opinions; or The History of Benignus* (1775), Melmoth offers a long, rambling satire against society, which drives his benevolent hero into misanthropy and retirement into the woods. As was seen in chapter two, however, Benignus bears no enmity towards mankind and retains his benevolence, but he does not turn satirist.[8] In his second novel, *Shenstone-Green* (1779), Melmoth returned to the theme he developed in *Liberal Opinions,* that man, if left to himself in the present situation of the world, will ordinarily choose vice over virtue.[9] Hence, the man of feeling, without protection, is doomed in the world to frustration and disappointment and will find his virtue rewarded only in the next world. But in this novel, Melmoth decided to save the man of feeling from destruction. The benevolent, but antisocial, misanthropy that drove Benignus to his death in the wilderness is now transformed into the active, benevolent misanthropy of Samuel Sarcastic. Samuel continually enunciates this same thesis about the world and the man of feeling, but his "speculative" misanthropy saves him from Benignus' destruction. Samuel's chief role is that of steward to the benevolent Sir Benjamin Beauchamp, and this stewardship includes being a satiric commentator on the folly Sir Benjamin's benevolence produces.

The novel is essentially a superficial allegory based on Genesis and *Paradise Lost*. Indeed, Melmoth significantly subtitles his work *The New Paradise Lost. Being a History of Human Nature*. Sir Benjamin thinks of Shenstone-Green as *Paradise Regained* and then lost again. Sir Benjamin's folly in attempting to establish a new society that would outwit man's natural appetites and remain in its original state of bliss is attributed to his benevolence and goodwill, but except in a few men like Sir Benjamin benevolence unfortunately "is in these days a tolerable economist" (I, 2). Thus, like *Liberal Opinions, Shenstone-Green* is a warning to men of feeling; it is written for those "few, and those chiefly a set of simpletons who work up their hearts to a warmth that mounts into the brain, and brings on the convulsions of sympathy" (I, 3). As a condemnation of the vices of man and society, the satire is as pungent as in *Liberal Opinions*, but, by putting the actual satire in the mouth of Samuel Sarcastic and by constantly contrasting his benevolent misanthropy with Sir Benjamin's foolish charity, *Shenstone-Green* loses the heavyhandedness of the satire in the former novel. As a case against society, however, it is just as effective.

Samuel accepts the position as steward to the Green, even though he "grinned a silent sarcasm on... [the] scheme in every lineament of his face" (I, 47). He intends, however, to use the job as a means of convincing Beauchamp of his folly. If Sir Benjamin plans to put his romantic scheme into action, Samuel warns that

he had better at least set up laws for his model community, for no society "can long preserve its harmony
without regulations" (I, 78). He attempts to make Beauchamp see that the half a hundred people he has assem-
bled have "at least half a thousand contrary passions"
(I, 78). On his journey to seek suitable inhabitants
for the Green, Samuel adopts Bramble's satiric "form"
when he sends satiric letters to Beauchamp that try to
prove to him that his benevolent schemes are really
"charitable abuses" (I, 72). As a satirist, Samuel expresses the pessimistic view of man, which in the context of the novel turns out to be the realistic one that
triumphs: "'For my part, sir,' said the steward, 'I
think one has more reason to cry at human nature than
to laugh, for I never yet found her four and twenty
hours in the same mind in my life'" (II, 5-6). The
gradual decay of the Green draws from Sarcastic only
such satiric remarks as "Let us shut our eyes for a
few hours—*against the species*" (II, 31). Samuel is
not, however, a complete Calvinist, for he does not contend that man is by nature evil. As a man of feeling,
Samuel holds that man does have innate benevolent feelings, but he also sees that man has passions that tend
to corrupt; both are equally natural. "Nature, I believe, sir, leads to a decent behaviour; but there are,
I fear, five perverted appetites, which lean to the
grossest pleasure, to one that is delicate or true to
the original bias of human feelings" (II, 162).
Melmoth elaborated Sarcastic into the completely low
comic misanthrope Partington in *Family Secrets* (1797),
which, chronologically, is almost the last work of literature to use the benevolent misanthropic satirist.[10]
The novel itself is a veritable treatise on benevolence
and feeling, covering in one manner or another nearly
every type of man of feeling available to the period.
If one can speak of structure in a work longer and more
rambling than *Liberal Opinions,* Partington represents
a balance between the morbid benevolence of Henry Fitzorton and the Timonian misanthropy towards which his
brother John tends (needless to say as a result of his
excessive feelings). Melmoth's triangle of feeling is
certainly not subtle; it is easy to hear what J.M.S.
Tompkins calls the gongs of antisentimentality that

sound from both Partington and John.[11] But, as Tompkins has also noted, the pages are drenched with tears,
and for all his antisentiment Melmoth approves of them.[12]
It is only fair to Melmoth, however, to say that the
tears are consistent with the excessive melodrama of
the story and are not merely decoration. The action
moves forward by a constant series of contrasts between
the benevolent Fitzortons and the malevolent Sir Guise
Stuart (who later adds a vicious wife and her followers
to his family group). In terms of this type of plot,
the villainy of Sir Guise tends to Gothic horror as the
benevolence of the Fitzortons tends to sentimentalism.
Partington weaves in and out of these two families as a
friend to the Fitzortons, an enemy to the Stuarts, and
a satiric commentator on the whole scene.

 Partington strikes the balance between the extremes of
Henry and John, protecting his sensitive heart with the
armor of misanthropy; Melmoth carefully observes that
Partington is thus a true man of feeling and not a mere
"sentimentalist":

> Mr. Partington had many peculiarities;—there was
> a rough honesty in his manner, and a freedom of ex-
> pression corresponding to it....beneath this unin-
> viting exterior, beat a heart, every pulsation of
> which was a genuine good-will to mankind, without
> the least alloy of *sentimentality,*—that shining
> dress which makes so much glitter in these tinsel
> times. (II, 1-2)

Partington shows his favor to people by addressing them
rudely and his disfavor by addressing them with great
civility. The extent of his favor and disfavor depends
on the violence of his language (I, 203). Melmoth's
addition of this rather strange trait heightens Partington's humor and readily places him in the realm of
low comedy. Characteristic of the benevolent misanthrope type, Partington aids in private those he rails
against in public; he puts active charity above mere
well-wishing. Melmoth's description of Partington is
almost archetypal:

> He never *talked* of doing any person a kindness, and
> yet was kindness itself. In truth, while other peo-

ple were *only* talking, he would be doing the very
thing they talked about; for he would slip out of
the company, on fifty different pretenses, none of
which you could suspect—and have had an interview
with the party he had heard commiserated,—then return to the company with no alteration in his general manner, but that of loading with exaggerated
scurrility the person to whom he was indebted for
the opportunity of being bountiful.... But more
frequently he would appear altogether inattentive
to tales of distress, or, if he *did* give ear to them,
would break out into—"Psah!—don't tell me! riff-
raff! stuff! a pack of beggars! I should not have
thought of their impudence! I say distress too!"...
yet he would be at the door, or at the bed-side of
the sufferers...before any other man of the party
thought of leaving the company. (II, 4-5).

The nature of Partington's satiric role is perhaps
best dramatized in a superb mock heroic trial, where
Melmoth adds legal strength to Partington's satiric
power. John Fitzorton and Partington sit in judgment
over Lady Stuart, Sir Guise, and their followers. "And
now, Sir John Fitzorton, and Edward Partington, Esq.,
two of his Majesty's justices, ordering two chairs of
judgment, sat themselves down" (VI, 20). Before the
case can be heard, however, Justice Barhim, Sir Guise's
corrupt friend, finds himself on the floor; in the description of the Justice and the brawl that ensues,
Melmoth significantly calls on Rabelais, Fielding, Le
Sage, and Smollett to assist his pen (IV, 24). When
order has been restored, Partington, who had been running to and fro enthusiastically encouraging his friends
to defeat Sir Guise in the fray, symbolically unites
justice and satire by taking his stand beside John; he
alternates sarcastic bows to Lady Stuart with John's
recitation of the legal charges (IV, 35ff.). This addition of legal power, recalling *Sir Launcelot Greaves*,[13]
points up Partington's satiric powers, for ultimately
the law is frustrated, and it is only satiric castigation that lashes the villains.
Melmoth's architectonic weaknesses are particularly
glaring in the light of the rather tight structural

unity of the novels of his contemporary Robert Bage. Bage's novels are, perhaps unfortunately, rarely read today; by modern standards they lack even much of the sophisticated architechtonic complexity of Richardson and Fielding. But in his own day Bage was extremely popular, and, except for Fanny Burney, probably the most technically competent novelist between Smollett and Jane Austen. His popularity and importance as an author can be judged merely by the fact that Sir Walter Scott included three of his novels in the Ballantyne Series. The inclusion is doubly significant, for Scott detested Bage's politics and morality, both of which he felt came out only too clearly in all of the novels. Like Melmoth, Bage constantly fought false and overrefined feelings, while he praised the true feeling that displayed itself in active charity. There are moments, indeed, when it is difficult to decide just where Bage draws the line between true and false feeling, for a rich irony pervades all of Bage's work and often places even true benevolence in an extremely precarious position.

In reviewing *Barham Downs,* the *Monthly* praised Bage's good sense but expressed considerable concern at his ironical presentation of benevolence and feeling: "The leading principle of this Author's novels is good sense, animated by a spirit of freedom and benevolence, and expressed in a style peculiarly pointed and sprightly. ...he is...chargeable with a levity of sentiment,which hath a strong cast of irreligion and infidelity." The reviewer, perhaps, more accurately gaged Bage's satiric method when he rather penetratingly commented on his irony of presentation: "...the Author's talent lies chiefly in striking and spirited touches, and such as convey lively images of objects under a light and ludicrous form. He is seldom serious: and his pathetic is sometimes dashed with an odd mixture of ridicule and irony."[14] Actually Bage attacks benevolence and feeling in such a manner that he preserves true feeling; his method involves a constant maintenance of ironic tension among the various men of feeling in his novels, who range from the morbid Henry type to the type tending towards Timonian misanthropy. He then heightens his irony with the addition of a benevolent misanthrope who can be a friend to the men of feeling and, as a satirist, can condemn, not only affected feeling, but the morbid and antisocial type of feeling as well.

Bage's first novel, *Mount Henneth* (1781), introduces the benevolent misanthrope to his work in an extremely striking way, for he is actually unknown to any of the characters; in fact he is dead before the story begins, and his life is narrated by one of the correspondents, John Cheslyn.[15] Sir Howell Henneth, the benevolent misanthrope, had been the owner of Mount Henneth and Henneth Castle, which Mr. Foston purchases at the misanthrope's death as a residence for himself and eventually for the other chief characters of the story. Mount Henneth itself becomes the symbolic focal point of the novel, and one character after another leaves the world to join Mr. Foston in creating a new community on the Mount. All of these characters are men and women of feeling who can find happiness in an unfeeling world only by banding together in a sort of model society, not unlike Shenstone-Green. Sir Howell's presence pervades the novel as a symbolic satiric commentator on the evils of a world that he himself finally had to desert to find peace of mind. Like himself, the characters of the novel ironically discover that Henneth Castle, a "large old castle, in good, though gloomy repair" (IX, 126), is really a place of happiness.

"Sir Howell Henneth, the great misanthrope, whose life and conversation may be classed in the number of Welch curiosities" (IX, 126), had begun life as a wealthy young man in high society, and, like the youth of most of these misanthropes, his had been a rather dissipated one. But, disgusted with the world, he finally "threw up his place with disdain, and retired to this castle, fully imbued with the surly spirit of misanthropy" (IX, 135). Sir Howell, however, is a benevolent misanthrope and in his retirement goes farther than most benevolent misanthropes, for he actually writes formal satire: "...he had lately made it his principal amusement to write bitter philippics against...[the world's] pleasures" (IX, 135). But for all his misanthropy and satire, Sir Howell was one of the most benevolent landlords of the country: "...you will be astonished at the strange mixture of genius, whim, misanthropy, and benevolence" (IX, 136).

In his benevolence he permitted his tenants to deceive him with their tales of woe, so that he usually ended up paying their taxes as well as their rent (IX, 136); he then went out of his way to provide work and wages for them:

> In the area that fronts the baronet's late apart-
> ment, we observed several heaps of the common peb-
> ble stone, and wondering for what use they could
> have been collected,—I believe, gentlemen, says an
> elderly labourer, I can give you some information.
> His honour that's dead and gone, God Bless him!
> neither liked to see a poor man starve, nor be idle.
> So when work was scant in the country, in winter
> time, when the brick-kilns could not gang, he sent
> as many of us as wanted employment to work in car-
> rying these same heaps of stone from one place to
> another; and you might see his honour peeping out
> of the window now and then, just to see if we kept
> in motion, and that was all he wanted. (IX, 136)

In the summertime, he had the men make more bricks, and then, when winter returned, either had them moved from place to place or even buried. Thus, Sir Howell "chose to do some good with his money, without injuring the country, or doing violence to his hermetical determina-tions" (IX, 136-137). Sir Howell's method of doing good deeds illustrates the essential ingredient of humor in his nature that makes him "risible" at the same time that it highlights his satiric contempt for the world. In the laborer's words, "He was a vast comical gentle-man, to be sure, at times..." (IX, 136). Sir Howell's resemblance to Matt Bramble is, of course, obvious. In-deed, Bage is probably the finest imitator of Smollet-tean humor in the last quarter of the eighteenth cen-tury.

The symbolic implications of Sir Howell and Mount Hen-neth are elaborated in Samuel Sutton, one of the char-acters who eventually retires to Henneth Castle. Sam-uel's conversion from Timonian misanthropy and his re-tirement to Henneth Castle structurally reflect Sir How-ell's own merger of satire and feeling and establish the Mount as the refuge for men of feeling. In Samuel,

the movement from benevolence to misanthropy and recon-
version to benevolence can be followed: "Samuel found
his arm-chair irresistible. The arm-chair engendered
weariness, weariness begot the spleen, and five year's
habit has confirmed him the most growling and ill-con-
ditioned tyrant within the bills of mortality" (IX,118).
Beneath this misanthropy, of course, lies a tender and
feeling heart, which the young Scots doctor, Gordon,
easily draws out, to the amazement of Sutton's nephew,
Tom: "Ay, gude troth, Maister Sutton is one o' the best
natured men in the world, 'gin he did na tak sic muckle
pains to conceal it" (IX, 178).[16]
In *Barham Downs* (1784), Bage explored the possibilities of the benevolent misanthrope in a principal role
instead of as the unifying symbol he is in *Mount Henneth*.[17] Although Bage continues to write in the epis-
tolary form, he creates essentially the same dramatic
situation Melmoth established in *Family Secrets,* a triangle of different types of men of feeling. Wyman is
his Partington, but without low comic accretions. As
a satirist, Wyman castigates affected benevolence and
overrefined feeling, while, as a friend of young Harry
Osmond, a morbid sentimentalist, he assists both him
and the other plot characters and ridicules their follies. In the character of George Osmond, Harry's older brother, Bage offers an analysis of a malicious cynic
eventually converted to benevolent misanthropy. Bage
stresses George's cynicism but leaves the actual railing to Wyman. Wyman is intellectually convinced of
human depravity, but his misanthropy is also the armor
that allows him to remain in the world and perform benevolent deeds without imposition. In this vein, he
castigates the retired Harry Osmond for permitting his
sensibilities to draw him from active and beneficial
participation in the affairs of the world:

> Thy letter, Harry, for awhile, deceived me into an
> opinion that thou wert justified in thy sentiments
> of the world, and right in secluding thyself from
> it. It was the momentary triumph of feeling over
> reason. I was betrayed, *against nature,* into a fit
> of *sensibility,* which, as thy brother says, leads
> to infinite absurdities. (IX, 250)

Harry has turned sensibility into the morbid luxuriating in feeling that destroys initiative and active charity.

The two brothers, Harry and George, represent two extremes in human nature. Harry, as a foolish man of
feeling, leaves himself open to every form of imposition and absurdity, until he hates mankind and rejects
society. Since, however, Bage thinks Harry worth sav-
ing, he permits his retirement from the busy world actually to serve the purpose of reforming him, teaching
him that the ability to act is as necessary as the ability to feel. At Barham Downs, Harry falls in love with
Annabella Whitaker, who serves as the cause of his reformation. In terms of the plot structure, her abduc-
tion by Lord Winterbottom finally moves Harry to transform his refined feelings into action. In a frantic
and hot pursuit after the melodramatic villain, Harry
learns that feeling and sensibility can be protected
and preserved in this world only by a paradoxically active confrontation and struggle with its evils.

Like Partington, Wyman walks the middle road between
two extremes and uses his armor of misanthropy to castigate both brothers and false sentiment in general.
Bage carefully points up Wyman's role as friend: "A
plague upon it! I am doomed, in spite of myself, to love
those animals the best, who have the greatest share of
this cursed sensibility, which I am at every hour wishing at the devil, with all the appurtenances thereunto
belonging" (IX, 250). His pity for the seduced Miss
Ross and his eventual marriage to her only affirm Harry's assertion that Wyman, despite his misanthropy, had
a heart "as soft and gentle as a virgin's" (IX, 257).
Harry's analysis of Wyman emphasizes the idea that misanthropy may be a psychological defense mechanism, an
incognito of feeling: "Whether thou assumest an air of
asperity, and stormest at the world and me, or endeav-
ourest to throw an air of playfulness or ridicule over
a tale of love and innocence, its [his heart] tenderness is conspicuous" (IX, 257).

As a satirist, however, Wyman can effectively analyze
excess in any direction, illustrating at the same time
his own attempt to maintain an ideal intermediate position:

I object equally to insensible, and to too sensible minds. There is a medium, a boundary, fixed by the nature of things, which it is folly to pass. Would you have mankind feel for themselves and others, till ease and happiness were banished the world? And would not this be the case if everyone could really say, what the affected lady says, "Alas! I feel too sensibly for my peace?"...One consolation is, the affection of it is at least ten times as great as the reality.... (IX, 274)

Wyman's hatred of excessive sensibility is closely allied to the ideal moral position of the man of feeling supported by contemporary periodical writers like Henry Mackenzie.[18]

The Fair Syrian, Bage's next novel (1787), does not make extensive use of the benevolent misanthrope as satirist.[19] He appears briefly as Mr. Warren, the "fair Syrian's" uncle, who is a satiric commentator on the lack of justice and charity in fashionable family life. His own "family of fashion ridiculed Mr. Warren as a morose and surly humourist, which his external appearance did not much contradict; and he, on his part, attacked their abundant pride, and little wisdom" (II, 26). But Mr. Warren is the only member of this "family on the rise" who has the charity to save the "fair Syrian's" father from financial ruin. After a short test in which the surly misanthrope bullies and abuses his nephew (II, 30ff.), he sets the young man up as a merchant—"so much did the benevolence of his heart counteract the harshness of his features" (II, 34). Mr. Warren then disappears from the book, but much later his function as benevolent misanthropic satirist is briefly taken up by a Scots nobleman, Lord Konkeith.

Lord Konkeith's poverty makes him somewhat of a social outcast, but fortunately "He has, it seems, other ill qualities; as a passion for truth, a turn for satire, a contempt for frivolity of every species, and an intrepidity which carries him directly to the point" (II, 192). Lord Konkeith maintains more detachment from the human scene than most of the other benevolent misanthropes thus far examined. Although he tries to mend Lady Bembridge's follies (II, 194-195) and saves the "fair Syrian" from the hands of Lord Bembridge (II, 231ff.), he is essentially a spectator of the world (II, 194) rather than an actor in it. Bage succinctly describes him as the benevolent spectator satirist who enters the human fray only when his benevolence can be of service: "He is not a polite man; and despises the manners of the age, perhaps too much. He can be silent upon occasion, and it is most frequently his choice; but if he speaks, he speaks what he thinks. His general look does not denote a heart turned to benevolence" (II, 230). Lord Konkeith's detachment recalls Goldsmith's Man in Black more closely than Matt Bramble. He probably derives more immediately, however, from Albany in Fanny Burney's *Cecilia*, which will be examined below.

In *James Wallace* (1788), on the other hand, Bage developed the benevolent misanthrope as satirist into the most important character of the novel.[20] Although this next novel centers to a certain extent on James Wallace himself, "one of the most carefully wrought figures...is that of Paul Lamounde,"[21] who is the benevolent satirist of the work. As in *Humphry Clinker*, an obvious influence on *James Wallace*, the main character is not the title character. In his plot role, Uncle Paul serves as Wallace's friend and adviser; his satiric role permits him to rail, however, both at Wallace's excessive benevolence and at benevolence in general, much like Wyman. His niece's description is perhaps the briefest and most pointed: "My uncle, by the aid of contracted eye-brows, and some asperity of language, conceals a kind and benevolent heart. He seldom speaks to please, and still more seldom acts to offend" (IX, 426). To Uncle Paul, benevolence consists in action and not words. As James's instructor he attempts to remove his pupil's extravagant notions of benevolence (without much success), as indicated in his letter to the captain of the ship James has agreed to serve on: "The young man has, moreover, a sound understanding, and, I suppose, a large stock of integrity. The fellow has damn'd fine sensibilities too, and a nice notion of honour; but his greatest extravagance is a romantic benevolence; a folly of the first magnitude, when there is nothing to support it" (IX, 453). Uncle Paul's attempts to teach James restraint are, of course, frustrated by his own secret benevolence and ironically recoil on the misanthrope. On his wedding day, James goes to the sponging houses of London to distribute a hundred pounds to the poor. In his letter to Sir Patrick Islay, Uncle Paul comments on this extravagance: "I abused him for it with all the authority of an uncle. What think you was the whelp's answer? Marry—that he prayed to God like other people, till I taught him this other mode of religion; and then retorted upon me with a late foolish charitable indiscretion of my own, which I thought a profound secret..." (IX, 506).

As a satirist, Uncle Paul is primarily concerned with denouncing universal benevolence: "The justice that soars above the laws...is romance. Universal benevolence is romance; and the affections you talk of, meaning, I suppose, the altitudes of love and friendship, the greatest romance of all" (IX, 419). In his denunciations, Uncle Paul usually combines the role of satirist and instructor, for more often than not his invective arises in an altercation with James over what Uncle Paul feels is some act of foolish benevolence. Indeed, Uncle Paul's whole role in the novel is revealed in just such an argument, where his savage denunciations of man and benevolence are followed by his private decision to help the distressed people James himself has tried to assist. Uncle Paul's invective participates in the vitriolic Juvenalian tradition: "No, sir, but man is an ass; these remote and improbable evils are upon his right hand and upon his left, whilst the fool, guided by passion or prejudice, will only look straight forward" (IX, 429-430). As far as benevolence is concerned, Uncle Paul reasserts Wyman's position: "I hate the cant of benevolence; books are full of it; it fills our mouth, and sometimes gets as far as the eye, but never reaches the heart" (IX, 430). But, as James reminds him, his private life of benevolence is a commentary on his public one as satirist; his misanthropy is only "speculative," as Wallace notes: "Will you have the goodness to pardon me, sir, if I suspect your assumed principles ill agree with your practice" (IX, 430).

Man As He Is (1792), the last novel in which Bage elaborates the benevolent misanthrope, is essentially *James Wallace* inverted.[22]   The purpose of the novel is to demonstrate that man in general is not basically good but must be led to virtue through misery: "Man—though the lord of the creation, for whom the sun and moon was made, and the bright galaxy above, and the sweet pretty galaxies below—is yet—I am sorry to tell it my fair readers—is yet an imperfect being" (IV, 182). Bage further assures the reader that "the principal part of our business is to conduct a rich high blooded young Englishman to the temple of wisdom, no small undertaking" (IV, 115). The rich young lord is Sir George Paradyne, and the priest of the temple of wisdom is the benevolent misanthrope Mr. Lindsay. Lindsay's role is much like that of Uncle Paul, only his satire aims more at the general evil of the world than specifically at affected benevolence. To Sir George's request that he become his tutor, Lindsay replies: "Disgusted with mankind—is it for me to introduce a gentleman into a proper commerce with it?" (I, 21). But Sir George, as foolish as he may be, realizes that just such a vision of the world is required if a young man is to succeed in living in reality and enter the "temple of wisdom":

Excellent...this is precisely what I want. I love the world too well, especially the fairer part of it. A gentleman of your misanthropic turn will mitigate the violence of this passion. It is through magnifiers I look at the world and its pleasures. You turn the glass the opposite way; who knows, but that by our mutual labours, we may at length construct the catoptric instrument, at which divines and philosophers have been labouring so long, and with so little success—the glass of truth; and see things as they are.   (I, 23)

Lindsay's role as satirist is highlighted again and again as the two men travel through the continent on the Grand Tour. Sir George even refers to Lindsay as his "inhuman satirist" (I, 78). As Sir George's tutor and friend, however, Lindsay seeks to steer him through the vices and follies of the world by means of kindness and benevolence: "Mr. Lindsay spoke his usual language; a language which could seldom fail to animate the hu-

man heart to virtue, if the human heart was always disposed to hear" (IV, 79). Like all of these benevolent
misanthropes, Lindsay turns to railing simply because
the world is not "disposed to hear" the voice of benevolence and reason. Thus Sir George says, with ironical
truth, that Lindsay "is most natural in the character
of a cynic philosopher; neither the moral fabric of man,
nor the silk fabric of woman, are to his taste" (II,
41).[23]

The Disintegration of the Benevolent Misanthrope Type

The precariously comic juxtaposition of hatred and
feeling in the benevolent misanthrope is difficult to
maintain. It is only too easy to charge the comedy
with tragic overtones. Such overtones almost overwhelm
Fanny Burney's *Cecilia* (1782),[24] a melodramatic novel
in which she introduces a character that has long puz-
zled readers. In George Sherburn's words, "there is a
mad moralist, Albany, who appears at the oddest moments
to utter diatribes against the follies of fashionable
life."[25] I think that Albany can be best explained in
the tradition of the benevolent misanthrope and as such
can be integrated more completely into the total structure of the novel. For a minor character, Albany is
rather well wrought. Described by Mrs. Harrell as a
"manhater" (I, 112), his character is more fully elaborated by Gosport: "He seems to hold mankind in abhor-
rence, yet he is never a moment alone, and at the same
time that he intrudes himself into all parties, he associates with none: he is commonly a stern and silent
observer of *all* that passes, or when he speaks, it is
but to utter some sentences of rigid morality, or some
bitterness of indignant reproof" (I, 117). On the other hand, all of his activities are spent in relieving
the poor, such as Mr. Belfield (II, 58ff.), and at the
end of the novel Cecilia appoints him her almoner (V,
395). "'I know not what he is,' said Cecilia, 'but his
manners are not more singular than his sentiments are
affecting...'" (I, 220).

As a misanthrope, Albany is even more detached than
Matt Bramble, but, as Gosport notes, he feels a compul-
sion to be in society, where he can use his satiric

powers most fully. Albany, at first glance, seems to be a rather awkward humor character in the midst of a carefully documented novel of manners. But it is precisely the manners of an overluxurious and overrefined society that Burney is exposing in the novel. In relation to the corrupt mores and morals of vicious London high life, Albany rises as a satirist, but he radiates the gloom and doom of an Old Testament prophet, suggesting a self-conscious moral superiority: "Oh times of folly and dissipation!...Oh mignons of idleness and luxury" (I, 112). His prophetic castigations, however, become symbolically fulfilled in the gambling and suicide of Mr. Harrel and in the extravagance of Mrs. Harrel (II, 7ff.; III, 138-182). Albany's own past history strengthens his role, for as a youth he had indulged in the same dissipations until they finally destroyed his happiness in the death of his fiancée (IV, 306ff.). As a reformed libertine, he thus tightens his connections with the follies he castigates, and his denunciations illuminate the moral seriousness involved in the vices of society. At the same time, he possesses too much of the air of the rigidly righteous. From one point of view, for example, Mrs. Harrel's luxury and extravagance can be seen as mere folly, but, when it drives her husband to gaming and finally to suicide, that extravagance becomes a vice implying moral consequences more serious than the mere fulfillment of Albany's prophecies. In his prophetic-satiric role, Albany undercuts the pretentiousness of society's refinement and pursuit of luxury, but the ethos of his satire and the social milieu in which he satirizes border on tragedy, raising questions about motivation and making individual moral progress seem almost hopeless.

Although Albany spends much time uttering satiric invectives on society, he plays a special role in relationship to Cecilia, thus fusing his role as satirist and plot character. Cecilia first meets Albany at Mr. Moncton's, where he sat "frowning in a corner of the room" (I, 20); he almost immediately sets himself up as Cecilia's private prophet: "...fixing his eyes upon Cecilia with an expression of mingled grief and pity," he cries, "Alas! poor thing!" (I, 28). No one in the room heeds him except Cecilia. Later, at the music hall,

after his denunciations of the folly of the times, he
again turns to Cecilia and tries to warn her of her precarious situation: "Poor simple victim! Hast thou already so many pursuers? Yet seest not that thou art
marked for sacrifice! yet knowest not that thou are
destined for prey!" (I, 115). Cecilia begins to see
Albany's purpose and refers to him as her "unknown mentor" (I, 120), which is exactly what he becomes in the
novel. Significantly, Cecilia meets Albany at Moncton's
house, for it is Moncton whom she has always regarded
as her adviser and "mentor," unaware that he is plot-
ting to marry her for her money as soon as his aged wife
dies. When Moncton realizes Albany's influence over
Cecilia, he attempts to interfere, and Miss Burney pointedly notes the contrast between the two characters, for
Moncton fears that Albany will dissipate Cecilia's
fortune in benevolence (V, 95ff.). Despite Moncton's
attempts to preserve Cecilia's fortune for himself,
Cecilia officially installs Albany as her "almoner and
her monitor" (V, 136).

In the progression of the plot, Albany is also useful
to promote much of Burney's famous method of *contre-
temps*; he is responsible for introducing Cecilia to Belfield and his sister, an acquaintance that causes most
of the misunderstanding between Cecilia and the Del-
vills. In Cecilia's personal distresses, Albany, as
her monitor, is always present. He pointedly arrives
when Cecilia is mourning the death of her friend, Mrs.
Morton, and chooses this opportunity to recite his life
history, which further establishes him in the benevolent
misanthrope tradition. His severe morality and satiric
invectives are an attempt to save others from the lib-
ertinism and folly he fell into as a youth, while his
benevolence is an attempt to expiate his sins (IV, 306
ff.). His recitation "almost surprised her out of her
peculiar grief, by the view which it opened to her of
general calamity; wild, flighty and imaginative as were
his language and counsels, their morality was striking,
and their benevolence was affecting" (IV, 322). Albany
is also the first to discover the identity of Cecilia
when she lies alone and mad, and he enters what he thinks
is her death chamber surrounded with poor children whom
he wants to pay a last tribute to their benefactress
(V, 331ff.).

Fanny Burney thus integrates Albany's role as satirist
into the total structure of the plot by making him serve
as both prophet and adviser to the young Cecilia, warning her of the dangers of the fashionable society he
denounces in his satiric role.   Burney also integrates
him into the low comedy of the novel when she uses his
role as a satiric spokesman to lash metaphorically the
humors of Briggs, Hobson, and even Delvill senior.   In
the well-known attainment of majority scene, she gath-
ers all of these humors characters   together, and Albany rails at each one in turn, denouncing Briggs for
his parsimony (V,62), Hobson for his meanness of spirit
(V, 63), and Delvill for his pride and "vile arrogance"
(V, 74). This purging of humors rather clearly relates
Albany to the Jonsonian satiric method, especially to
Every Man Out Of His Humour, where affinity between Albany and Asper is evident.
  Giving tragic overtones to the role of the benevolent
misanthrope immediately threatens the viability of the
character type, for the old suspicions of motivation
arise again, and man's capacity for moral evil begins
to overshadow the affirmation of the individual's capacity for moral progress. Equally threatening, however, is reducing him to the mere abstraction of a character sketch, as Henry Mackenzie does in the *Lounger*
papers (1785).   In No. 4, Mackenzie, finally acting on
his own suggestion about misanthropy, in the *Man of
Feeling*, introduces one of his most famous characters,
Colonel Caustic, who appears from time to time in order
to satirize the follies of city life. Caustic, in an
extremely pale imitation of Matthew Bramble, now and
again leaves his country retreat to enter the world of
the busy city. The vice and folly he sees there force
him to vent his spleen in satiric invectives on man and
society. Scott, in his "Life of Henry Mackenzie," used
Caustic and another of Mackenzie's *Lounger* characters
to indicate the nature of Mackenzie's satire: "The
Northern Addison, who revived the art of periodical
writing, and sketched, though with a light pencil, the
follies and the lesser vices of the times, has shown
himself a master of playful satire.... Colonel Caustic
and Unfraville are masterly conceptions of the *laudator
temporis acti*...."26 Mr. Lounger himself was fascinated
by the nature of his "conceptions of the laudator" and

gave his readers an interesting character analysis, lest they be displeased with the surly colonel's strictures on society.

Since Caustic does not serve as a character in the plot of a novel, Mackenzie dwells more on the reasons that drive Caustic to satirize than on showing that his private life is in some way connected with many other people. In this respect, Caustic is a throwback to Goldsmith's Drybone, but he does not even enjoy the complexity of presentation Drybone received. He serves merely as a detached commentator and guide for another abstraction, Mr. Lounger. The *Critical Review*, however, noted the satiric use of Caustic and favored him over Addison's famous Sir Roger de Coverly: "...in some of the scenes, the pointed shrewdness of his remarks, with his good-natured severity, form a pleasing contrast to the mild unobtrusive benevolence of Sir Roger."27 In this role, he stands at a distance in public assemblies and satirizes the manners of the men and women present (No. 4); ridicules the theatre for stupid plays, and the audience for bad manners (No.6); shows Mr. Lounger the disgusting table manners of the young generation (No. 14); ridicules the modern taste for Gothic houses and gardens (No.31); and takes Mr. Lounger to a dinner which displays the pride and hauteur of the *nouveau riche* (No. 33). His own quiet and peaceful life in the country presents an idyllic contrast to the mad pursuits of vanity and folly (No. 31).

Mr. Lounger, however, is disconcerted by the paradox he finds in Caustic's character; at first he attributes the Colonel's satire to his retirement:

A person who, after living a number of years in retirement returns again into society, is somewhat in the situation of the foreigner. Like him, he is apt to be misled by prejudices; but like him, too, he remarks many things which escape the observation of those whose sensations are blunted by habit, and whose attention is less awake to the objects around him. (No. 6, p. 101)

The Lounger's accurate estimation of Caustic's satiric abilities of penetration, does not, however, seem to ex-

plain why the Colonel is "a determined batchelor, with
somewhat of misanthropy, and a great deal of good-nature
about him" (No. 4, p. 33).   The misanthropy obviously
explains the satire, but the good nature does not seem
to explain the misanthropy. After a visit to Caustic's
residence in the country, Mr. Lounger finds that it is
not retirement alone that explains the misanthropy, but
indeed the good nature itself:

> I am now assured of what before I was willing to
> believe, that Caustic's spleen is of that sort which
> is the product of the warmest philanthropy.... the
> lover of mankind, as his own sense of virtue has
> painted them, when he comes abroad into life, and
> sees what they really are, feels the disappointment
> in the severest manner; and he will often indulge
> in satire beyond the limits of discretion.... (No.
> 32, p. 220)

Scott's connection of Mackenzie's satiric talent with
Shakespeare's Jaques places both Mackenzie and Caustic
clearly in the benevolent misanthrope tradition: "...
although his [Mackenzie's] peculiar vein of humour may
be much more frequently traced, yet it is so softened
down, and divested of the broad ludicrous, that it harmonizes with the more grave and affecting parts of the
tale, and becomes, like the satire of Jaques, only a
more humourous shade of melancholy."[28]
  Colonel Caustic is not chronologically the last of the
benevolent misanthropes (since both Bage and Melmoth
extend farther into the end of the century), but the
brevity of his presentation and his lack of complexity
as a plot character lead easily to his final appearance
as a satirist (at least so far as I have been able to
determine) and complete deterioration in Sir Walter
Scott.[29]   In *The Black Dwarf* (1816), Scott presents a
misanthropic railer in the central character, Elshie.[30]
Elshie's history as a bridegroom whose bride has run off
with his best friend is more consistent with the Timonian misanthrope who is later reformed than with the benevolent misanthrope tradition itself, in which he is
more often a rake than a jilted lover. Nevertheless,
Scott does not set out to reform Elshie but rather insists that he is basically benevolent already; his mis-

anthropy is the result of his "morbid and excessive
sensibility" (V, 350), as was the misanthropy of John
in Melmoth's *Family Secrets.*

   The Black Dwarf, however, was not a success in its own
day and certainly is not one today.[31]   The essential
failure of the character can, I think, be attributed to
Scott's mixture of the Timon and Jaques character types.
The real nature of Elshie's character is not revealed
until the very end of the novel,[32] so for the most part
all that is seen of his character is his public stance
as misanthropic railer, a Timon who appears in his blackest hue. All that is known of his private life indicates
that it is as vile as his public denunciations, so that,
like Timon, he appears to be the satirist whose own ex-
cesses are an object of ridicule; the few good deeds he
does perform, he attributes to his desire to promote
misery.[33] When Scott finally reveals Elshie's true nature, the surprise element of this dramatic revelation,
which takes place in a charnel house, militates against
even the credibility that would arise, for example, from
gradual revelation,[34] as in Cumberland's Penruddock,
whose final metamorphosis into a benevolent misanthrope
results from a gradual resolution of tortured internal
struggle. Penruddock can be seen dramatically moving
from Timon to Jaques; the reader sees Elshie acting in
the tombs only once and then in an atmosphere not very
conducive to benevolence. In contrast to Cumberland's
dramatic presentation of Penruddock's struggle, Scott
merely relates Elshie's history and the reasons for his
misanthropy. This confusion of roles is essentially an
attempt to have both Timonian and benevolent misanthropy
at the same time. Either kind of misanthrope will provide the satire desired, but Timonian misanthropy will
not provide the benevolence available to a character
fusing feeling and misanthropy. Ultimately such a confusion of types also leads to a blurring of the satirist's role. With Timon we have a satirist satirized and
with Jaques we have a benevolent satirist. Scott would
seem to want to have both at once, a combination that
appears to be dramatically unconvincing, as Smollett
discovered in *Peregrine Pickle.*

   In *The Fortunes of Nigel* (1822), Scott abandoned the
combination and returned to the malcontent of the Renais-

sance convention in the character of Sir Mungo Malagrowther.[35] Sir Mungo possesses all the malicious qualities of the cynic malcontent as well as those of the traditional malicious satirist; he has a "bitter, caustic, and backbiting humour, a malicious wit, and an envy of others" (IX, 100). Sir Mungo's "satire ran riot, his envy could not conceal itself" (IX, 100). He spends his time in typical Renaissance malcontent manner, "indulging his food for satire in public walks, and in the aisles of St. Paul's" (IX, 101). Sir Mungo does, however, have some degree of benevolence, which he displays to Nigel: "...he was about to leave Nigel very hastily, when some unwonted touch of good-natured interest in his youth and inexperience, seemed suddenly to soften his habitual cynicism" (IX, 268). In terms of the historical novel, Sir Mungo's type of cynical melancholy, of course, fits chronologically within the framework of *Nigel*, since the action occurs during the reign of James I. But Sir Mungo is clearly a reversion to the Renaissance misanthrope who is a satirist satirized; his benevolence does not counteract his misanthropy, nor is he in any way a man of feeling. Symbolically, Sir Mungo completes a cycle and returns the misanthrope to the Renaissance satirist satirized tradition and, indeed, beyond it to the whole tradition of misanthropic satire extending from Lucian's *Timon of Athens*. In one sense, the benevolent misanthrope as satirist died with Scott's Elshie, for in Elshie can be discerned the decline of the man of feeling as an ideal all men could easily realize.[36] The benevolent misanthrope as satirist depended on the man of feeling's popularity as such an ideal, for both his satiric power and his benevolence were generated by the benevolist doctrine of natural goodness. In his role as satirist, the benevolent misanthrope enjoys corrective force only because his character as a man of feeling assures that benevolence underlies his misanthropic attitude toward the world. As a humorist, the benevolent misanthrope creates a comic-satiric ethos that draws sympathetic affection to himself and ridicule to the world that causes his misanthropy.

The peculiar nature of the benevolent misanthrope's role as satirist emerges more boldly when he is con-

trasted with the many *bourrus bienfaisants,* the can-
tankerous splenetic humorists who appear everywhere in
the literature of the late eighteenth century and extend well into the nineteenth. The *bourru bienfaisant,*
the mere amiable humorist with a gruff exterior and a
moderate case of the spleen, is, of course, a benevolent
misanthropic satirist in embryo. In a limited way, such
characters, if they are not merely amiable humorists,
simply eccentrics, already possess implied satiric sta-
ture. Smollett's *Peregrine Pickle,* for example, obviously juxtaposes Commodore Trunnion and the Timonian
misanthrope Crabtree and satirizes the latter character
merely by the contrast. Indeed, the contrast with the
commodore does more to place Crabtree in the satirist
satirized convention than all Perry's denunciations of
him. But, like the works that focus on the process of
reforming the misanthrope instead of on his railing, the
bourru does not achieve the status of a fully developed
and clearly delineated misanthropic satirist. He remains a satirist only by implication and ironic contrast
with other characters.

The deeper irony of the benevolent misanthrope also
depends on his status as a man of feeling, for benevolent misanthropy ultimately represents a major solution
to the man of feeling's problem of surviving in a vicious world. By assuming benevolent misanthropy, the
man of feeling can remain in the world and participate
in its activities. In this limited sense, misanthropy
is a mask that helps to protect the man of feeling
against unwilling imposition. But benevolent misanthropy is far more than a mere mask, for it definitely
arises from disappointed benevolence and a conviction
of the general corruptness of man. The misanthropy is
immediately the result of the man of feeling's disappointment, but it also represents a philosophic vision
that rejects mankind but accepts the individual as a
person deserving sympathy and ultimately salvation. The
disappointment itself, of course, arises from the conflict between man as he is and man as he should and supposedly could be according to benevolist theory. The
benevolent misanthrope thus recoils on himself, for he
is the proof that benevolent feeling, however natural
to man, will hinder rather than advance worldly happi-

ness.   At the same time, he represents a standard of
virtue in opposition to the vice he castigates. The
irony of his situation is in some ways more complex than
the satirist satirized convention, for the man of feeling retreats into the satirist's role not from wounded
pride or self-love but to protect benevolent feeling
open to imposition. He is a socially oriented man who
must assume an antisocial philosophical position.

 The benevolent misanthrope as satirist probably lacks
the satiric power of the satirist satirized, since, as
Paulson points out, his satire is often "so generalized
that it lacks bite," and "much of the time...functions
mainly to characterize the speaker."[37] If, however, the
satire emerging from benevolent misanthropy is mitigat-
ed and qualified rather than intensified, it also brings
into startling focus the conflict between the individual and society inhering in the human condition. Jacques
Maritain observes, "on the one hand, life in society is
natural to the human person, and..., on the other hand
—because the person as such is a root of independence
—there will always exist a certain tension between the
person and society. This paradox, this tension, this
conflict are themselves something both natural and inevitable."[38] Conflict between the individual and society is made inevitable, claims Reinhold Niebhur, "by
the double focus of the moral life. One focus is in the
inner life of the individual, and the other in the ne-
cessities of man's social life. From the perspective of
society the highest moral ideal is justice. From the
perspective of the individual the highest ideal is unselfishness."[39] The satire of benevolent misanthropy
highlights this double focus by exposing the injustice
in society and by advocating the unselfishness the benevolent misanthrope exemplifies in his own personality.

 So bound up with the man of feeling, however, the benevolent misanthrope inevitably disappeared as a satirist when the man of feeling lost his appeal for society
in general. As long as benevolent feeling remained even
an affectation, as Mackenzie and the other periodical
writers claimed it had become by the end of the century,
the benevolent misanthrope could continue, for he represented at least the ideal man of true benevolence op-

posed to the man of "drawing-room" benevolence. But, as the "Society of Gentlemen at Exeter" complained in 1796, benevolent feeling had become, not merely affected, but affected for criminal purposes. They argued that "delicate sensibility, and refined ideas, are more frequently pretended than real: they are every day assumed, as the pretext for some criminal design."[40] The "Gentlemen" are pointing to the man of feeling's decay into the criminal of feeling inhabiting Gothic literature. This is not the place to discuss the development of the Gothic, but some note must be taken of the man of feeling's transformation into a morbid hero.[41] As feeling became an end in itself, all connections with benevolent actions were obscured by the cultivation of feeling for its own inherent pleasures. Luxuriating in feeling increased in morbidity as heroes and heroines began to relish pain, sorrow, misery, terror, and death as exquisite pleasures. The delight in death and misery may, of course, assume the more classical form of the "complaint of life," the plaintive melancholy that Eleanor Sickels so well describes in *The Gloomy Egoist.*[42] In this form, the man of feeling's loneliness turns to brooding introspection that leads to a catalogue and repudiation of the miseries and vanities of this life. Such a position, for example, probably most characterizes Mackenzie's man of feeling, Harley. On the other hand, the complaint of life may easily degenerate into the mysterious, morbid introspection of a Childe Harold or of a Manfred, so-called Byronic Heroes, and finally into the misanthropy of the antisocial criminal of feeling, who also claims to be a man of feeling disappointed by an evil society.[43]

The benevolent misanthrope is a delicate balance between benevolence and misanthropy, a balance that merges the antisocial tendencies of misanthropy with the social tendencies of benevolence. The criminal of feeling destroys this balance; essentially he represents the man of feeling who has become a Timonian misanthrope and remained one, that "unnatural" creature repudiated continually in the second half of the eighteenth century. The transformation of the misanthropic man of feeling into the criminal of feeling, usually in a Gothic novel, undermined the whole status of the man of

feeling as an ideal. In the first place, such a situation stripped benevolence of its social orientation
and immediately disposed of the man of feeling's very
purpose for existence. In the second place, and perhaps more significantly for the man of feeling's literary demise, it opened the door for a satiric attack on
the whole concept of misanthropy as a major refuge for
the man of feeling.

  This dual attack on feeling and misanthropy occurs most
clearly in probably the most masterful satire ever written on Gothic literature, Thomas Love Peacock's *Nightmare Abbey*.[44] The novel satirizes Gothic literature in
general, of course, but it also attacks the man of feeling as misanthrope. According to Mr. Flosky, the reading public at first delighted in "ghosts, goblins, and
skeletons" to spice the imagination, but now "the delight of our spirits is to dwell on all the vices and
blackest passions of our nature, tricked out in a masquerade dress of heroism and disappointed benevolence"
(p. 382). Flosky's "recipe for a modern novel" follows
in the eighteenth-century tradition of literary "reci-
pes" and clearly illustrates the criminal tendencies
now associated with the misanthropy arising from disappointed benevolence: "...if a man knocks me down, and
takes my purse and watch by main force, I turn him to
account, and set him forth in a tragedy as a dashing
young fellow, disinherited for his romantic generosity,
and full of a most amiable hatred of the world in general, and his own country in particular, and of a most
enlightened and chivalrous affection for himself" (p.
383). A few pages later Mr. Hilary disposes of nearly
the whole concept of misanthropy as a result of disappointed benevolence: "Misanthropy is sometimes the
product of disappointed benevolence; but it is more frequently the offspring of overweening and mortified vanity, quarreling, with the world for not being better
treated than it deserves" (p. 392). It no longer seemed
very "natural," as Coleridge sneered, to find in literature that "all our very generous, tender-hearted
characters *are* a little rude or misanthropic, and all
our misanthropes very tender-hearted."[45]

  The decay of feeling into affectation, morbidity, and
finally criminality is the negative and probably the

most significant cause for the disappearance of the benevolent misanthrope as satirist. On the positive side,
however, Byron revived verse satire in *Don Juan,* and
the satiric novel of manners was also receiving new
life; as one critic has commented, satire gradually en-
croached on the novels of the first thirty years of the
nineteenth century, "until finally the satiric novel
was reborn, and satire took its place in realistic fiction."[46] The new century witnessed a revived form of
the satiric novel of manners in Jane Austen and later
in Dickens and Thackeray. A satiric character type associated with the "unrealistic" spokesman of formal
satire did not fit very well into the "realistic" por-
trayal of life in the novel of manners.[47]

The great social movements of the nineteenth century
also seemed to demand something new of the satirist. As
a satirist, the benevolent misanthrope required a certain amount of psychological distancing from the society that fell under his censure. The writer of realistic fiction, on the other hand, appeared to need an
intense involvement in the society he was depicting, if
he hoped to reform social evils. Perhaps Dickens symbolizes this change in attitude and approach most clearly. His movement from the eighteenth-century characters
that brighten the Pickwickian world of the early novels
to what Stuart Tave aptly calls the "wilderness" of *Little Dorrit* and the novels of social reform reflects the
new direction of the novel.[48] The benevolent satirist
sees the vices of the world as something to be ridiculed
and corrected—but corrected only to a limited degree.
After all, mankind is, in the main, emersed in evil;
whatever limited virtue is possible, and only rarely
will it be as complete as in the man of feeling, occurs
in individuals. The benevolent misanthrope's philosophic vision generates a healthy pessimism suggesting
that social reform, while perhaps necessary, also generates new, different, and usually unanticipated kinds
of moral evil. The social reformer may often employ
satire of the most scathing kind, but his intimate involvement and belief in the value of reforming social
measures discourage the use of an intermediary spokesman
like the benevolent misanthrope.

The man of feeling, considered historically, was the

literary manifestation of an eighteenth-century moral ideal. Stripped of his eighteenth-century trappings, however,particularly of his tears and emotionalism,the external signs of his virtue, the man of feeling represents the virtuous man of any era attempting to live in and make his peace with a world of reality--a world in which virtue is not always even an ideal. The peculiar solution the second half of the English eighteenth century evolved for the virtuous man's problem of survival, benevolent misanthropy, is at times cumbersome and artificial in artistic presentation, but, even then, it offers a viable philosophical and even religious position, as Dr. Johnson clearly suggests; it is, perhaps, one of the few open to the virtuous man. Certainly, some such philosophical stance seems to support much of what is rather carelessly called modern existentialism. If Dr. Johnson, Matt Bramble, and the gloomy fraternity were supplanted by the Romantic fraternity of Gothic heroes,perhaps that gloomy fraternity has reappeared and is actually flourishing once again in modern literature. Its current members may be less stereotyped than their eighteenth-century forerunners; they may reflect the various existential philosophies that the nineteenth and twentieth centuries have produced; and yet perhaps the benevolent misanthrope's major features can be discerned. Here is Tarrou talking to Dr. Rieux in Albert Camus' *The Plague:*

> I know positively--yes,Rieux, I can say I know the world inside out, as you may see--that each of us has the plague within him; no one, no one on earth is free from it.... Yes, Rieux, it's a wearying business,being plague-stricken.But it's still more wearying to refuse to be it. That's why everybody in the world today looks so tired; everyone is more or less sick of the plague. But that is also why some of us, those who want to get the plague out of their systems,feel such desperate weariness, a weariness from which nothing remains to set us free except death.

When Dr. Rieux asks Tarrou to name the "path to follow for attaining peace," the "misanthrope" Tarrou gives the eighteenth-century answer, "The path of sympathy."[49]

Notes

Introduction

1. Swift to Pope, September 29, 1725, in *Correspondence of Jonathan Swift*, ed. F. Elrington Ball (London, 1912), III, 277. Swift's letter was published by Pope in 1741.
2. Swift to Pope, November 26, 1725, in *Correspondence*, III, 293.
3. The phrase comes from Northrop Frye, "Towards Defining an Age of Sensibility," in *Eighteenth Century English Literature*, ed. James L. Clifford (New York, 1959), pp. 311-318.
4. See especially Ernest Tuveson, *Millennium and Utopia* (New York, 1964). Also of importance are Ronald S. Crane, "Anglican Apologetics and the Idea of Progress, 1699-1745," *MP*, 31 (1934), 273-306, 349-382; and Lois Whitney, *Primitivism and the Idea of Progress* (Baltimore, 1934).
5. The terms come from Samuel H. Monk, "The Pride of Lemuel Gulliver," *SR*, 63 (1955), 48. See also Henry Vyverberg, *Historical Pessimism in the French Enlightenment*, Harvard Historical Monographs, No. 36 (Cambridge, Mass.; 1958).
6. See Peter Thorslev, *The Byronic Hero* (Minneapolis, 1962).
7. *Essential Works of David Hume*, ed. Ralph Cohen (New York, 1965), p. 260.

Chapter 1

1. See R.C. Elliott, *The Power of Satire* (Princeton, 1960), pp. 130-184. My discussion of the "satirist satirized" convention in the great literary misanthropes to a large extent summarizes points made by Elliott. For the popularity of the Timon figure in the Renaissance, see J.

C. Maxwell, "Introduction," in *Timon of Athens* (Cambridge,1957).Lesser known Renaissance literary treatments of Timon are discussed in Willard Farnham,*Shakespeare's Tragic Frontier* (Berkeley and Los Angeles, 1950), pp. 50-67.

2. *Plutarch's Lives*,Englished by Sir Thomas North,Intro. George Wyndham (London, 1896), VI, 73.
3. *Timon, or The Misanthrope*, trans. A.M. Harmon (London, 1915), II, 367.
4. All quotations are from the *Complete Works,* ed. G.B. Harrison (New York, 1958).
5. Absolutely speaking, as Montaigne noted,there is a vast difference between a misanthrope and a professional cynic, but in practice this difference is usually ignored (see Farnham,pp. 65-67).For various discussions of the melancholy character type, see Oscar J. Campbell,*Shakespeare's Satire*(New York,1943),and "Jaques," *HLB*, 8 (1935), 71-102; Theodore Spencer, "The Elizabethan Malcontent," in *Joseph Quincy Adams Memorial Studies* (Washington,1948); John W. Draper,*The Humours and Shakespeare's Characters* (Durham, 1945); Lawrence Babb, *The Elizabethan Malady* (East Lansing, 1951). On the character books in general, see Benjamin Boyce,*The Theophrastan Character in England to 1642* (Cambridge, Mass.,1942).
6. *The Complete Works of Samuel Rowlands,* ed.Edmund Gosse (Glasgow, 1829), II, 7.
7. *My Ladies Looking Glass* (London, 1616), p. 53.
8. *Characters of Virtues and Vices* (London,1608), pp. 99-104.
9. *More Fools Yet* (London, 1610), sig. E_2.
10. *The Power of Satire,* p. 141.
11. See Eleanor M. Sickels, *The Gloomy Egoist* (New York, 1932), pp. 21ff. and p. 351, n. 45.
12. "Concerning Humour in Comedy" (1695), in *Dramatic Essays of the Neo-Classic Age,* ed. Henry Hitch Adams and Baxter Hathaway (New York, 1950), pp. 172-173.
13. See George Converse Fiske, *Lucilius and Horace,* University of Wisconsin Studies, No. 7 (Madison, 1920), pp. 99-147; and C.W. Mendell, "Satire as Popular Philosophy," *Classical Philology,* 15 (1920), 138-157.
14. *Lives of Eminent Philosophers,*trans. R.D. Hicks (London, 1925), II, 27.
15. See Lucius R. Shero, "The Satirist's Apologia," in *Classical Studies,* University of Wisconsin Studies, 2nd series, No. 15 (Madison, 1922), pp. 148-367; and

Maynard Mack, "The Muse of Satire," *YR*, 41 (1951-52), 80-92.

16. Fiske, p. 99.

17. Mary Claire Randolph, "The Neo-Classic Theory of the Formal Verse Satire in England, 1700-1750," Diss. University of North Carolina (Chapel Hill) 1939, p. 41. See also her "The Structural Design of the Formal Verse Satire," *PQ*, 21 (1942), 369-384.

18. Fiske, p. 104.

19. Quoted in Fiske, p. 115.

20. The distinction between the satirist's private and public life is made by Alvin Kernan, *The Cankered Muse* (New Haven, 1959), pp. 16ff.

21. Cicero is quoted in Fiske, p. 87. See also Elliott's discussion of Timon and Gulliver.

22. See Kernan, pp. 54-63; Elliott, pp. 3-100; and Rose Zimbardo, *Wycherley's Drama* (New Haven, 1965), pp.61-68.

23. See Kernan, pp. 81-140; Zimbardo, pp. 65-68, 103-126; and Randolph, "Structural Design."

24. *The Dialogues of Plato,* trans. Benjamin Jowett (Oxford, 1953), 1, 445-446.

25. In addition to Elliott, see Campbell, *Shakespeare's Satire;* J.C. Maxwell, "Introduction"; and William Empson, *The Structure of Complex Words* (London, 1952), pp. 177-178.

26. All quotations are from Dialogue XVII, in *Fables and Dialogues of the Dead* (London, 1722).

27. *Gulliver's Travels,* ed. Robert A. Greenberg (New York, 1961), p. 257.

28. Ibid., p. v.

29. G. Wilson Knight, using the faint hints in the play, presents this view of Shakespeare's Timon in his now famous essay, "The Pilgrimage of Hate: An Essay on Timon of Athens," in *The Wheel of Fire* (New York, 1957), pp. 207-239.

30. Zimbardo, pp. 127-147, 77-90. See also Norman Holland, *The First Modern Comedies* (Cambridge, Mass., 1959), pp. 96-113. All quotations from *The Plain Dealer* are from the text in *British Dramatists From Dryden to Sheridan,* ed. George H. Nettleton and Arthur E. Case (Boston, 1939).

31. For some less negative views of Manly, see Ian Donaldson, "'Table Turned': *The Plain Dealer*," *EIC*, 17 (1967), 304-321; and A.M. Friedson, "Wycherley and Molière: Satirical Point of View in *The Plain Dealer*," *MP*, 64

(1967), 189-197.

32. All quotations are from Richard Wilbur's translation, *The Misanthrope and Tartuffe* (New York, 1954).

33. *The Amiable Humorist* (Chicago, 1960).

34. E.N. Hooker, "Humour in the Age of Pope," *HLQ*, 11 (1948), 363.

35. *Essential Works*, p. 222.

36. On the English proneness to the spleen, see Cecil A. Moore, "The English Malady," in *Backgrounds of English Literature, 1700-1760* (Minneapolis, 1953), pp. 179-235; and Oswald Doughty, "The English Malady of the Eighteenth Century," *RES*, 2 (1926), 257-269. For the European attitude towards the English, see Harry Kurz, *European Characters in French Drama of the Eighteenth Century* (New York, 1916), especially pp. 186ff.

37. "Sur la comédie," in *Lettres philosophique, Oeuvres completes de Voltaire* (Paris, 1899), XXII, 158:

> Pour qu'il y eût de faux dévots, il faudrait qu'il y en eût de véritables.... La Philosophie, la liberté, et le climat, conduisent à la Misanthropie: Londres, qui n'a point de Tartuffes, est plein de Timons.

38. Classic treatments of Benevolism and the man of feeling are found in R.S. Crane, "Suggestions towards a Genealogy of the 'Man of Feeling,'" *ELH*, 1 (1934), 205-230; Cecil A. Moore, "Shaftesbury and the Ethical Poets," in *Backgrounds*; Ernest Tuveson, "The Importance of Shaftesbury," *ELH*, 20 (1953), 267-299. See also Norman Sykes, *Church and State in England in the XVIIIth Century* (Cambridge, 1934), especially pp. 257ff.

39. *An Inquiry into the Original of our Ideas of Beauty and Virtue*, rev. ed. (London, 1726), p. 196.

40. *An Enquiry Concerning the Principles of Morals*, in *Essential Works*, pp. 194-195.

41. *An Essay on the Freedom of Wit and Humour*, in *Characteristics*, ed. John M. Robertson (New York, 1964), I, 74.

42. "The Long Rules," in *Ascetical Works*, trans. Sister M. Monica Wagner, C.S.C., The Fathers of the Church Series (New York, 1950), IX, 239-241.

43. "On Nature and Grace" and "On the Spirit and the Letter," in *Anti-Pelagian Works*, trans. Peter Holmes (Edinburgh, 1872), I, 292, 159.

44. *The Writings of Clement of Alexandria*, trans. William Wilson, Ante-Nicene Christian Library (Edinburgh, 1872)

IV, 118-120, 164-173; XII, 57-60. For other early Christian benevolist writings, see in The Fathers of the Church Series, St. Clement of Rome, "Letter to the Corinthians," trans. Francis X. Glimm, I, 47ff.; St. Ignatius of Antioch, "Letter to the Smyrnaeans," trans. Gerald G. Walsh, S.J., I, 120; The Shepherd of Hermas *Works*, trans. Joseph M.-F. Marique, S.J., I, 288ff.

45. "Objections against the True Religion Answered," in *The Works of the Most Reverend Dr. John Tillotson*, 9th ed. (London, 1728), pp. 255, 256.

46. *An Inquiry concerning Virtue or Merit*, in *Characteristics*, I, 250.

47. *The Sermons of Mr. Yorick*, Shakespeare Head Edition (Oxford, n.d.), I, 82.

48. *Eight Charges Delivered to the Clergy of the Dioceses of Oxford and Canterbury*, 5th ed. (London, 1799), pp. 216-218.

49. Ibid., pp. 18-19.

50. *Inquiry*, in *Characteristics*, I, 272. Fielding, of course, satirizes the exemplary character in the opening chapter of *Joseph Andrews*. Alan McKillop provides some penetrating insight into the theory of exemplary characters in an unpublished lecture delivered at Duke University, 1959. For the concept of candor, see Mary Claire Randolph, "Candour in Eighteenth Century Satire," *RES*, 20 (1944), 45-62.

51. *A Collection of Moral and Instructive Sentiments, Maxims, Cautions, and Reflexions Contained in the Histories of Pamela, Clarissa, and Sir Charles Grandison* (London, 1755), p. 259.

52. *The Novels of Samuel Richardson* (London, 1902), XX, 330-331.

53. *Several Discourses Preached at the Temple Church* (London, 1764), "Discourse XI," III, 312.

54. *Inquiry*, in *Characteristics*, I, 260.

55. Ibid., 261, 292.

56. *Essays on Shakespeare's Dramatic Characters*, 6th ed. (London, 1818), pp. 76, 119-120.

57. See St. Thomas Aquinas, *Summa Theologica*, trans. Fathers of the Dominican Province, First Complete American Edition, 3 vols. (New York, 1947), II-II, Q. 55, A. 1-2. On the virtue of prudence itself, see II-II, Q. 47-52.

58. *Inquiry*, pp. 174-175.

59. "The Power of Charity to Cover Sin," in *Sermons and*

Discourses on Several Subjects and Occasions, 5th ed.
(London, 1740), I, 61-62.

60. Preface to the *Miscellanies,* in *Works of Henry Field-ing,* ed. W.E. Henley (London, 1903), XII, 238.

61. *Works,* XIII, 110. Fielding's use of the serpent-dove allusion was not unusual. See, for example, its use in Addison's *Spectator,* No. 245; in Bishop Sherlock's "Discourse VII," *Several Discourses,* IV, 207-208; and by Richardson's Lovelace as quoted in *A Collection of Moral and Instructive Sentiments,* p. 143. For the use of the prudence theme by Fielding generally, see Henry Knight Miller, *Essays on Fielding's Miscellanies* (Princeton, 1961). For its use in the novels espe-cially, see Eleanor Hutchens, "'Prudence' in *Tom Jones:* A Study in Connotative Irony," *PQ,* 39 (1960),486-570; Martin Battestin, *The Moral Basis of Fielding's Art* (Middletown, Conn., 1959); and "Fielding's Definition of Wisdom: Some Functions of Ambiguity and Emblem in *Tom Jones,*" *ELH,* 35 (1968), 188-217; Glenn W. Hatfield, "The Serpent and the Dove: Fielding's Irony and the Prudence Theme of *Tom Jones,*" *MP,* 65 (1967), 17-32.

62. *Connoisseur,* No. 98, in *British Essayists,* ed. Alex-ander Chalmers (Boston, 1856), Vol. XXVI.

63. *British Essayists,* Vol. XXX.

64. Ibid., Vol. XXXI. See also the *Looker-On,* No. 62, Vol XXXVI.

65. See the relevant chapters in Eleanor M. Sickels, *The Gloomy Egoist;* and J.M.S. Tompkins, *The Popular Novel in England, 1770-1800* (London, 1931).

66. See Robert B. Pierce, "Moral Education in the Novels of the 1750's," *PQ,* 46 (1965), 73-87.

67. *William Thornbourough, The Benevolent Quixote,* 4 vols. (London, 1791). All quotations are from this edition.

68. See Robert Hoopes, *Right Reason in the English Renais-sance* (Cambridge, Mass., 1962), especially p. 162.

69. *Works* (London, 1830), I, pp.171-172; Hutchens, "'Pru-dence' in *Tom Jones.*"

70. *Collection of Moral Sentiments,* pp. 233, 234.

71. Quoted in Alan D. McKillop, *The Early Masters of Eng-lish Fiction* (Lawrence, Kan., 1956), p. 92.

72. Sec. III, "Of Self-Command" (London, 1875), p. 360.

73. See Sickels on the varieties of melancholy. Suicide was an evil particularly attributed to the English. See Roland Bartel, "Suicide in Eighteenth-Century Eng-land: The Myth of a Reputation," *HLQ,* 23 (1960), 145-158.

74. All quotations are from the Norton edition (New York, 1958).
75. Walter Allen, *The English Novel* (New York, 1958), p. 89.
76. *British Essayists,* Vol. XXVIII.
77. See *Kierkegaard's Concluding Unscientific Postscript,* trans. David F. Swenson (Princeton, 1944), especially pp. 48-58.

Chapter 2

1. *Inquiry,* in *Characteristics,* I, 315, 332.
2. Ibid., 64. See Epictetus, *The Discourses,* trans. W.A. Oldfather (Cambridge, Mass., 1952), II, 137-163.
3. Ibid., II, 38-39.
4. *Essays Moral, Political, and Literary,* ed. T.H. Green and T.H. Grose (London, 1912), I, 151.
5. *Letters,* ed. Matthew Montagu (London, 1813), III, 263-265.
6. All quotations are from *Politics and the Arts,* trans. Allan Bloom (Glencoe, Ill., 1960).
7. All quotations are from *The Library: or Moral and Critical Magazine,* 2 vols. (London, 1761-1762).
8. All quotations from Goldsmith are from *Collected Works,* ed. Arthur Friedman, 5 vols. (Oxford, 1966).
9. *Mémoires de [Carlo] Goldoni,* intro. M. Moreau (Paris, 1822), II:

> La bienfaisance est une vertu de l'âme; la brus-querie n'est qu'an défaut du tempérament; l'une et l'autre sont compatibles dan le même sujet. (p. 241)

> ...j'avais eu le bonheur de retrouver dans la nature un caractère qui était nouveau pour le théâtre; un caractère qu'on recontre partout, et qui cependant avait échappé à la vigilance des auteurs anciens et modernes. (p. 240)

Voltaire had created a benevolent misanthropic satirist for his play *L'Ecossaise* (which will be treated in the next chapter), and Goldoni had translated the play rather freely into Italian. See his comments, ibid.,135-143.
10. All quotations are from the 6th edition (London, 1818).
11. All quotations are from the 4 vol. edition (London, 1783).

12. *Primitivism and the Idea of Progress*, p. 66.
13. *Monthly Review*, 52 (June 1775), 471.
14. All quotations are from the first edition.
15. "The Misanthrope Corrected," trans. C. Dennis and R. Lloyd (London, 1781), included in the *Novelist's Magazine* (London, 1782), VI, 219-234. All quotations are from the *Novelist's Magazine*. Marmontel's claim that even the misanthropy of a Timon is "factitious" and can, therefore, presumably be corrected received literary support in the character of Chaubert, who appears as the hero of a tale written by Richard Cumberland for the *Observer*, Nos. 15-16 (1785) and of a tedious verse drama written by John Villiers, *Chaubert, or The Misanthrope* (London, 1789). Cumberland also rewrote Shakespeare's *Timon of Athens* (1771) to have Timon repudiate his malevolence at the end of the play. Penruddock, the hero of Cumberland's *The Wheel of Fortune*, follows this same pattern and will be considered in chapter six.
16. All quotations are from the first edition.
17. *The Characters of Jean de la Bruyère*, trans. Henri von Laun (London, 1929), pp. 287-288. I am indebted for this reference to T.O. Wedel, "On the Philosophical Backgrounds of *Gulliver's Travels*," *SP*, 23 (1926), 434-450.
18. Etienne Gilson, *The Spirit of Mediaeval Philosophy*, trans. A.H.C. Downes (New York, 1936), pp. 195ff. See St. Thomas Aquinas, *Summa Theologica*, I, Q. 29, A.3.
19. Emmanuel Mounier, *Personalism* (London, 1952), p. xiv.
20. *Fear and Trembling*, trans. Walter Lowrie (New York, n.d.), p. 66.
21. *An Essay concerning Human Understanding*, ed. Alexander Campbell Fraser (Oxford, 1894), I, 448-449, 456-457. For the opposition of the divines, see, for example, Bishop Butler's "Dissertation of Personal Identity," in *Whole Works of Joseph Butler* (London, 1835), pp. 263-267.
22. Mounier, p. 30.
23. All quotations are from *British Essayists*, Vol. XXXI.
24. *Collected Works*, ed. Sir William Hamilton (Edinburgh, 1877), VI, 337-338.
25. All quotations are from *Mrs. Inchbald's British Theatre* (London, 1808), Vol. XXIV.
26. All quotations are from the revised edition (London, 1832).

Chapter 3

1. See Andrew Wilkinson, "The Decline of English Verse Satire in the Middle Years of the Eighteenth Century," *RES*, N.S., 3 (1952), 222-223; Stuart Tave, *The Amiable Humorist*, pp. 22ff; Peter K. Elkin, *The Augustan Defence of Satire* (Oxford, 1973), pp. 44-70, 185-201.
2. *Collection of Moral Sentiments*, pp. 200-201.
3. *The History of English Poetry*, ed. W.C. Hazlitt, IV (London, 1871), 409.
4. *British Essayists*, IV, 267.
5. See the *Cankered Muse*, pp. 150-163; and *Wycherley's Drama*, pp. 70-75.
6. *The Nature and Destiny of Man* (New York, 1941), I, 220.
7. *The Works of the English Poets*, ed. Alexander Chalmers (London, 1810), XVII, 204, 207.
8. (London, 1798), pp. v, 4. See also Charles Abbot, *An Essay on the Use and Abuse of Satire* (Oxford, 1786); Elkin, pp. 90-117.
9. (New Haven, 1967), p. 309.
10. All quotations are from the Henley edition.
11. "Some Recent Views of *Tom Jones*," *CE*, 21 (1959), 19. On the theme of prudence in *Tom Jones*, see the works cited in chapter one, n. 59; and Allan Wendt, "The Moral Allegory of *Jonathan Wild*," *ELH*, 24 (1957), 306-320.
12. McKillop, "Recent Views," 19.
13. All quotations are from *An Essay towards Fixing the True Standards of Wit, Humour, Raillery, Satire, and Ridicule* (1744), rptd. in the *Augustan Reprint Society*, ed. James L. Clifford, 1st series, No. 4 (Los Angeles, 1947).
14. Morris argues that "If a *Person* in real Life, discovers any odd and remarkable *Features* of Temper or Conduct, I call such a Person in the *Book of Mankind*, a *Character*. So that the chief Subjects of Humour are Persons in real Life, who are *Characters*." A few pages later Morris makes it quite clear that his humorist is only one species under the genus character; he writes that a man of humor is one "who can happily exhibit and expose the Oddities and Foibles of an *Humourist*, or of other *Characters*" (ibid., p. 15). See the discussion in Tave, pp. 118ff.
15. *The Frenchman in London*, trans. [anon.] (London, 1755), p. 26.
16. Ibid., p. iv.
17. All quotations are from *Works of Samuel Foote, Esq.*, ed. Jon Bee, Esq. (London, 1830), Vol. I. See the *Critical Review*, 1 (Feb: 1756), 83-85.

18. *Oeuvres complètes*, V, 439, 445-446:

    ...les hommes ne sont pas bons à grand'chose: fripons
    ou sots, voilà pour les trois quarts: et pour l'autre
    quart, il se tient chez soi.

19. All quotations are from the 1768 edition.
20. *Lessings Werke*, ed. Franz Vornmuller (Leipzig, n.d.),
    IV, 56.

    Wir lieben seine plumpe Edelmütigheit, und die Eng-
    länder selbst haben sich dadurch geschmeichelt gefund-
    en.

21. All quotations are from *The Adventures of David Sim-
    ple*, 2nd ed., 2 vols. (London, 1744).
22. The honor is shared with Mary Collyer, *Letters from
    Felicia to Charlotte*. See the discussion in James R.
    Foster, *History of the Pre-Romantic Novel in England*
    (New York, 1949), pp. 85ff, and n. 3.
23. Miss Fielding is not, however, above mildly satirizing
    David himself at times. See her depiction of David's
    reaction to being jilted by Miss Johnston (I, 61).
24. All quotations are from the Friedman edition.
25. I cannot agree with Robert Hopkins that Lien Chi is
    the object of serious satire,and I agree even less with
    his attempt to show ridicule of the Man in Black. Both
    are amiable humorists evoking sympathetic laughter at
    their inconsistencies rather than corrective ridicule.
    In the scenes with the beggar and the sailor, for ex-
    ample, the whole point seems to be that the Man in
    Black knows he is being duped and knows Lien Chi knows.
    He is being *willingly* imposed upon. See *The True Gen-
    ius of Oliver Goldsmith* (Baltimore, 1969), pp. 96-
    123, 124-137.
26. See Michael E. Adelstein, "Duality of Theme in the *Vic-
    ar of Wakefield*," *CE*, 22 (1961), 315-321; and Curtis
    Dahl, "Patterns of Disguise in *The Vicar of Wakefield*,"
    ELH, 25 (1958), 90-104. The structure of the novel is
    handled at some length by Sven Bäckman, *This Singular
    Tale*, Lund Studies in English, No. 40 (Lund,1971), pp.
    40-84.
27. See the many fine comments of W.O.S. Sutherland, Jr.,
    The Art of the Satirist (Austin, 1965), pp. 83-91.
28. *Critical Review*, 21 (1766), 441.
29. All quotations are from the Norton edition.

Chapter 4

1. See Fred W. Boege, *Smollett's Reputation As A Novelist* (Princeton, 1947), chapters 3, 4; and McKillop, *Early Masters*, p. 180.
2. Lewis Knapp, *Tobias Smollett: Doctor of Men and Manners* (Princeton, 1949), p. 314.
3. All quotations from Smollett's novels are from the *Works*, ed. George Saintsbury, 12 vols. (London, 1903).
4. McKillop, *Early Masters*, p. 149. See also the chapter on Smollett in Robert Alter, *Rogue's Progress* (Cambridge, Mass., 1964). Robert Spector explores the whole picaresque tradition as Smollett uses it in *Tobias Smollett* (New York, 1968), pp. 39-145.
5. See the excellent study of the country as a symbol for moral and physical harmony in Jeffrey L. Duncan, "The Rural Ideal in Eighteenth-Century Fiction," *SEL*, 8 (1968), 517-535.
6. Quoted in George M. Kahrl, *Tobias Smollett: Traveller-Novelist* (Chicago, 1945), p. 84.
7. *Works of Tobias Smollett,* ed. John Robert Moore (London, 1797), I, 196, 208, 211.
8. My discussion of Smollett's novels assumes the excellent work of Ronald Paulson in *Satire and the Novel* and in his earlier "Satire in the Early Novels of Smollett," *JEGP*, 59 (1960), 381-402. Where Paulson focuses on satire alone, I attempt to relate satire to Smollett's use of the man of feeling. Spector's fine study treats Smollett's early heroes primarily as rogues, though he admits the possibility of some virtue in them. See pp. 47-48.
9. See M.A. Goldberg, *Smollett and the Scottish School* (Albuquerque, 1959), p. 40. Also illuminating is the discussion of "Aventure et Morale," in *Roderick Random* by P.-G. Boucé, *Les Romans de Smollett* (Paris, 1971), pp. 155-177.
10. McKillop, *Early Masters,* p. 152.
11. *Scottish School*, chapter two.
12. On Lady Vane's "Memoirs" and the moral development of Peregrine, see Rufus Putney, "The Plan of *Peregrine Pickle*," *PMLA*, 60 (1945), 1051-65. See also Boucé, pp. 177-195.
13. Paulson, *Satire and the Novel,* pp. 173ff. See also Mary Claire Randolph, "The Medical Concept in English Renaissance Satiric Theory," *SP*, 38 (1941), 125-157.

14. Paulson, *Satire and the Novel*, p. 184.
15. *Letters of Tobias Smollett, M.D.*, ed. Edward S. Noyes (Cambridge, Mass., 1926), Letter 38 (to John Moore, Sept. 28, 1758), p. 55.
16. *Works*, VIII, xviii.
17. Even from the time of its first publication *Fathom* has been viewed as an imitation of *Wild*. See Knapp, pp. 318ff.; and Goldberg, pp. 194ff.
18. *Lives of Eminent Novelists and Dramatists* (London, 1887), p. 465.
19. *Works*, VIII, xiii.
20. See *Works*, VIII, xiii; and Wendt, "Moral Allegory." Spector uses the Iago image to discuss Fathom's character (See pp. 87-106).
21. All quotations are from the Henley edition.
22. Knapp, p. 304.
23. See, for example, VIII, 20-22, 26-27, 31, 35-39, 54, 56, 58, 63, 91, 97, 113, 119, 125, 150-151, 175, 178-179, 214, 218; IX, 29-31, 41-42, 46, 51, 64, 66, 76, 89, 109, 162.
24. On Fathom as a satirist satirized, see *Satire and the Novel*, pp. 187-188; and "Satire in the Early Novels," 399-400.
25. For Smollett's use of theatrical conventions, see George M. Kahrl, "The Influence of Shakespeare on Smollett," *Parrott Presentation Volume*, ed. Hardin Craig (Princeton, 1935), pp. 399-420; and my essay "'The Dramatic Passions'and Smollett's Characterization," *SP*, 71 (Jan. 1974), 105-125.
26. Goldberg, pp. 99ff.
27. *Satire and the Novel*, p. 188.
28. *Inquiry*, in *Characteristics*, I, 274.
29. Quotations from the *Faerie Queene* are from *Complete Poetical Works of Spenser*, ed. R.E. Neil Hodge (Boston, 1908).
30. In *Harrison's British Classicks* (London, 1785), VIII, 63.
31. *Characters*, ed. A.R. Waller (Cambridge, 1908),p. 469.
32. *Works*, ed. Moore, I, 204.
33. See Kahrl, pp. 125ff.; Knapp, pp. 306-307, 322.
34. See Matt's other comments on the spleen, XI, 42, 74. William Park gives an interesting psychological interpretation of the Matt-Humphry relationship in "Fathers and Sons—*Humphry Clinker*," *Literature and Psychology*, 16 (1966), 166-174.

35. Matt uses theatre imagery at least twice (XI, 73, 130); Lydia is, of course, in love with an actor, and she uses theatre imagery once (XI, 52); Wilson uses it once (XI, 18); Tabby, once (XI, 164); Winifred, once (XI, 54); Sir Thomas Bulford, once (XII, 164). The novel closes with the group planning to act the *Beaux' Stratagem* (XII, 207).

36. According to Diogenes Laertius, the Cynics produced the railing of Diogenes and the laughing satire of Menippus and Crates. Of Menippus, Diogenes Laertius writes, "There is no seriousness in him; but his books overflow with laughter" (II, 103). Lovejoy and Boas quote from Plutarch's *De Animi Tranquilitate:*"Crates, though he carried a beggar's wallett and wore a threadbare coat, went through life joking and laughing like one who is at a festival" (*Primitivism and Related Ideas in Antiquity* [Baltimore, 1935], p.130). See also Donald R. Dudley, *Cynicism* (London, 1937), pp.42-46. For other aspects of the comic in *Clinker*, see Sheridan Baker, "*Humphry Clinker* As Comic Romance," *Papers of the Michigan Academy of Science, Arts, and Letters*, 46 (1961), 645-653.

37. McKillop, *Early Masters*, pp. 152-153.

38. See W. J. Hughes, *Wales and the Welsh in English Literature* (London, 1924), chapter 7 and passim; Wallace Nottestein, *The Scot in History* (New Haven, 1946), pp. 327ff.

39. *Rambler*, No. 95, in *British Essayists*, XVII, 203-204.

40. M. Formey, *A Concise History of Philosophy and Philosophers*, trans. Oliver Goldsmith [?] (London, 1766), p. 124.

41. "The Vanity of Human Wishes," in *Poems of Samuel Johnson*, ed. David Nichol Smith and E.L. McAdam (Oxford, 1941), ll. 367-368.

42. Goldberg discusses the novel in terms of primitivism and progress, *Scottish School*, pp. 143-180.

43. From Dio Chrysostom, as quoted in Lovejoy-Boas, *Primitivism*, p. 132.

44. See XII, 83, 92.

45. See Maren-Sophie Røstvig, *The Happy Man* (Oslo, 1958), II, 13-59.

46. On this point, see the excellent essay by B.L. Reid, "Smollett's Healing Journey," *VQR*, 41 (1965), 549-570.

47. I agree with Boucé that in the final analysis *Humphry Clinker* is not "un roman pessimiste." See Boucé, p. 298.

48. The phrase is from Emmanuel Mounier, *Be Not Afraid*, trans. Cynthia Rowland (New York, n.d.), p. 11.

Chapter 5

1. *Sermons*, in *Works of Samuel Johnson* (Oxford, 1829), IX, 332.
2. *The Rambler*, ed. W.J. Bate and Albrecht Strauss, The Yale Edition of the Works of Samuel Johnson (New Haven, 1969), V, 146.
3. Yale Edition, V, 160.
4. *Johnsonian Miscellanies*, ed. George B. Hill (Oxford, 1897), II, 256.
5. James Boswell, *Life of Johnson*, ed. George B. Hill, rev. L.F. Powell (Oxford, 1934-1950), I, 443-444.
6. James Boswell, *Journal of A Tour to The Hebrides*, ed. R.W. Chapman (Oxford, 1924), p. 300.
7. *Works*, I, 73.
8. See *Miscellanies*, II, 251, 168-169; Sir John Hawkins, *Life of Samuel Johnson* (London, 1787), pp. 400, 408-409; "Sermon XIX," in *Works*, IX, 467.
9. Hawkins, *Life*, p. 413.
10. Boswell, *Life*, IV, 239.
11. Yale Edition, V, 162. See also *Adventurer*, No. 120, Yale Edition, II, 466-470.
12. Yale Edition, II, 42. For discussions of Johnson's moral purpose in writing, see Robert Voitle, *Samuel Johnson The Moralist* (Cambridge, Mass., 1961), pp.44-45; Paul Alkon, *Samuel Johnson and Moral Discipline* (Evanston, Ill., 1967), pp. 146-179.
13. *Works*, IX, 331. For discussions of Johnson's religious purpose in writing, see Alkon, pp. 176-179; and Arieh Sachs, *Passionate Intelligence* (Baltimore,1967), passim.
14. Yale Edition, II, 469.
15. *Works*, IX, 314. For the religious dimension of Johnson's life and works, see, in addition to Alkon and Sachs, Maurice Quinlan, *Samuel Johnson: A Layman's Religion* (Madison, 1964); and Chester Chapin, *The Religious Thought of Samuel Johnson* (Ann Arbor, 1968).
16. All quotations from *Rasselas*, hereafter cited in the text, are from the R.W. Chapman edition (Oxford,1927).
17. See especially Nicholas Joost, "Whispers of Fancy; or the Meaning of *Rasselas*," *Modern Age*, I (Fall 1957),

166-173.

18. For a summary of critics who have written on the Ethi-
    opian background and for a pinpointing of precisely
    which works Johnson probably used, see Donald Lockhart,
    "'The Fourth Son of the Mighty Emperor': The Ethiopian
    Background of Johnson's *Rasselas,*" *PMLA,* 78 (Dec.1963),
    516-528. Johnson was also, I contend, using material
    from Bishop Simon Patrick's *Paraphrase upon the Book
    of Ecclesiastes* (1685). See my "The Biblical Context
    of Johnson's *Rasselas,*" *PMLA,*84 (March 1969),274-275.

19. For a more extended but slightly different treatment
    of the Happy Valley as a false paradise, see Bernard
    L. Einbond,*Samuel Johnson's Allegory* (The Hague,1971),
    pp. 83-96. The satiric nature of the plot of *Rasselas*
    is treated by W.O.S. Sutherland, Jr., *The Art of the
    Satirist* (Austin, 1965), pp. 92-104; see also Harold
    E. Pagliaro, "Structural Patterns of Control in *Ras-
    selas,*" in *English Writers of the Eighteenth Century,*
    ed. John H. Middendorf (New York, 1971), pp. 208-229.

20. "The Importance of Imlac," in *Bicentenary Essays on
    Rasselas,*supplement to *Cairo Studies in English* (Cairo,
    1959), p. 39.

21. *Posthumous Works* (London, 1807), I, 109-110.

22. *The Vision of Theodore,* in *Johnson,* ed. Mona Wilson,
    2nd ed. (Cambridge, Mass.,1957), p. 152. All further
    quotations from *The Vision* are from this edition and
    are cited in the text.

23. Boswell, *Life,* I, 341-342. George Saintsbury also as-
    sociates *Rasselas* with Ecclesiastes in the *Peace of
    the Augustans* (London, 1916), p. 190; and the Rev. H.
    C. Beeching, preaching at the bicentenary of Johnson's
    birth, entitled his sermon *Johnson and Ecclesiastes*
    (London, 1909).

24. Boswell, *Life,* IV, 301, n.2.

25. To my knowledge, the most complete discussion of these
    two schools of interpretation, as well as the rabbin-
    ical school, is by Christian D. Ginsburg, *Coheleth*
    (London, 1861), pp. 1-255.

26. Boswell, *Life,*III, 58.

27. See "The Biblical Context," 274-278.

28. Michael Jermin, *Commentary upon the Whole Book of Ec-
    clesiastes...* (London, 1639), p. 2.

29. Bishop Patrick's *Paraphrase,* in *A Commentary on the
    Books of the Old Testament* (London, 1853),III, 112.

30. Ibid., 116.

31. Samuel Clarke, *A Survey of the Bible*... (London,1693), pp. 289, 299.
32. Patrick, III, 114.
33. Ibid, 113.
34. Jermin, p. 6. See also William Lowth, *Directions for the Profitable Reading of the Holy Scriptures* (London, 1708), p. 88.
35. Patrick, III, 113.
36. Ibid., 155.
37. Ibid., 113.
38. Ibid., 116.
39. William Sherlock, *A Discourse Concerning the Divine Providence*, 7th ed. (London, 1694), pp. 280-281.
40. Boswell, *Life*, I, 342.
41. Boswell, *Life*, II, 124.
42. "The Importance of Imlac," p. 41. See also the fine essay by Sheridan Baker, *"Rasselas:* Psychological Irony and Romance," *PQ*, 45 (Jan. 1966), 249-261.
43. *Works*, IX, 395.
44. Ibid., 400.
45. See Donald M. Korte, "Johnson's *Rasselas*," Forum,*PMLA*, 87 (Jan. 1972), 100-101; and my reply, Forum, *PMLA*,87 (March 1972), 312-314.
46. *Works*, IX, 402.
47. Ibid., 403.
48. See Johnson's translation of Father Lobo's *Voyage to Abyssinia* (London, 1735), p. 208.
49. *Works*, IX, 402-403.
50. Boswell, *Life*, II, 22.
51. Patrick, III, 115.

Chapter 6

1. All quotations are from *Perth Magazine*, 1(Edinburgh, 1772), 2-7.
2. *London Magazine*, 51 (July 1782), 322, 323.
3. *Bell's British Theatre* (London,1797), Vol. XVIII. All quotations are from this edition.
4. Thomas Davies, *Memoirs of the Life of David Garrick* (London, 1808), II, 296.
5. All quotations are from *The Natural Son* (London,1785).
6. All quotations are from *Inchbald's British Theatre* (London, 1808), Vol. XVIII. Other examples of "converted" Timonian misanthropes are Marmontel's "The Misanthrope Corrected," *Novelist's Magazine* (London,

1782), VI, 219-234; Richard Cumberland's Chaubert, in *Observer*,Nos.15-16 (1785); John Villiers' verse drama, *Chaubert* (London, 1789); and Cumberland's rewrite of Shakespeare's *Timon* (London, 1771).

7. *Memoirs of Richard Cumberland* (London, 1807), I, 274.
8. See *Liberal Opinions*, 2 vols. (London, 1775).
9. All quotations are from *Shenstone-Green; or, The New Paradise Lost*, 3 vols. (London, 1779).
10. All quotations are from *Family Secrets*, 5 vols. (London, 1797).
11. *The Popular Novel in England, 1770-1800* (London,1931), pp. 110-111.
12. Ibid., p. 110.
13. See the discussion of *Launcelot Greaves*,chapter four.
14. *Monthly Review*, 71 (Sept. 1784), 223-224, 223.
15. Ballantyne Novel Series, ed. Sir Walter Scott (London, 1824), Vol. IX. All quotations are from this edition.
16. Gordon is a typical Scots doctor come to London for financial advancement. He can also speak excellent English. Gordon marries Sutton's niece and retires with her to Mount Henneth.
17. All quotations are from the Ballantyne Series.
18. See *Lounger*, No. 77, in *British Essayists*, ed. Alexander Chalmers (Boston, 1856), XXI, 295. For other examples, see in this same series, *Connoisseur*, No. 98; *Lounger*, No. 20; *Looker-On*, No. 62, Vols. XXVI, XXX, XXXVI.
19. All quotations are from *The Fair Syrian*, 2 vols.(London, 1787).
20. All quotations are from the Ballantyne Series.
21. *The Popular Novel*, p. 204.
22. All quotations are from *Man As He Is*, 4 vols.(London, 1782).
23. Bage abandoned the benevolent misanthrope as satirist in *Hermsprong, or Man As He Is Not*. The main satirist is the narrator Gregory Glen, who is a mixture of the naif and the conscious ironist.
24. All quotations are from *Cecilia, or Memoirs of an Heiress*, 5 vols. (London, 1782).
25. George Sherburn, "The Restoration and Eighteenth Century," in *A Literary History of England*, ed. Albert C. Baugh, et. al. (New York, 1948), p. 1034.
26. Sir Walter Scott, *Biographical Memoirs*,in *The Miscellaneous Prose Works* (Edinburgh, 1834), IV, 17.

27. *Critical Review,* 64 (Aug. 1787), 127. All quotations from the *Lounger* are from *British Essayists,*Vols. XXX-XXXI.

28. *Memoirs,* IV, 18-19.

29. The benevolent misanthrope as satirist makes a very brief appearance as Lord Belmount in Susanne Harvey Keir, *The History of Miss Greville,* 3 vols. (London, 1787), III, 169-180. In a much diluted form he appears as Job Thornbury in the younger George Colman's *John Bull; or The Englishman's Fireside* (London,1803).

30. All quotations are from *The Black Dwarf,* in *Works,*ed. Andrew Lang (Boston, 1894), Vol. V.

31. See Lang's historical preface, V, 175-180.

32. Ratcliffe tells the dwarf's history to Isabella, V, 350ff.

33. See V, 229ff.

34. Ibid., 364ff.

35. All quotations are from the Lang edition, Vol. IX.

36. See Erick Erämetsä, *A Study of the Word 'Sentimental' and of Other Linguistic Characteristics of Eighteenth Century Sentimentalism in England,* Annales Academiae Scientiarum Fennicae, Ser. B, LXXIV, No. 1 (Helsinki, 1951).

37. Paulson, *Satire and the Novel,* p. 218. Paulson is referring to my Rice University doctoral dissertation, "The Good-Natured Misanthrope: A Study of Satire and Sentiment of the 18th Century," 1962.

38. *The Rights of Man and Natural Law,*trans. Doris C. Ansom (New York, 1943), p. 18.

39. *Moral Man and Immoral Society* (New York, 1932), p.257.

40. *Essays by a Society of Gentlemen, at Exeter* (Exeter, 1796), p. 325.

41. Excellent discussions of the man of feeling's decay into the Byronic hero and the criminal of feeling can be found in Mario Praz, *The Romantic Agony* (New York, 1956),chapters 2,4; Peter Thorslev, *The Byronic Hero,* especially chapters 3-5; Lowry Nelson, Jr., "Night Thoughts on the Gothic Novel," *YR,* 52 (1962), 236-257.

42. See especially pp. 18-21.

43. See Thorslev, chapters 4-5. The "Romantic" Timonian misanthrope is treated also in the final chapter of Bill Harris Casey, "The Misanthrope in English Literature of the Eighteenth Century," Diss. University of Texas 1962, evidently in progress about the time my "Good-Natured Misanthrope" was registered (Jan. 8, 1962).

44. All quotations are from *Nightmare Abbey,* in *The Novels of Thomas Love Peacock,* ed. David Garnett (London, 1948).
45. "Satyrane's Letters," in *Biographia Literaria,* ed. John C. Metcalf (New York, 1926), Letter III, p. 339.
46. Winfield H. Rogers, "The Reaction Against Melodramatic Sentimentalism in the English Novel, 1796–1830," *PMLA,* 49 (1934), 98.
47. See the fine discussion in Paulson, *Satire and the Novel,* pp. 266–310.
48. Tave, *Amiable Humorist,* p. 243.
49. *The Plague,* trans. Stuart Gilbert (New York, 1948), pp. 229–230.

Bibliography

Abbey, Charles J., and John N. Overton. *The English Church in the Eighteenth Century.* 2 vols. London, 1878.

Abbot, Charles, Lord Tenterdon. "On the Use and Abuse of Satire (1786)." *The Oxford English Prize Essays.* 2nd ed. Vol. I. Oxford, 1836.

Adams, Thomas. *Mystical Bedlam, or The World of Mad-Men.* London, 1615.

Adelstein, Michael E. "Duality of Theme in *Vicar of Wakefield.*" *CE*, 22 (1961), 315-21.

Aikin, J. "On the Humour of Addison, and the Character of Sir Roger de Coverley." *The Monthly Magazine,* 9 (Feb. 1, 1800), 1-3.

Alkon, Paul. *Samuel Johnson and Moral Discipline.* Evanston, Ill., 1967.

Allen, Walter. *The English Novel.* New York, 1958.

Alter, Robert. *Rogue's Progress.* Cambridge, Mass., 1964.

Anon. *The Benevolent Man; or the History of Mr. Belville.* 2 vols. London, 1775.

_____. *The Placid Man.* 2 vols. London, 1770.

Aquinas, St. Thomas. *Summa Theologica.* Trans. Fathers of the English Dominican Province. 3 vols. New York, 1947.

Atterbury, Francis, Bishop of Rochester. *Sermons and Discourses on Several Subjects and Occasions.* 5th ed. Vol. I. London, 1740.

Augustine, Aurelius. *The Anti-Pelagian Works.* Trans. Peter Holmes. Vol. I. Edinburgh, 1872.

Babb, Lawrence. *The Elizabethan Malady.* East Lansing, 1951.

Babcock, R.W. "William Richardson's Criticism of Shakespeare." *JEGP*, 28 (1929), 117-36.

Bäckman, Sven. *This Singular Tale.* Lund Studies in English, No. 40. Lund, 1971.

Bage, Robert. *Barham Downs* [1784]. Ballantyne Novel Series. Vol. IX. London, 1824.

_____. *Hermsprong, Or Man As He Is Not.* Ed. Vaughn Wilkins. New York, 1951.

_____. *James Wallace* [1788]. Ballantyne Novel Series. Vol. IX. London, 1824.

_____. *Man As He Is.* 4 vols. London, 1792.

_____. *Mount Henneth* [1781]. Ballantyne Novel Series. Vol. IX. London, 1824.

Baker, Sheridan. "Humphry Clinker as Comic Romance." *Papers of the Michigan Academy of Science, Arts and Letters,* 46 (1961), 645-53.

_____. "*Rasselas:* Psychological Irony and Romance." *PQ,* 45 (Jan. 1966), 249-61.

Bartel, Roland. "Suicide in Eighteenth Century England: The Myth of a Reputation." *HLQ,* 23 (1960), 145-58.

Battestin, Martin C. "Fielding's Definition of Wisdom: Some Functions of Ambiguity and Emblem in *Tom Jones.*" *ELH,* 35 (1968), 188-217.

_____. *The Moral Basis of Fielding's Art.* Middletown, Conn., 1959.

Boattie, James. *Dissertations Moral and Critical.* 2 vols. Dublin,1783.

Beeching, Rev. H.C. *Johnson and Ecclesiastes.* London,1909.

Boege, Fred W. *Smollett's Reputation as a Novelist.* Princeton, 1947.

Boissy, Louis de. *Le François à Londres* (1727). *Chefs-d'oeuvre dramatique de Boissy. Répertoire du théâtre français.* 2nd series. Vol. XVII. Paris, 1824.

_____. *The Frenchman in London.* Trans. Anon. London, 1755.

Boscawen, William. *Progress of Satire.* London, 1798.

Boswell, James. *The Hypochondriack.* Ed. Margery Bailey. 2 vols. Stanford, 1928.

_____. *Journal of A Tour To The Hebrides.* Ed. R.W. Chapman. Oxford, 1924.

_____. *Life of Samuel Johnson.* Ed. George B. Hill, rev. L.F. Powell. 6 vols. Oxford, 1934-50.

Boucé, P-G. *Les Romans de Smollett.* Paris, 1971.

Boyce, Benjamin. *The Theophrastan Character in England to 1642.* Cambridge, Mass., 1947.

Bredvold, Louis I. "Some Basic Issues of the Eighteenth Century." *Michigan Alumnus Quarterly Review,* 64 (1957), 45-54.

Brewer, Wilmon. *Shakespeare's Influences on Sir Walter Scott.* Boston, 1925.

Buck, Howard Swazey. *A Study in Smollett, Chiefly Peregrine Pickle, with a Complete Collation of the First and Second editions.* New Haven, 1925.

Burney, Fanny. *Cecilia, or Memoirs of an Heiress.* 5 vols. London, 1782.

Butler, Joseph, Bishop of Durham (1750-52). *The Whole Works of Joseph Butler.* London, 1835.

Butler, Samuel. *Characters.* Ed. A.R. Waller. Cambridge, 1908.

Campbell, Oscar James. "Jaques." *HLB*, 8 (1935), 71-102.

_____. *Shakespeare's Satire.* New York, 1943.

Camus, Albert. *The Plague.* Trans. Gilbert Stuart. New York, 1948.

Casey, Bill Harris. "The Misanthrope in English Literature of the Eighteenth Century." Diss. Univ. of Texas, 1962.

Chapin, Chester. *The Religious Thought of Samuel Johnson.* Ann Arbor, 1968.

Chapone, Hester. *Posthumous Works.* 2 vols. London, 1807.

Charity Schools and Sermons. A Collection of Accounts and Sermons from 1704 to 1718. 2 vols. London, n.d.

Chorney, Alexander H. "Wycherley's Manly Reinterpreted." *Essays Critical and Historical Dedicated to Lily Campbell.* Berkeley, 1950.

Clarke, Samuel. *A Survey of the Bible....* London, 1693.

Clement of Alexandria. *The Writings of Clement of Alexandria.* Trans. William Wilson. Ante-Nicene Christian Library. Vols. IV and XII. Edinburgh, 1867.

Clement, St. of Rome. "Letter to the Corinthians." Trans. Francis X. Glimm. *The Apostolic Fathers.* The Fathers of the Church Series. Vol. I. New York, 1947.

Coleridge, Samuel Taylor. "Satyrane's Letters." *Biographia Literaria.* Ed. John C. Metcalf. New York, 1926.

Colman, George. *The English Merchant.* London, 1768.

Colman, George, the younger. *John Bull; or The Englishman's Fireside* [1803]. London, 1805.

Congreve, William. "Concerning Humour in Comedy" [1695]. *Dramatic Essays of the Neoclassic Age.* Ed. Henry Hitch Adams and Baxter Hathaway. New York, .950.

The Connoisseuer. The British Essayists. Ed. Alexander Chalmers. Vol. XXVI. Boston, 1856.

Crane, Ronald S. "Anglican Apologetics and the Idea of Progress, 1699-1745." *MP*, 31 (Feb. and May, 1934), 273-306; 349-82.

_____. "The Plot of *Tom Jones*." *Journal of General Education*, 4 (1950), 112-30.

_____. "Suggestions toward a Genealogy of the 'Man of Feeling.'" *ELH*, 1 (1934), 205-30. Rpt. *Studies in the Literature of the Augustan Age*. Ed. Richard C. Boys. Ann Arbor, 1952.

Critical Review. "Review of Foote's *Englishman Returned from Paris*." 1 (Feb. 1756), 83-85.

_____. "Review of *Vicar of Wakefield*." 21 (June 1766), 439-41.

_____. "Review of *Shenstone-Green*." 47 (March 1779), 207-10.

_____. "Review of *The Lounger*." 64 (Aug. 1787), 125-30.

Cumberland, Richard. *The Fashionable Lover* [1772]. Rpt. *Bell's British Theatre*, Vol. XVIII. London, 1797.

_____. *Memoirs of Richard Cumberland*. 2 vols. London, 1807.

_____. *The Natural Son*. London, 1785.

_____. *Timon of Athens*. London, 1771.

_____. *The Wheel of Fortune* [1795]. Rpt. *Inchbald's British Theatre*. Vol. XVIII. London, 1808.

Dahl, Curtis. "Patterns of Disguise in *The Vicar of Wakefield*." *ELH*, 25 (1958), 90-104.

Davies, Thomas. *Memoirs of the Life of David Garrick*. 2 vols. London, 1808.

Diogenes Laertius. *Lives of Eminent Philosophers*. Trans. R.D. Hicks. 2 vols. London and New York, 1925.

Donaldson, Ian. "'Table Turned': *The Plain Dealer*." *EIC*, 17 (1967), 304-21.

Doughty, Oswald. "The English Malady of the Eighteenth Century." *RES*, 2 (July 1926), 257-69.

Draper, John W. *The Humours and Shakespeare's Characters*. Durham, N.C., 1945.

_____. "The Theory of the Comic in Eighteenth-Century England." *JEGP*, 37 (1938), 207-23.

Duncan, Jeffrey L. "The Rural Ideal in Eighteenth-Century Fiction." *SEL*, 8 (1968), 517-35.

Einbond, Bernard L. *Samuel Johnson's Allegory*. The Hague, 1971.

Elkin, Peter K. *The Augustan Defence of Satire*. Oxford, 1973.

Elliott, Robert C. *The Power of Satire*. Princeton, 1960.

Empson, William. *The Structure of Complex Words*. London, 1951.

"Enquirer No. IV." "Is Private Affection Inconsistent with Universal Benevolence." *Monthly Magazine*, 4 (May 1796), 273-76.

Epictetus. *The Discourses*. Trans. W.A. Oldfather. 2 vols. Cambridge, Mass., and London, 1952.

Erämetsä, Erik. *A Study of the Word 'Sentimental' and of other Linguistic Characteristics of Eighteenth Century Sentimentalism in England*. Annales Academiae Scientiarum Fennicae, Ser. B, Vol. LXXIV, No. 1. Helsinki, 1951.

Essays by a Society of Gentlemen, at Exeter. Exeter, 1796.

"Examiner No. IX." "Ought Sensibility to be Cherished or Repressed." *Monthly Magazine*, 9 (Oct. 1796), 706-09.

Fenelon, Archbishop François. *Fables and Dialogues of the Dead*. Trans. Anon. London, 1722.

Fielding, Henry. *The Complete Works of Henry Fielding*. Ed. W.E. Henley. 16 vols. London, 1903.

Fielding, Sarah. *The Adventures of David Simple*. 2nd ed. 2 vols. London, 1744.

Fiske, George Converse. *Lucilius and Horace*. University of Wisconsin Studies in Language and Literature, No. 7. Madison, 1920.

Foote, Samuel. *The Englishman Returned from Paris*. *The Works*. Ed. Jon Bee, Esq. Vol. I. London, 1830.

Formey, M. *A Concise History of Philosophy and Philosophers*. Trans. Oliver Goldsmith [?]. London, 1766.

Foster, James R. *History of the Pre-Romantic Novel in England*. New York, 1949.

Friedson, A.M. "Wycherley and Molière: Satirical Point of View in *The Plain Dealer*." *MP*, 64 (1967), 189-97.

Frye, Northrop. "Towards Defining an Age of Sensibility." *ELH*, 23 (1956), 144-52.

Gallaway, W.F. "The Sentimentalism of Goldsmith." *PMLA*, 48 (1933), 1167-81.

Gentleman's Magazine. "The Force of Ridicule in Writing." 8 (Oct. 1738), 529-30.

Gibson, Edmund, Bishop of London. *The Bishop of London's Pastoral Letter to the People of his Diocese*. London, 1730.

_____. *The Bishop of London's Second Pastoral Letter to the People of His Diocese*. London, 1730.

Gilson, Etienne. *The Spirit of Medieval Philosophy*. Trans. A.H.C. Downes. New York, 1936.

Ginsburg, Christian D. *Coheleth*. London, 1861.

Godwin, William. *Fleetwood*. Rev. ed. London, 1832.

Goldberg, M.A. *Smollett and the Scottish School*. Albuquerque, 1959.

Goldoni, Carlo. *Le Borru Bienfaisant* [1771]. Trans. Barret H. Clark. London, 1915.

_____. *Mémoires de Carlo Goldoni*.   Intro. M.   Moreau.
Vol. II.   Paris, 1822.

Goldsmith, Oliver.   *The Collected Works of Oliver Goldsmith*.   Ed. Arthur Friedman.   5 vols.   Oxford, 1966.

Gordon, Thomas.   *The Humourist* [1720].   3rd ed.   2 vols.
London, 1725.

Gray, Kirkman.   *A History of English Philanthropy*.   London, 1905.

Hall, Joseph.   *Characters of Virtues and Vices*.   London,
1608.

Hatfield, Glenn W.   "The Serpent and the Dove: Fielding's
Irony and the Prudence Theme of *Tom Jones*."   *MP*, 65
(1967), 17-32.

Hawkins, Sir John.   *Life of Samuel Johnson*.   London, 1787.

Hayley, William.   *The Triumph of Temper; A Poem*.   London,
1781.

Hazard, Paul.   "Les origines philosophiques de l'homme de
sentiment."   *Romantic Review*, 28 (1937), 318-41.

Heilman, Robert B.   "The Sentimentalism of Goldsmith's
Good Natured Man."   *Studies for William A. Reed*.   Ed.
Nathaniel M. Caffee and Thomas A. Kirby.   Baton Rouge,
1940.

Hermas, The Shepherd of. *Works of the Shepherd of Hermas*.
Trans. Joseph M.-F. Marique, S.J. *The Apostolic Fathers*.
The Fathers of the Church Series.   Vol. I.   New York,
1947.

Hill, George B.   *Johnsonian Miscellanies*.   Vol. II.   Oxford, 1897.

Holland, Norman N. *The First Modern Comedies*.   Cambridge,
Mass., 1959.

Hooker, Edward Niles.   "Humour in the Age of Pope."   *HLQ*,
11 (1948), 361-85.

Hoopes, Robert.   *Right Reason in the English Renaissance*.
Cambridge, Mass., 1962.

Hopkins, Robert.   *The True Genius of Oliver Goldsmith*.
Baltimore, 1969.

Hughes, W.J.   *Wales and the Welsh in English Literature*.
London, 1924.

Hume, David.   *Essays Moral, Political, and Literary*.   Ed.
T.H. Green and T.H. Grose.   2 vols.   London, 1912.

_____.   *Essential Works*. Ed. Ralph Cohen. New York,1965.

_____.   *A Treatise of Human Nature*. Ed. L.A.Selby-Bigge.
Oxford, 1888.

Humphreys, A.R.   "Fielding's Irony: Its Methods and Effects."   *RES*, 18 (April 1942), 183-96.

_____. "'The Friend of Mankind' (1700-60)—An Aspect of Eighteenth-Century Sensibility." *RES*, 24 (1948), 203-18.

Humphry, R.H. "Literature and Religion in Eighteenth-Century England." *Journal of Ecclesiastical History*, 3 (Oct. 1952), 159-90.

Hutchens, Eleanor. "'Prudence' in *Tom Jones*: A Study in Connotative Irony." *PQ*, 39 (1960), 486-570.

Hutcheson, Francis. *An Inquiry Into the Original of Our Ideas of Beauty and Virtue*. 2nd ed. London, 1726.

Ignatius, St. of Antioch. "Letter to the Smyrnaens." Trans. Gerald G. Walsh, S.J. *The Apostolic Fathers*. The Fathers of the Church Series. Vol. I. New York, 1947.

"Imaginary Dialogue between Walter Shandy and Matthew Bramble." *London Magazine*, 51 (1782), 322-23.

Jermin, Michael. *Commentary upon the Whole Book of Ecclesiastes....* London, 1639.

Johnson, Samuel. *Rasselas*. Ed. R.W. Chapman. Oxford, 1927.

_____. *Works.* Ed. Mona Wilson. 2nd ed. Cambridge, Mass., 1957.

_____. *Works.* Vol. IX. Oxford, 1829.

_____. *Works.* Gen. Ed. Allen T. Hazen. The Yale Edition. New Haven, 1958-.

Jones, Claude E. "The English Novel: A Critical View, 1756-1785." *MLQ*, 19 (1958), 147-59; 213-24.

Jones, M.G. *The Charity School Movement.* Cambridge, 1938.

Joost, Nicholas. "Whispers of Fancy; or the Meaning of *Rasselas.*" *Modern Age*, 1 (Fall 1957), 166-73.

Kahrl, George M. "The Influence of Shakespeare on Smollett." *Parrott Presentation Volume.* Ed. Hardin Craig. Princeton, 1935. Pp. 399-420.

_____. *Tobias Smollett: Traveller-Novelist.* Chicago, 1945.

Keir, Susanne Harvey. *The History of Miss Greville.* 3 vols. London, 1787.

Kernan, Alvin. *The Cankered Muse.* New Haven, 1959.

Kierkegaard, Søren. *Concluding Unscientific Postscript.* Trans. David F. Swenson. Princeton, 1944.

_____. *Fear and Trembling.* Trans. Walter Lowrie. New York, n.d.

Knapp, Lewis M. *Tobias Smollett: Doctor of Men and Manners.* Princeton, 1949.

Knight, G. Wilson. *The Wheel of Fire.* New York, 1957.

Knudson, Albert C. *The Philosophy of Personalism.* New York, 1927.

Korte, Donald M. "Johnson's *Rasselas.*" *PMLA*, 87 (Jan.

1972), 100-01.

Kotzebue, Augustus. *Misanthropy and Repentance*. Trans. Anon. 1798 (as *The Stranger.*). *Inchbald's British Theatre*. Vol. XXIV. London, 1808.

Kurz, Harry. *European Characters in French Drama of the Eighteenth Century*. New York, 1916.

La Bruyère, Jean de. *The Characters*. Trans. Henri von Laun. London, 1929.

Landa, Louis A. "Jonathan Swift." *EIE* (1946 [1947]), pp. 20-40. Rpt. *Studies in the Literature of the Augustan Age*. Ed. Richard C. Boys. Ann Arbor, 1952.

Lascelles, Mary. "Johnson and Juvenal." *New Light on Dr. Johnson*. Ed. Frederick W. Hilles. New Haven, 1959.

Lessing, Gotthold. *Hamburgische Dramaturgie*. *Lessings Werke*. Ed. Franz Vormuller. Leipzig, n.d.

Link, Frederick M. "Rasselas and the Quest for Happiness." *Boston University Studies in English*, 3 (1957), 121-23.

Locke, John. *An Essay Concerning Human Understanding*. Ed. Alexander Campbell Fraser. 2 vols. Oxford, 1894.

Lockhart, Donald. "'The Fourth Son of the Mighty Emperor': The Ethiopian Background of Johnson's *Rasselas.*" *PMLA*, 78 (Dec. 1963), 516-28.

Lombardo, Agostino. "The Importance of Imlac." *Bicentenary Essays on Rasselas*. Supplement to *Cairo Studies in English*. Cairo, 1959. Pp. 31-49.

The Looker-On. *The British Essayists*. Ed. Alexander Chalmers. Vol. XXXVI. Boston, 1856.

Lovejoy, Arthur O., and George Boas. *Primitivism and Related Ideas in Antiquity*. Baltimore, 1935.

Lovejoy, Arthur O. *The Great Chain of Being*. New York, 1960.

Lowth, William. *Directions for the Profitable Reading of the Holy Scriptures*. London, 1708.

Lucian. *Works*. Trans. A.M. Harmon. Vol. II. London and New York, 1915.

McKillop, Alan D. *The Early Masters of English Fiction*. Lawrence, Kan., 1956.

_____. "Some Recent Views of *Tom Jones*." *CE*, 21 (1959), 17-22.

_____. "Unpublished Lecture Delivered at Duke University." 1959.

Mack, Maynard. "The Muse of Satire." *Yale Review*, 41, No. 1 (1951), 81-92. Rpt. *Studies in Literature of the Augustan Age*. Ed. Richard C. Boys. Ann Arbor, 1952.

Mackenzie, Henry. *The Lounger*. *The British Essayists*. Ed.

Alexander Chalmers. Vols. XXX-XXXI. Boston, 1856.
_____. *The Man of Feeling*. Intro. Kenneth C. Slagle. New York, 1958.
_____. *The Mirror*. *The British Essayists*. Ed. Alexander Chalmers. Vol. XXVIII. Boston, 1856.
_____. *The Works*. 8 vols. Edinburgh, 1808.
Maritain, Jacques. *The Rights of Man and Natural Law*. Trans. Doris C. Ansom. New York, 1943.
_____. *True Humanism*. New York, 1938.
Marmontel, Jean François. "The Misanthrope Corrected." *Novelist's Magazine*. Vol. VI. London, 1782.
Martz, Louis T. *The Later Career of Tobias Smollett*. Yale Studies in English, 97. New Haven, 1942.
Maxwell, J.C. "Introduction" to *Timon of Athens*. Cambridge, 1957.
Melmoth, Courtney [Samuel Jackson Pratt].*Family Secrets*. 5 vols. London, 1797.
_____. *Liberal Opinions, or the History of Benignus*. 4 vols. London, 1783.
_____. *Shenstone-Green; or, The New Paradise Lost*. 3 vols. London, 1779.
Melmoth, William. *Letters on Several Subjects* [1776]. *Harrison's British Classicks*. Vol. VIII. London, 1785.
Mendell, C.W. "Satire as Popular Philosophy." *Classical Phil.*, 15 (1920), 138-57.
"M-H." "Letter on Novel Writing." *Monthly Magazine*, 4 (Sept. 1797), 180-81.
Miller, Henry Knight. *Essays on Fielding's Miscellanies*. Princeton, 1961.
"The Misanthrope." *Perth Magazine*, 1 (Edinburgh, 1772), 2-7.
"Of Misanthropy." *Library*, 1 (Oct. 1761), 359-64.
Molière. *The Misanthrope and Tartuffe*. Trans. Richard Wilbur. New York, 1954.
Monk, Samuel Holt. "The Pride of Lemuel Gulliver." *SR* (Winter 1955), 48-71. Rpt. *Eighteenth Century English Literature*. Ed. James L. Clifford. New York, 1959.
Montagu, Mrs. Elizabeth. *Letters*. Ed. Matthew Montagu. Vol. III. London, 1813.
Monthly Review. "Review of *Liberal Opinions*." 52 (June 1775), 468-72.
_____. "Review of *Mount Henneth*." 66 (Jan. 1782), 129-31.
_____. "Review of *Barham Downs*." 71 (Sept.1784), 223-24.

_____. "Review of *James Wallace*." 80 (June 1789), 498-502.

Moore, Cecil A. *Backgrounds of English Literature, 1700-1760*. Minneapolis, 1953.

More, Hannah. "Sensibility." *Works*. Vol. I. London, 1830.

Morris, Corbyn. *An Essay towards Fixing the True Standards of Wit, Humour, Raillery, Satire, and Ridicule* [London, 1744]. *The Augustan Reprint Society Publications*. 1st series: Essays on Wit. No. 4. Ed. James L. Clifford. Los Angeles, 1947.

Mounier, Emmanuel. *Be Not Afraid*. Trans. Cynthia Rowland. New York, n.d.

_____. *Personalism*. Trans. Philip Mairet. London, 1952.

Myers, Sylvia Harcstark. "Ideals, Actuality, and Judgment in the Novels of Tobias Smollett: A Study in Development." Diss. Univ. of California (Berkeley), 1955.

Nelson, Lowry, Jr. "Night Thoughts on the Gothic Novel." *YR*, 52 (1962), 236-57.

Niebhur, Reinhold. *Moral Man and Immoral Society*. New York, 1932.

_____. *The Nature and Destiny of Man*. Vol. I. New York, 1941.

Notestein, Wallace. *The Scot in History*. New Haven, 1946.

The Observor. The British Essayists. Ed. Alexander Chalmers. Vol. XXXIII. Boston, 1856.

Pagliaro, Harold E. "Structural Patterns of Control in *Rasselas*." *English Writers of the Eighteenth Century*. Ed. John H. Middendorf. New York, 1971. Pp. 208-29.

Park, William. "Fathers and Sons—*Humphry Clinker*." *Literature and Psychology*, 16 (1966), 166-74.

Patrick, Simon, Bishop of Ely. *Paraphrase upon the Book of Ecclesiastes* (1685). *A Commentary on the Books of the Old Testament*. Vol. III. London, 1853.

Paulson, Ronald. *Satire and the Novel in Eighteenth-Century England*. New Haven, 1967.

_____. "Satire in the Early Novels of Smollett." *JEGP*, 59 (1960), 381-402.

Peacock, Thomas Love. *Nightmare Abbey*. *The Novels of Thomas Love Peacock*. Ed. David Garnet. London, 1948.

Pierce, Robert B. "Moral Education in the Novels of the 1750's." *PQ*, 46 (1965), 73-87.

Plaquevent, Jean. "Individu et Personne: Esquisse Historique Des Notions." *Esprit*, 64 (Jan. 1938), 578-608.

Plato. *Phaedo*. *The Dialogues of Plato*. Trans. B. Jowett.

Vol. I. Oxford, 1953.

Praz, Mario. *The Romantic Agony*. New York, 1956.

Preston, Thomas R. "The Biblical Context of Johnson's *Rasselas*." *PMLA*, 84 (March 1969), 274-81.

_____. "Disenchanting the Man of Feeling: Smollett's *Ferdinand Count Fathom*." *Quick Springs of Sense*. Ed. Larry S. Champion. Athens, Ga., 1973.

_____. "'The Dramatic Passions' and Smollett's Characterization." *SP*, 71 (Jan. 1974), 105-25.

_____. "The Good-Natured Misanthrope: A Study of Satire and Sentiment of the 18th Century." Diss. Rice Univ., 1962.

_____. "Johnson's *Rasselas* Reconsidered." *PMLA*,87 (March 1972), 312-14.

_____. "Smollett and the Benevolent Misanthrope Type." *PMLA*, 79 (March 1964), 51-57.

"Publicola." "Against Whitefield." *Gentleman's Magazine*, 21 (June 1751), 274.

_____. "Further Arguments Against Whitefield." *Gentleman's Magazine*, 21 (July 1751), 304-05.

Putney, Rufus. "The Plan of *Peregrine Pickle*." *PMLA*, 60 (1945), 1051-65.

Quinlan, Maurice. *Samuel Johnson: A Layman's Religion*. Madison, 1964.

Randolph, Mary Claire. "Candour in Eighteenth Century Satire." *RES*, 20 (1944), 45-62.

_____. "The Medical Concept in English Renaissance Satiric Theory." *SP*, 38 (1941), 125-57.

_____. "The Neo-Classic Theory of the Formal Verse Satire in England, 1700-1750." Diss. Univ. of North Carolina (Chapel Hill), 1939.

_____. "The Structural Design of the Formal Verse Satire." *PQ*, 21 (1942), 368-84.

Reid, B.L. "Smollett's Healing Journey." *VQR*, 41 (1965), 549-70.

Rich, Barnaby. *My Ladies Looking Glass*. London, 1616.

Richardson, Samuel. *A Collection of Moral Sentiments*.... London, 1755.

_____. *The Novels of Samuel Richardson*. Vol. XX. London, 1902.

Richardson, William. *Essays on Shakespeare's Dramatic Characters*. 6th ed. London, 1818.

Rodgers, Betsy. *The Cloak of Charity*. London, 1949.

Rogers, Winfield II. "The Reaction Against Melodramatic Sentimentalism in the English Novel, 1796-1830." *PMLA*,

49 (1934), 98-122.

Røstvig, Maren-Sofie. *The Happy Man*. 2 vols. Oslo, 1958.

Rousseau, Jéan Jacques. *Politics and the Arts*. Trans. Allan Bloom. Glencoe, Ill., 1960.

Rowlands, Samuel. *The Complete Works*. Ed. Edmund Goose. 3 vols. Glasgow, 1829.

Sachs, Arieh. *Passionate Intelligence*. Baltimore, 1967.

Saintsbury, George. *The Peace of the Augustans*. London, 1916.

Scott, Sir Walter. *Biographical Memoirs. The Miscellaneous Prose Works of Sir Walter Scott*. Vol. IV. Edinburgh, 1834.

_____. *Lives of Eminent Novelists and Dramatists*. London, 1887.

_____. *The Works*. Ed. Andrew Lang. Vols. V and IX. Boston, 1894.

Secker, Thomas, Archbishop of Canterbury. *Eight Charges Delivered to the Clergy of the Dioceses of Oxford and Canterbury*. 5th ed. London, 1799.

Shaftesbury, Anthony A. Cooper, Third Earl of. *Characteristics*. Ed. John M. Robertson. Vol. I. New York, 1964.

Shakespeare, William. *The Complete Works*. Ed. G.B. Harrison. New York, 1958.

_____. *Timon of Athens*. Ed. J.C. Maxwell. Cambridge, 1957.

Sharpe, Roger. *More Fools Yet*. London, 1610.

Sherbo, Arthur. *English Sentimental Drama*. Lansing, Mich., 1957.

Sherburn, George. "The Restoration and Eighteenth Century." *A Literary History of England*. Ed. Albert C. Baugh. New York, 1948.

Sherlock, Thomas, Bishop of London. *Several Discourses Preached at the Temple Church*. 4 vols. London, 1764.

Sherlock, William. *A Discourse Concerning the Divine Providence*. 7th ed. London, 1694.

Shero, Lucius R. "The Satirist's Apologia." *Classical Studies*. 2nd series. Univ. of Wis. Studies, No.15. Madison, 1922.

Sickels, Eleanor M. *The Gloomy Egoist*. New York, 1932.

Silvester, Tipping. *Moral and Christian Benevolence, A Sermon Containing Some Reflections upon Mr. Balguy's Essay on Moral Goodness*. London, 1734.

Smith, Adam. *Theory of Moral Sentiments*. London, 1875.

Smollett, Tobias. *Letters of Tobias Smollett, M.D.* Ed. Edward S. Noyes. Cambridge, 1926.

_____. *Works*. Ed. John Robert Moore. Vol. I. London, 1797.

_____. *The Works of Tobias Smollett*. Ed. George Saintsbury. 12 vols. London, 1903.

_____. "New Smollett Letters." *TLS*, July 24, 1943.

The Spectator. Ed. D. F. Bond. 5 vols. Oxford, 1965.

Spector, Robert. *Tobias Smollett*. New York, 1968.

Spencer, Theodore. "The Elizabethan Malcontent." *Joseph Quincy Adams Memorial Studies*. Washington, 1948.

Spenser, Edmund. *Complete Poetical Works*. Ed. R.E. Neil Hodge. Boston, 1908.

Steele, Sir Richard. *The Tatler*. *The British Essayists*. Ed. Alexander Chalmers. Vol. I. Boston, 1856.

Sterne, Laurence. *The Sermons of Mr. Yorick*. 2 vols. Shakespeare Head Edition. Oxford, n.d.

Stewart, Dugald. *The Collected Works of Dugald Stewart*. Ed. Sir William Hamilton, Bart. 11 vols. Edinburgh, 1877.

Stockdale, Percival. *An Essay on Misanthropy*. London, 1783.

Stoll, Edgar Elmer. "Shakespeare, Marston, and the Malcontent Type." *MP*, 3 (1905-06), 281-303.

Sutherland, John H. "Robert Bage: Novelist of Ideas." *PQ*, 36 (1957), 211-20.

Sutherland, W.O.S., Jr. *The Art of the Satirist*. Austin, 1965.

Swift, Jonathan. *The Correspondence of Jonathan Swift*. Ed. F. Elrington Ball. 6 vols. London, 1912.

_____. *Gulliver's Travels*. Ed. Robert A. Greenberg. New York, 1961.

Sykes, Norman. *Church and State in England in the XVIIIth Century*. Cambridge, 1934.

Tave, Stuart M. *The Amiable Humorist*. Chicago, 1960.

Theophrastus. *Characters*. Trans. and ed. J.M. Edmonds. London, 1929.

Thorslev, Peter. *The Byronic Hero*. Minneapolis, 1962.

Tillotson, John. "A Sermon Preach'd before the Queen at Whitehall, March the 7th, 1689/90." London, 1690.

_____. *The Works of the Most Reverend Dr. John Tillotson*. 9th ed. London, 1728.

Tompkins, J.M.S. *The Popular Novel in England, 1770-1800*. London, 1931.

Tuveson, Ernest. *The Imagination as a Means of Grace*. Berkeley, 1960.

_____. "The Importance of Shaftesbury." *ELH*, 20 (1953), 267-99.

_____. *Millennium and Utopia*. New York, 1964.

"Verax." "The Dignity of Man's Nature." *Gentleman's Magazine*, 21 (Oct. 1751), 457.

Villiers, Rt. Hon. John Charles. *Chaubert, or the Misanthrope*. London, 1789.

The Visitor. [Essays in *Public Ledger*, 1760-61]. 2 vols. London, 1764.

Voitle, Robert. *Samuel Johnson the Moralist*. Cambridge, Mass., 1961.

Voltaire, François Marie. *Oeuvres complètes de Voltaire*. 52 vols. Paris, 1899.

_____. *The Works of Voltaire*. Ed. Tobias Smollett. Rev. William F. Flemming. 22 vols. New York, 1901.

Vyverberg, Henry. *Historical Pessimism in the French Enlightenment*. Harvard Historical Monographs, No. 36, Cambridge, Mass., 1958.

Warton, Thomas. *The History of English Poetry*. Ed. W. C. Hazlitt, Vol. IV. London, 1871.

Wasserman, Earl R. "The Sympathetic Imagination in Eighteenth-Century Theories of Acting." *JEGP*, 46 (1947), 264-72.

Watt, Ian. *The Rise of the Novel*. London, 1957.

Wedel, T.O. "On the Philosophical Background of *Gulliver's Travels*." *SP*, 23 (1926), 434-50.

Wendt, Allan. "The Moral Allegory of *Jonathan Wild*." *ELH*, 24 (Dec. 1957), 306-20.

Whitehead, William. "Poems of William Whitehead." *The Works of the English Poets*. Ed. Alexander Chalmers. Vol. XVII. London, 1810.

Whitford, Robert C. "Satire's View of Sentimentalism in the Days of George the Third." *JEGP*, 18 (1919), 155-204.

Whitney, Lois. *Primitivism and the Idea of Progress*. Baltimore, 1934.

Wilkinson, Andrew M. "The Decline of English Verse Satire in the Middle Years of the Eighteenth Century." *RES*, N.S., 3 (1952), 222-33.

William Thornbourough, The Benevolent Quixote. 4 vols. London, 1791.

Winspear, Mary. "The English Man of Feeling." Diss. Univ. of Toronto, 1942.

Wycherley, William. *The Plain Dealer*. *British Dramatists From Dryden to Sheridan*. Ed. George H. Nettleton and Arthur E. Case. Boston, 1939.

Zimbardo, Rose. *Wycherley's Drama*. New Haven, 1965.

Index

210

Shaftesbury
*Essay on the Knowledge of
the Characters of Men.
See* Fielding, Henry
Essay on Wit and Humour
(Morris), 55
*Essays on Shakespeare's
Dramatic Characters*
(William Richardson),
21, 35-37

Fair Syrian, The. See
Bage, Robert
Family Secrets. See
Melmoth, Courtney
*Fashionable Lover, The.
See* Cumberland,
Richard
Fathers, The. See
Fielding, Henry
Feeling, man of, 15-19,
172-76; as exemplary
hero, 19-20, 24-26,
58-61; disenchanted,
26-28, 86-88. *See
also* Benevolism; Mis-
anthropy, benevolent
Fenelon, Archbishop Fran-
çois, 10-11
*Ferdinand Count Fathom.
See* Smollett, Tobias
Fielding, Henry, 59; and
Smollett, 87-94, 100.
Works: *Enquiry into the
Causes of...Late In-
crease of Robbers,* 22-
23, 90; *Essay on the
Knowledge of the Char-
acters of Men,* 22, 88-
94, 100; *The Fathers,*
54; *Jonathan Wild,* 87-
88; *Tom Jones,* 52-54
Fielding, Sarah, 58-61

Fitzosborne, Thomas. *See*
Melmoth, William
Fleetwood (Godwin), 46-47
Foote, Samuel, 56-57, 107,
146
*Fortunes of Nigel, The.
See* Scott, Sir Walter
Foster, James R., 186 n. 22
Frye, Northrop, 177 n. 3

*Gentleman Returned from
Paris* (Foote), 56-57,
107
Gentleman's Magazine,
18-19
Gentlemen, Society of, at
Exeter, 173
Gilson, Etiènne, 41
Ginsburg, Christian, 191
n. 25
Godwin, William, 46-47
Goldberg, M.A., 77, 99,
189 n. 42
Goldoni, Carlo, 34-35,
183 n. 9
Goldsmith, Oliver. Works:
Asem, 34; *Citizen of
the World,* 33, 61-63,
81,125,167; *Public Ledger,*
33; *Vicar of Wakefield,*
63-68
Gothic novel, 96, 173-76
Gulliver's Travels, 11

Hall, Bishop Joseph, 6
Hamburgische Dramaturgie
(Lessing), 58
Hamlet. See Shakespeare
Harris, James, 39
Hawkins, Sir John, 122
Hayley, William, 38-39
Hermsprong. See Bage,Robert
History of Miss Greville,